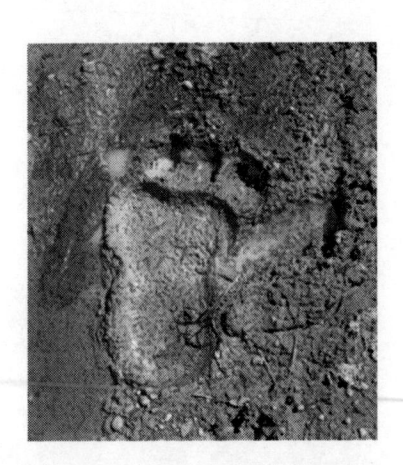

"Given the scientific evidence that I have examined, I'm convinced there's a creature out there that is yet to be identified..."
Jeff Meldrum, Professor of Anatomy and Anthropology at Idaho State University.

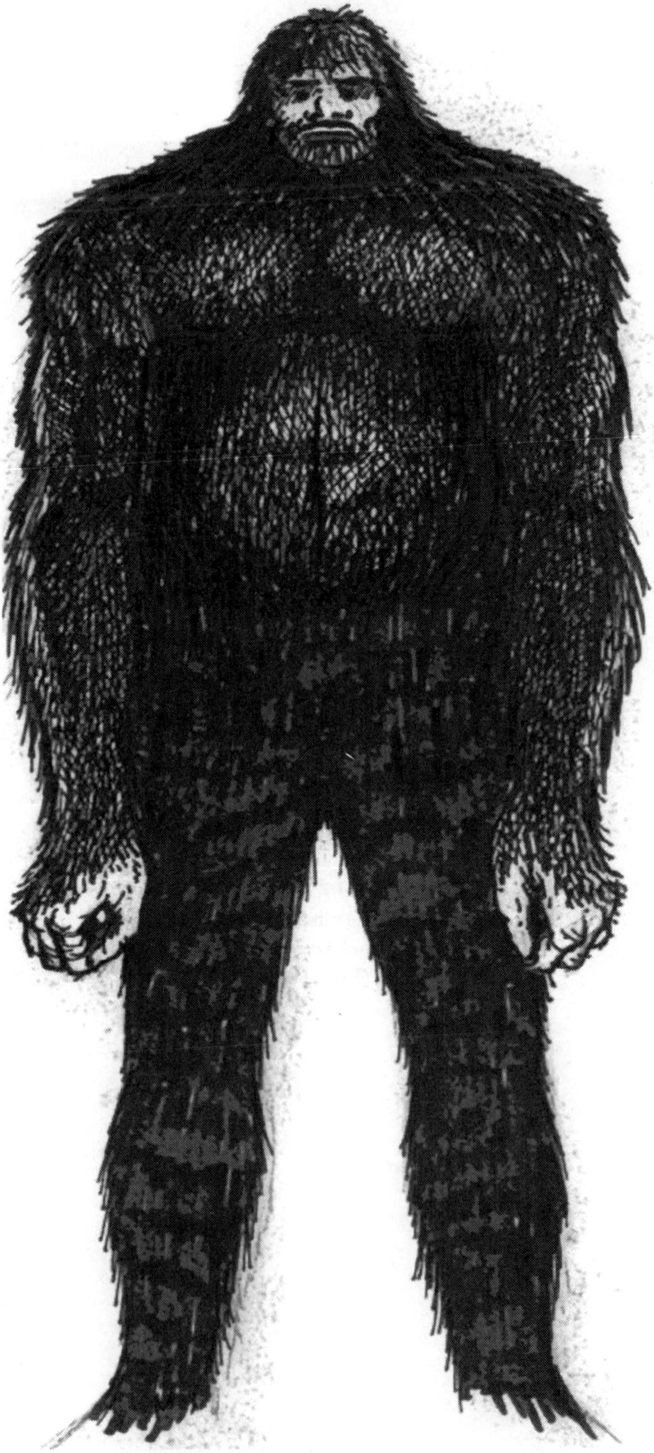

MYSTERIOUS PLACES FROM WHITECHAPEL PRESS

BIGFOOT IN KENTUCKY
ON THE TRAIL OF GIANTS IN THE BLUEGRASS STATE
BY B.M. NUNNELLY

A WHITECHAPEL PRESS BOOK FROM DARK HAVEN ENTERTAINMENT

© Copyright 2011 by B.M Nunnelly
All Rights Reserved, including the right to copy or reproduce this book, or portions thereof, in any form, without express permission from the author and publisher

Original Cover Artwork Designed by
© Copyright 2007 by Michael Schwab & Troy Taylor
Visit M & S Graphics at http://www.manyhorses.com

Original Photographs and Illustrations by B.M. Nunnelly
Additional Photograph Credits Noted in the Text

Editing and Proofreading Services: Jill Hand

This Book is Published By:
Whitechapel Press
A Division of Dark Haven Entertainment, Inc.
Chicago, Illinois
(312) 666-5255 / 1-888-GHOSTLY
Visit us on the internet at http://www.whitechapelpress.com

First Edition -- January 2011
ISBN: 1-892523-72-8

Printed in the United States of America

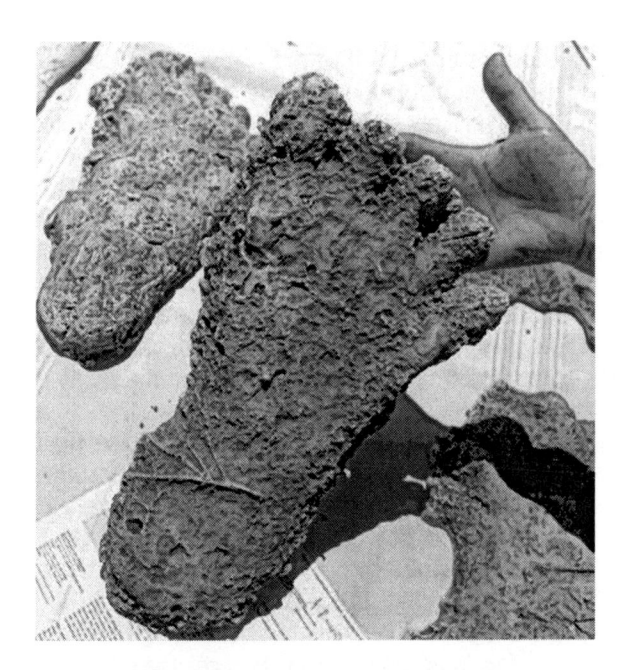

FOREWORD

Bigfoot is alive and well in Kentucky!

The purpose of this volume is to examine the curious proliferation of the Bigfoot phenomenon in the Bluegrass State. Why are these cryptids so common here? What is it about the state that attracts hairy humanoids like moths to a flame? As a Fortean researcher and investigator, I've been looking for the answer to that question for the past twenty-five years, and what I've found may surprise you.

Most skeptics find it difficult to believe that large, hairy, bipedal, apelike monsters of any origin could exist completely undiscovered anywhere in modern America. They will quickly tell you that there simply is not enough isolated wilderness left to support sizeable breeding populations of creatures of this statue. They will tell you that since no Bigfoot bones or bodies have ever been found, they simply cannot be. These assumptions are quite common - but still completely wrong. Millions of square acres of pristine wilderness and wetlands still exist in North America, areas large enough to easily support the physical needs of any number of undiscovered animals. The author sincerely believes that the existence of Bigfoot will be proved in the near future.

The Bluegrass State alone consists of roughly 42,500 square miles - much of it unexplored wilderness and watershed areas. While it is true that no bones have ever officially been recognized as belonging to the legendary creature, alleged Bigfoot skeletal remains have reportedly been found by a number of people, including a resident of Hebbardsville in Henderson County. Giant anomalous skeletal remains were also found with some frequency during the eighteenth and nineteenth centuries in many of the burial mounds attributed to the Native Americans that exist throughout the state. However, as no control specimen is on hand for easy reference by the zoological community, it is unlikely that any single bone, even if it did, in fact, actually belong to a Bigfoot, will ever be afforded this classification. This is curious, considering the fact that *Gigantopithicus blacki*, an early ancestor of the modern gorilla thought by many leading researchers to be the most likely candidate for the possible identity of Bigfoot, is known and officially recognized by academia merely from a handful of fossilized teeth found in apothecary shops in China.

The fossil record suggests they were the largest apes that ever lived, standing up to 9.8 feet tall and weighing 1,200 pounds. They are believed to have existed from roughly one million to as recently as 300 thousand years ago. It is possible that they never became extinct at all!

The single biggest mistake made by the detractors of the Bigfoot phenomenon is the all-too-casual dismissal of the thousands of eyewitness accounts and the reams of printed material, some dating back centuries, that describe very real appearances by these mysterious beasts. It has been estimated that only about 1 in 10 individual eyewitnesses of these creatures ever come forward and tell their astonishing tale to the public, out of fear of being ridiculed. Rural dwellers, by far the most common group to spot a Bigfoot, are even less likely to share their experience with anyone but their closest friends and family members. For this reason, the author surmises that a more accurate percentage would be around 1 in 20, or higher. That being the case, silent witnesses to this unexplained phenomenon must number in the tens of thousands. It seems the height of folly to simply write off all these sightings as hallucinations, misidentifications or downright lies.

Notwithstanding, the number of believers in Bigfoot grows with each newly reported sighting. Researchers have long held that these mysterious creatures utilize rivers and creeks as a means of travel, just as we do roads. There are hundreds of reported sightings of these creatures either wading or swimming in the water or dashing into it to make their escape; so many, in fact, that it might be reasonably conjectured that the beasts might even be aquatic in nature and not land animals at all. After all, as of this writing, no one actually *knows* anything concerning the habits of the Bigfoot. In any event, if waterways really are "Bigfoot roads," the state of Kentucky is ideally suited for such creatures, with more miles of navigable waterways and shorelines than any other state save for Alaska.

Many other researchers feel that it is entirely possible that Bigfoot are subterranean in nature, living in underground tunnels and caves and only briefly coming topside to forage or hunt. Again, the Bluegrass State is ideally suited as a habitat for such creatures, with the largest known cave system in the entire world, Mammoth Cave, located in Edmonson County in the south-central portion of the state. Over 360 miles of tunnels, passageways and caverns have been found in Mammoth Cave so far, radiating outward in all directions like spokes on a wheel. This vast network is covered by hundreds of miles of rough and mountainous terrain containing thousands of cave openings - some known and many others still undiscovered - dotting the landscape like entrances to another world, as indeed they are. I've personally explored a few caves in the region and it is not an activity for the faint of heart. If these creatures truly are subterranean it might even be hypothesized that many if not all of them might have emerged from this vast cave system at some point and traveled to other parts of the country. When nothing is known for certain, anything is possible.

So, without doubt, Kentucky has enough space for large numbers of Bigfoot to exist undetected with room to spare. It has ample food sources in the form of bountiful wildlife and edible flora. It has the waterways that these creatures may use for traveling and plentiful underground caverns in which they might hide and make their homes undetected by humans. Small wonder then, that Bigfoot activity has been reported in over 100 of the state's 120 counties. It must surely be only a matter of time before credible reports of these creatures come in from every county in the commonwealth. It is interesting to note that considering the large tracts of wilderness available for habitation, tracts so extensive that these creatures could disappear into them and remain unseen and undiscovered for many decades, they don't seem all that interested in hiding from humans. They haunt the fringes of civilization, appearing to startled people seemingly from out of nowhere , and then vanishing back into the darkness without a trace. It seems almost as if they *want* to be seen. Imagine a carload of travelers driving down an isolated stretch of country road late at night. Somewhere up ahead a Bigfoot waits in the trees at the edge of the road. As the car approaches, the creature steps out into the glow of the headlights and races across the road, nimbly jumping a ditch and disappearing up a wooded slope. This scenario has been repeated scores of times in nearly every state in the U.S. and throughout the world. If the creatures desire to remain undiscovered, why don't they simply wait in concealment a few more seconds before leisurely crossing the road *behind* the vehicles, thereby avoiding being seen?

And then there are the atypical reports, the ones that suggest that Bigfoot may not be a normal, flesh and blood animal but something more akin to zooform manifestations that appear as physical entities capable of leaving footprints or a few tufts of hair or of killing the family dog - but are transitory in nature, disappearing back into some mystical plane of existence, some "otherwhere," once they have done whatever it is they do. I find it scientifically untenable to automatically disregard or ignore such reports. Therefore, I have included each report in its entirety, regardless of which paradigm the data may support or challenge.

Readers are invited to review the data and form their own conclusions as to the validity, or lack thereof, in each case. As a seasoned Fortean investigator, however, I have often found that many seemingly unrelated unexplained phenomena, including that of hairy hominids, tend to overlap repeatedly in certain locations. Paranormal researchers call these places "window areas," and it seems there are many in the Bluegrass State. Even if there were only one such window area in the entire world, the fact that multiple anomalies frequently manifest in the same locations does seem to suggest some type of connection. It might also be pointed out that a race of eight- to ten-foot-tall giants, in order to survive, must surely be omnivorous, but to my knowledge not a single report has ever been logged which mentions the discovery of an area inexplicably stripped of flora and fauna, as might be expected if that were the case. Over and over I've listened to Kentucky witnesses tell me that they have shot at the monsters to no apparent effect, or that the creatures disappear before their eyes. They often leave no footprints when they pass, even in soft dirt or mud, as if they were weightless. Other times they leave deep impressions in extremely hard or frozen ground, as if their weight is impossibly immense - even for an eight-foot giant. Certainly these aspects do not fit in with what we might expect from ordinary creatures, regardless of how elusive or sly they might be.

For one thing is clear: thousands of interesting incidents involving these so-called apemen have quietly been taking place in the commonwealth for as long as there have been people here to record them. The question, then, is not whether or not these hirsute giants exist here - for they surely do - but what are they? Are they flesh and blood animals or are they merely part of the human experience, manifestations of some primitive, Jungian wild man archetype, such as the mythological woodwose of medieval Europe? Are they transitory will-'o-the-wisps with no real, lasting substance? Or are they hallucinations, as many claim them to be? This question has been hotly debated for decades with no definitive answer expected any time soon, but for the witnesses who actually encounter these creatures, there can be no doubt as to their very real nature. They kill livestock, chase vehicles, rummage through garbage bins and sometimes leave behind hair, footprints or scat - things that no mere hallucination has ever been accused of doing. That said, the purpose of this work is not to attempt to solve the Bigfoot mystery, but rather to present data in an unbiased manner and let the readers decide for themselves the value of each report.

Whatever the origins of these oversized anomalies may turn out to be in the end, one thing is clear regarding Bigfoot in Kentucky: they *are* here!

ADAIR COUNTY (SOUTH CENTRAL KY)

From the Jan. 30, 1876 edition of the *Louisville Courier-Journal* comes this curious article:

Columbia, Ky.-- Two young men named White, while idly wandering in a large tract of wild, dense forest, in the southeastern part of our county, discovered what they supposed to be a sink-hole or fox-den, and with that idea proceeded to explore it. After a little trouble in making their way through the entrance, the cave (for such it proved to be) became large enough to admit of their walking upright. They had proceeded thus in this passage probably 150 yards, when they emerged into a large and picturesque gallery, the beauty and grandeur of which will rival that of the old Mammoth itself. The room, according to their calculations, is about 150 by 100 feet, and abounds in all the varieties of the stalactite and stalagmite.

But it is not the things we naturally expect to find in caves that we wish to mention particularly, but the curious remains that we discovered therein. In the northeast corner of the first gallery, (which there are five that we will speak of) about five feet from the ground, they noticed some strange characters, or hieroglyphics, neatly carved in the wall, which, upon close examination, proved to be the head-rock of a vault. A few minutes prying served to loosen this and disclose to view the interior of an enclosure in the solid rock of about five by ten feet, which contained the remains of three skeletons which measure eight feet seven and a half inches, eight feet five inches and eight feet four and three quarter inches in length respectively. The heads were lying toward the East, each body parallel to the other. Beside them lay three huge (what looked to be) swords, but they were so decayed that, upon being touched, they crumbled to dust.

After examining the remains closely, but finding nothing that would serve to throw any light on the question as to who and from whence they are, they closed the vault, but in doing so, knocked their torch out, which they had contrived before entering, leaving them in anything but a pleasant predicament. After searching some time for their lost treasure, they concluded to try to escape by feeling their way out, but in this they made the matter worse. They stated that after leaving the first large room they struck a good sized branch, and continued following it until forced to turn into another passage, the stream disappearing suddenly in a huge perpendicular gulch which led them into another spacious hall, the size of which they believe to be quite as large as the first.

Out of this second opening, and through what they conceived to be three others similar at least in size their way seemed to gradually ascend, until their hearts were made glad by the discovery of light ahead, and [they] finally emerged from their ugly confinement through a hole about midway, the cliff of Russell's Creek, having been confined in their subterranean discovery over thirty-eight hours. The whole country *thereabouts is rife with speculations concerning the interesting discovery, and numbers of citizens will visit it as soon as the Messrs. White finish their work of rendering the entrance less difficult to pass.*

The above is a correct account and may be replied on, as the young men are of unimpeachable veracity. With a party from town, your correspondent will start in the morning to further explore and should new curiosities present themselves, will give you the account of an eyewitness."

Nine-foot-tall humanoids bearing immense swords? Could these "people" have devolved over the centuries into a more savage state, making them responsible for some of the reported Bigfoot sightings in Kentucky today? According to the Jan. 5, 1858 edition of the *Adair County News*, another old "Indian" mound located on the farm of one Harrison Robinson was excavated and yielded giant human skeletal remains. If these anomalous skeletal remains are related to the Bigfoot mystery, then the race of creatures that left them have by no means died out.

The following incident was reported to have happened between Columbia and Knifley during the last week of May 2008 involving a big, hairy, manlike creature.

"I am a sixty-three-year-old housewife and caregiver to thirty abused animals," stated Sharon J. (full name on file), a firm believer in the existence of Bigfoot. "My husband and I have been taking care of abused animals out of our own money for thirty-three years. On one of our many trips back and forth to the Adair County Animal Hospital on Route 55 in Columbia I was headed back home to Knifley on 504. I was on the hill going down to cross the bridge over the Green River. I was at the top of this hill and I saw this big, hairy creature cross on the other side of the bridge about halfway up the hill. It looked like a big man, but was covered in hair. It came out of a very heavy [sic] wooded area, crossed the road, then went back to the middle of the road and just sort of stared at me. It then went back to the right side of the road and disappeared into the woods. I was really stunned and said to myself, *I think I have just seen a Bigfoot.* Its arms seemed much longer than any person's would be and the creature just swayed them back and forth.

Well, I wasn't sure I should tell anybody. I did tell my husband. Then I was talking to my very best friend here in Kentucky and I told her what I had seen. What she told me next really shook me up. She claimed she has an uncle who lives very close to this same area where I had the sighting and he often told her he had seen what he thought to be a Bigfoot in the area. I am very sure of what I had seen. That's my story. Every word is true."

Another Adair County resident, this time one who asked to remain anonymous, reportedly saw a similar manlike creature while turkey hunting in Sparksville in 2009. He described the figure as, "a massive thing."

ALLEN COUNTY

Like many other places in Kentucky, Allen County has a long and varied history of high strangeness of just about every sort. The Scottsville area in particular seems especially prone to appearances by hairy humanoids, locally called the Monkey Man. Some locations are even named after them, Monkey Man Hollow, for instance, and Monkey Cave Hollow, mentioned in Loren Coleman's classic *Mysterious America*, (first published by Faber & Faber in 1983). These names were given by the early settlers and reflect the presence of apelike creatures in the area.

An elderly Allen County woman reported she saw one of the strange creatures on two separate occasions in the spring of 2002 outside her home on Durham Springs Road. Both sightings took place at night as the monster, which the witness described as tall and upright, covered in white, somewhat curly hair, entered her front yard and reclined beneath a large beech tree. After a few moments, the woman said, it simply got up and walked "on two feet just like a person would do" back into the woods.

On the second occasion, the woman said she got a shotgun, intending to shoot the thing but was stopped and pulled back into the house by her grandson out of concern for her safety. According to the grandson, a neighbor who lived down the road encountered a similar creature, this one covered in shaggy, brown hair, in broad daylight. When his dogs gave chase the thing leaped over a fence and disappeared into the valley below. It is said that the creature's mournful screams have been heard in the area for generations.

At around 9:00 p.m. one evening in the fall of 2006 yet another lone motorist got a glimpse of the unknown. Neil A. (full name on file) was taking a shortcut to his home in rural Scottsville when the event unfolded.

"I was driving down Bridge Hollow Road, which is a shortcut I take to get from the Barren River Lake area to my house. I was driving slow [sic] because it was night on a one- lane road," he recounted.

As his vehicle topped a small hill, Neil was shocked to see a huge animal dart down an embankment on the right-hand side of the road and cross directly in front of him. It turned briefly and looked back, then struck out across a creek bottom on the left side of the road and disappeared into the woods.

"It stood around seven to eight feet tall," he claimed, "with long, mangy hair all over its body. It was definitely male because, as it turned to look at my car, I could see a protrusion in the genital area." Neil said he did not feel threatened because despite its size, the creature did not act aggressive.

"Every other description I have read makes this creature out to be very aggressive," he said. "I don't think that is the case. When the animal turned and looked at me the only emotion I saw in his eyes was peace. It reminded me of the movie, *Harry and the Hendersons.*" The 1987 film, starring John Lithgow, is about a family who encounters a friendly Bigfoot.

From his brief glimpse, Neil said the creature seemed "very intelligent and humanlike, with feelings and emotions, perhaps even thought." He said the creature appeared calm and did not make any sounds, but he felt sure that he had heard its howls in the area on several occasions. For what it's worth, Scottsville has a history of UFO activity and unexplained animal disappearances.

ANDERSON COUNTY

Deer hunters are often prime witnesses to Bigfoot activity. They are usually in the thickest parts of the woods well before daylight, sitting silently in tree stands high above the forest floor, well camouflaged right down to their scents, awaiting their unwary prey. We will meet several of them in this work. Although some of them hesitate to admit it, more than a few brave Kentucky hunters have been scared out of the woods on occasion.

Anderson County is particularly rich in such stories. In 1993, a huge creature some eight feet tall and covered with long, tangled, brown hair was seen emerging from a large cedar thicket In Lawrenceburg just before dusk. The witnesses, Lynn Hutton and his eight-year- old son, bolted for the safety of their truck when the monster stepped back into the woods. They claimed they could hear it following them and wasted no time exiting the area of Bods Mill Road.

"The appearance of the thing was just as I have seen on TV stories and descriptions I have heard," Hutton stated. "As far as the behavior of it, it was very shy as it appeared not to want to be seen. My son and I had been deer hunting on a local farm. When time came to leave we met up and started back to my truck."

The two had walked about fifty yards down the path when things took a dramatic turn for the surreal. They heard what sounded like something large coming out of the cedar thicket. Then they both saw it.

"It stood approximately eight feet tall and had long, brown hair all over it. We stopped and it stopped at the same time. We didn't know what to say or do," Hutton said.

Father and son were both relieved when the hulking figure stepped back into the thicket and disappeared.

"We got back to my truck as fast as we could, but we could hear something following us the whole time," Hutton said. Luckily, the creature never stepped out again from its concealment. "I haven't told too many people about this because they always laugh at us or start making jokes. I know I'll never forget it as long as I live. It was really scary. That thing was huge," he said.

The Huttons had been hunting on a 100-acre farm near Bypass 127 when the sighting took place. The incident was investigated by my good friend and fellow Bigfoot researcher professor Tony Gerrard, who was able to speak with both father and son.

"Both said that it appeared as if they startled the creature," Gerrard said. "The creature was walking toward them on a path and gave a small jerk when it sighted them. There was no associated odor with the creature. They described the hair as being dirty brown, tangled-looking and "messed up" (the father's words). The son said the hair looked like it was "in dreads" (dreadlocks or locs).

Both witnesses said no facial details were visible due to the hair hanging down in its face. Lynn Hutton estimated the body hair to be about eight inches long. The arms hung to below knee level. He estimated the weight to be 300-plus pounds and described the build as "bigger than the biggest football player but not fat." Neither witness could see anything to indicate gender. The son assumed it was male. The father described the creature's stance as being "very upright, not hunched over. Almost at attention." Both witnesses agreed that the thing had quietly walked backwards until it turned and re-entered the thicket. The father described the creature's gait as being "just like a man."

In 2008 Hutton, 57, a lifelong resident of Anderson County, appeared on a local television documentary concerning the mysteries of the area and spoke of his encounter.

"I was deer hunting with my son. He was eight years old at the time. We were bow hunting, but I had an illegal firearm, a pistol, under my coveralls. I don't like to go into the woods without one, for many reasons."

It was beginning to get dark so Hutton decided it was time to call it a day.

"I told my son we better get back to the truck before it got too dark. All of a sudden, about twenty feet from us -- there's no other words to call it -- a Bigfoot stepped out from the cedar trees."

Hutton said he grabbed his son and pushed him behind him while he locked eyes with the hairy monster. The two stared at each other for a couple of seconds until Hutton decided it was time to take action. As he put it, "By that time I realized I better get my gun out."

Fortunately the creature stepped backwards into the cedar thicket out of which it had emerged, never taking its eyes off the two hunters. Thoroughly unnerved, Hutton said he grabbed his son and wasted no time getting back to his vehicle.

"When we got back to the truck, we got in and left and I haven't been back since," he said.

When asked to describe the creature he claimed that it was very tall, thick and heavy looking, covered with long, matted, dark hair.

"Its face was the same as its whole body, covered in long hair. You could make out its eyes and mouth. Not so much the nose. The hair was just real long, at least a foot long, all over its body. It never took its eyes off us. Never. Not once. It just stepped out of the cedars, we looked at each other for a second or two, then it just stepped right back."

Neither Hutton nor his son said they recalled any other details in association with the sighting.

"I was so scared I didn't notice anything else. My son didn't either. Him being eight years old it didn't scare him as much as it did me. He didn't have any idea what it was. I knew what it was as soon as I saw it. It had to be. It just couldn't have been nothing else [sic]. It was just like looking at a big ape. It was massive, just huge. I'll

never forget it. It scared me so bad I'll remember it for the rest of my life," Hutton said.
He seemed unconcerned that anyone might call him crazy or ridicule his experience.
"They can laugh at me all they want," he said. "It was real. I would walk into any church, put my hand on a stack of Bibles and swear to God that what we saw was real."

Another Anderson County encounter took place in November of 2000 in Lawrenceburg to a witness who wishes to remain anonymous.
"I was deer hunting off of Wildcat Road on the edge of an old field when I heard something large crashing through the woods toward me on the other side of the field. Not a deer. [It] sounded much bigger and deer don't snap off branches and large sticks the way this thing was doing. Just before it would have entered the field where I could see it, the thing stopped and issued the loudest, scariest scream I have ever heard - and I've been roaming the woods for over forty years now. [The] best description I can give would be somewhere between an elk bugling and a wild pig squealing - and it sounded angry. I know that's applying human attributes to it but that's just how it sounded. That first scream lasted maybe five to ten seconds. Then another scream began and I heard whatever it was crashing through the woods back in the direction it had come from, moving very fast and continuing that second, long scream. It was moving so fast that you could hear the sound of the scream fade as it moved away - kind of like the whistle of a train. I could hear it maybe fifteen to twenty seconds before the scream and crashing faded away."
The man claimed that his dogs always became frightened when he took them out by the old tobacco barn on the property and that he'd once found a large pile of scat, full of fur and possibly persimmon seeds, that he couldn't identify.

In June of 2006 another motorist got a glimpse of the elusive creature as he was driving down a lonely road in Lawrenceburg at around 11:00 p.m.
"I was driving down a back road," said Zachary Y. (full name on file). "As I came over a hill I saw a big animal on the side of the road. As I slowed down to see what it was it slowly walked across the road. I went home and right away my mom knew something was wrong. I was pale and was soaked with sweat."
Zachary claimed that the figure was "tall and black." He said he is sure that it wasn't a bear or any other animal native to the region. He also noted that it had long arms and walked slowly. "I can swear on it. I saw what I saw," he said.

Lawrenceburg deer hunter Aaron S. (full name on file) got a pretty good scare just before dawn on the cold, foggy morning of December 5, 2006 as he walked to his deer stand near Wildcat Road. It was about 6 a.m. when Aaron said he heard footsteps behind him.
"I then heard what sounded like screaming - real low-pitched sounding - almost a growl. I got to the stand and climbed up. For about ten minutes whatever this thing was circled the tree I was in and made these sounds. I would have shot at it but I

never could see it because of the dense fog. I don't think it was any animal I know of. I stayed there until about 10 a.m. then left. On the trail back I noticed there were branches broken off about chest high and I felt like someone was watching me the whole way."

The witness recalled that he smelled a "terrible skunk smell" while the creature was prowling in the area. During the previous summer he said he had camped nearby on a farm near Wildcat Road and smelled the same smell and heard what sounded like footsteps tromping around the campsite late at night. He said he was so frightened that he didn't dare look outside of his tent. He said he doesn't feel safe going back there without a gun.

Bigfoot investigator Philip Spencer wrote about a series of unexplained events that took place in Anderson County near Panther Rock in *The Wildman of Kentucky* (Reality Press, 2008). He later made a documentary with the same title. Spencer, a native of the area, claims that in 1970 he found humanlike footprints measuring twenty inches in length near Panther Rock and that he and a group of friends actually observed the creature standing along the edge of a field near a herd of deer one evening.

According to him, one afternoon in the early 1990s a boy and girl who were walking near the Salt River unexpectedly came upon a huge, hairy, man-like creature sitting on a log. They claimed that even while sitting down, the creature was taller than a grown man. The incident allegedly frightened the children's family so badly that they ended up moving away from the area.

Spencer said an anonymous Anderson County man claimed many encounters with the monster over the past decade. He told of hearing his dogs barking excitedly one night, causing him to step outside to see what was going on. He could see his three dogs apparently fighting with something "significantly larger" than they were across a field, just at the edge of his light. The figure, which appeared to have a low-hanging belly, swatted at the dogs as it retreated into the woods. The dogs, still fighting, followed the beast. The witness chose to go back inside his house. The next day he said he found two of his dogs beaten and bloodied in their pens. No trace of the third dog was ever found.

The witness claimed to have heard nocturnal noises that he could not identify many times over the last ten years, and has even managed to record some of them. Many other residents of the area have made similar claims. In 2007 a local farmer and his sons reportedly heard strange sounds in the creek near their house. The sounds were described as being "like deep breathing and a large creature walking in the creek." The next day a twenty-inch track was reportedly found in the creek bed.

At about the same time, Bruce Young and a friend claimed they saw the creature moving along the top of a hill while they were driving down Hammond Creek Road. It was just after sunset, Young said, but still light enough to see the thing. He described the creature as standing at least seven feet tall, massively built, hairy, and man-like in appearance. For an estimated thirty seconds he stood watching it from fifty yards away. He said he got goose bumps when he realized what he was seeing. The figure moved along at an "easy gait" and was covered with long, dark-brown hair.

In the eastern part of the county, just a few miles from Panther Rock, another man-like monster is rumored to haunt the Cedar Brook area. This creature, called "The Cedar Brook Howdy" or simply "Red Eyes," is said to have glowing red eyes and is prone to startling couples parked on lonely roads late at night. Locals say the creature's mournful wails are often heard at night. So powerful and frightening are the cries that it is said that every dog in town howls in fear.

BALLARD COUNTY

Bill M. (full name on file) described an encounter with a Bigfoot that happened during a 1964 family vacation trip to Alabama.

"Myself and two brothers [sic} were asleep in the back seat when we were awakened by my mother's screams. My dad, now ninety-one, and Mom, eighty-six, have told this story many times. It goes like this: While driving, this tall, hairy, man-like thing walked out onto the highway. Dad hit his brights and slammed on the brakes and just missed the thing. As it turned and my dad swerved to miss it, it raised one arm and the long hair on the arm brushed over the windshield on my mom's side of the car. We stopped and it was gone. After my mom calmed down we were on our way. I did not see it but I can say that my mom and dad are not prone to make up tales. I do believe that story they tell to this day."

In January of 1993, at about 2:30 a.m., two more motorists saw an eight-foot-tall, hairy, man-like creature while driving about twenty miles outside of Mayfield. According to the witnesses the "thing" had long, shiny, dark hair covering its entire body. Despite this fact, they both noticed that it had very pronounced muscle definition in its arms and legs. The face was described as humanlike, especially the eyes. It turned its head and watched them as their vehicle passed by a scant two or three feet away.

Both witnesses felt sure that the entity they saw was not a bear or any other known animal. "Its face was what startled me the most," one of the witnesses later stated, "because it had humanlike features, especially the eyes. [They were] not like any animal's eyes I'd ever seen before. Its eyes followed us as we passed."

BARREN COUNTY

Nighttime "yowler" activity was reported from the five-star Diamond Caverns Resort & Golf Club in Mammoth Cave State Park in the summer of 2003. Hairy humanoid monsters are often described as making "yowling" sounds. As an aside, the Colorado

Avalanche mascot is a Bigfoot named Yowler.

Nearly four years after the report of eerie noises at the golf club, a deer hunter named Chris (full name on file) saw something he said he would never forget near Cave City at around 4 a.m. on the morning of January 3, 2007. He was getting ready to come down from his deer stand, looking everything over to make sure that he had gathered all his deer-hunting equipment, when he heard an ungodly high-pitched scream come from the nearby woods.

"Then I smelled this awful smell, like something was dead," Chris later stated. "It was then that I caught sight of this thing out of the corner of my eye." The "thing" was a man-like, hairy giant that stood eight feet-tall. Chris remained in his stand, which was situated fifteen feet above the ground in a wooded area of Lazy Acre Estates, and watched the creature. After the thing screamed, he said everything became extremely quiet. The rotten stench that filled the air was so strong that he felt nauseous. The dark-colored, hairy creature was walking from left to right in front of his stand. Chris said it walked upright, like a man, swinging its arms much more dramatically than a human would.

Chris said the thing's hands hung down to around knee level. It had broad shoulders and a big, bulky body. Due to the minimal lighting conditions he couldn't make out any facial details nor could he approximate its hair length. The creature paused a moment directly in front of his location then proceeded to walk quietly away from his tree stand. The witness later claimed that he has heard similar screams five or six times over the past two years while hunting on this private property located near Mammoth Cave.

Four months later, on May 7, 2007, another Barren County hunter got more than he bargained for when he saw something that he could not identify approaching his hunting area.

"I had went up [sic] to where I deer hunt," the anonymous witness said, "and was checking the area to look for any deer movement, like trails or rubs, and I noticed that several trees were moved into, like huts, or shelters and I smelled an awful smell. Then I heard something walking so I laid down and crawled under some brush. The smell got worse, and I seen this tall animal, almost like a gorilla. I laid as still as possible. I had brought my gun just in case I ran into a bobcat, but I was so scared that I didn't move. After around ten minutes it walked off. I waited around three more minutes and went to get up and this scream that sounded like the gates of Hell had opened. I took the safety off my gun and slowly walked to my car then left the area as fast as I could."

He later described the animal as about eight feet tall with a slightly slumped-over posture, arms that reached to knee level, and covered with hair the color of tree bark.

At around midnight on July 25, 2007, a couple intending on taking a late-night stroll near a wooded pond in Cave City had their outing cut unexpectedly short. Amber and Chris Page were driving near Mammoth Cave and decided to take a moonlight stroll around a pond trail.

A Kentucky Bigfoot illustration by the author, drawn from witness descriptions of the elusive giants.

"As we pulled up the lights hit something red and it moved, like a pair of red eyes," Chris later stated. "We thought nothing about it. We got out of the car and heard this grunt."

The grunt was followed by the sound of heavy footsteps running in their direction. Unnerved, the two nature lovers dashed back to their car and beat a hasty retreat.

BATH COUNTY

The elusive creature showed up in Bath County on June 15, 2007. On that day, two brothers, who wish to remain anonymous, were returning after a long day of setting tobacco in Sharpsburg when something strange attracted their attention.

"My brother and I were coming in from the fields when we saw something running across the hay field heading toward the creek. But it stopped and rolled around in the grass for about fifteen minutes like it was trying to scratch its back," one of the men said. They claimed the creature was seven feet tall and covered with brown hair. It stood on two legs and walked like a human.

BELL COUNTY

In the late 1950s two teenage boys spotted what they later realized was a Bigfoot high in the mountains of Cary, near the mouth of an old coal mine. Speaking in 1998, one of the witnesses described the creature as being eight or nine feet tall and apelike, with gray or white hair.

"[We] noticed something standing right at the mouth of the mine. It appeared to be a gray or white-looking ape-type animal on two legs, with one arm hanging over a wooden cross timber, which would be about eight to nine feet tall," he said.

The two ran to tell adults what they had seen but when they returned the animal was long gone.

"I was born in Cary and never saw anything like what I saw that day with a neighbor boy. We both saw the same thing at the same time. The thing scared us to death. It watched us and we watched it. No mistake. Whatever it was, [it] was alive! We may have been young but we both know what we saw that day, and I still remember like it happened yesterday," he said.

Also in the Bell County, this time in 1966, hairy monsters were encountered on Booger Mountain near Brown's Creek in Hen Holler, near Pineville. One witness, who said he had disturbed the thing as it was raiding a fruit orchard early in the morning around 2 or 3:00 a.m., described the creature as extremely tall and hairy with "green, glowing eyes that reflected red in the moonlight." It stood there on two legs like a man and stared back at him. Then it "started to grunt real low in its chest," the man said.

It gave off a loud whistling sound then took off, still walking upright on two legs, across the field and into the woods. His mother didn't believe him when he told the story, he said, until she saw it herself as she was walking home from church that following Sunday night. It was sitting down like it was eating, she later claimed. When it saw her it stood straight up and took off running like a person. It moved so quickly that it was gone before her eyes could follow it into the woods. She also described it as having green eyes, its body covered with hair that was "moving around with the wind." She also stated that she heard it whistling to another creature, which answered back.

Could these creatures be the reason Booger Mountain got its name?

According to two anonymous Bell County men, Chenoa residents have been aware of the presence of the hirsute creatures for generations. In the late fall of 1982 the men saw one of the creatures peering at them from behind a tree not fifteen feet away. It was eight feet tall, one of the witnesses claimed, with a mix of human and ape characteristics. It had long arms that hung down to its knees and large, black hands "about five times the size of human hands."

It was dusk, though not yet dark when the incident occurred, but strangely, the thing's eyes were glowing red. Most of the face was covered with dark-colored fur, and the skin around the thing's deep-set eyes appeared black. The ears were visible as well, and were of a lighter color.

According to this witness, the area has a history of creature sightings and activity. He said something powerfully strong broke into a root cellar, tearing the door off its hinges. He said two men he knew were chased down off the mountain and their pack of hunting dogs were whipped by something that was "screaming and making a terrible commotion." These same dogs had killed a bear and were not usually afraid of any animal, the witness stated.

"One of the men was a two-term Vietnam vet and it scared him so bad he threw his gun down and ran! It took them two weeks to find their dead dogs or recover the ones still alive," he said.

The creature was seen yet again in Pineville in 2002 by two late-night motorists, one of whom, eyewitness Joey C. (full name on file), wrote: "At the time me and a friend [sic] were working third shift in Corbin, Kentucky. We would meet up at my house and carpool to work. We pulled out onto Highway 25 toward Corbin, and about a mile before crossing the Bell County/Knox County line we saw something. I was driving along not really paying attention too much when all of a sudden my friend almost jumps in my lap as we pass by something big and hairy walking on two legs. I swerved my truck across two lanes, almost running back off the road on the other side. We were too scared to turn back and have really kept this to ourselves because we thought people would think we're crazy."

Joey could only describe the thing as big, with dark fur.

Bell County was also the reported scene of a very bizarre 2004 incident involving a mysterious something being struck by an automobile driven by a woman named Angela Barth.

Date: First week of December, 2004
Time: Shortly after 9 p.m.
Location: Route 461 between Somerset and Mount Vernon.

"My friend and I left Somerset and were looking for 461," Mrs. Barth later told me. "I missed the turn as the road was pitch black." She said there were no streetlights and hardly any houses around to provide some light.

"I decided to do a U-turn since there was no way around to go back to the road. I started pulling over to the shoulder and saw a dead cat. The very next instant I saw what I can only describe as a huge boulder with hair! There was no way to avoid impact [but] impact did not happen. Instead my car went up and over. Instantly after my car came to a stop a gagging smell filled the car. It was not the smell of hitting a rotten animal. It was a combination of smells but very nauseating. My friend and I became very ill in the days after. She was a month in recovering from the cough and lung congestion. We did not stay to inspect anything because of the smell. It was absolutely horrific."

Mrs. Barth described the object as "white-ish" with no visible legs, arms, head, or feet.

"There was only a very large ball of fur. I pulled over at the first gas station and there was hair hanging off my tail pipe. The smell of the car filled up the parking lot and was very embarrassing. My car sustained seven hundred dollars worth of damage to the underneath and my husband fixed everything. I believe I hit a Bigfoot. No doubt in my mind."

Mrs. Bart said she knows two people who witnessed Bigfoots "balled up" by the side of a road and beside a bike trail, respectively.

After speaking to Mrs. Barth many times over the course of the next couple of months I was shocked to learn that the most bizarre aspect of her experience was not running over a possible Bigfoot, but something else entirely. She was keeping something about the encounter to herself that she thought was too unbelievable to tell anyone. Luckily, my unequaled Southern charm and rugged good looks soon won her over. I asked her to tell me again what had happened that night, and this time to not leave anything out. She wrote: "Only a very few people know about this. Having read what you and your family endured I know you will be interested."

She was referring to my family's harrowing 1975 encounters with a giant, hairy, red-eyed creature called the Spottsville Monster. The episodes continued for nearly a year and were so frightening that my parents moved the family out of our home on Mound Ridge Road in Henderson County.

She continued, "Two years ago in December I was coming back from the hospital in Somerset, Kentucky. My daughter had back surgery and we were leaving about 9 p.m. I was driving this pitch-black road to get to [Interstate] 75. I missed my turn and thus had to turn around. I was going to make a U-turn and started to leave the road onto the shoulder to negotiate the turn. I saw a dead cat and then a HUGE furry ball. I mean it was huge! It was too late; I hit it. If you have ever had an accident you know the helpless feeling. After I came to a stop the stench filled my car. It was nauseating beyond belief. Not rotten just nasty. My friend started gagging and begged me to hurry up and leave. I didn't even know if the car would start! It did and I made the turn. I cannot tell you how bad the car smelled and continued to smell." The pair went to the nearest gas station to inspect the damage.

"I was so embarrassed because my car was stinking so badly you could smell it all over the parking lot," Mrs. Barth wrote. "I looked under the car and there was hair hanging off my tail pipe. Gads! It all stunk so bad!"

At this point, her story made a strange turn, even stranger than running over a giant, stinking, mound of fur.

"I looked at the clock and we had left the hospital an hour and a half before. It was ten thirty and we had only gone about thirteen miles since leaving that hospital! We didn't do one thing but leave the hospital, miss the road we needed by a few hundred feet, hit something, and then turn around!

"Now not being able to account for that much time is unnerving. We tried every way to figure it out. We both got serious lung congestion after this and I was sick for a week or more. My friend was sick for a month or longer."

Mrs. Barth said her friend's lungs recovered after someone recommended that she take medicinal herbs.

"My car had seven hundred dollars worth of damage to the exhaust system and whatever that is that holds the wheels on underneath. My husband could not understand how I could hit something so big and not see it! I saw the cat but not the big, furry ball," she said, concluding, "This was hands-down my strangest experience."

Mrs. Barth was responsive to further questioning and even added some new insight. She reported, "In the seconds before impact I saw the dead kitty and then the big furry ball. It was whitish, rather like a polar bear and all one color. I saw absolutely nothing but the ball. No legs, arms [or] head. It looked like a huge ball of hair. It was as high as the hood [of the car] and ball-shaped. I had no idea at the time what it was. I didn't even think about it, which I now find very unusual.

"I didn't actually turn around to see anything. I was in the process of leaving the road to make a U-turn when I hit it. I merely finished the U-turn after the smell started and found the car actually would start. I do recall wondering if the car was too messed up to even run but I didn't care. I just wanted to get away from the smell. I wasn't concerned one iota what was out there!"

Mrs. Barth said she and her friend weren't at all frightened. In fact they were laughing hysterically.

"It was just weird. Neither one of us looked to see what I hit or even thought about it! We didn't suspect anything was strange at all until all the time was missing. We thought the smell was a bit excessive but that was all. It was a calm kind of thing. I cannot describe it. Ninety unaccounted-for minutes and we were both calm upon discovering it!

"I have no idea when we realized it was most probably a Sasquatch we hit. We certainly didn't even entertain the thought at first. It was on the way home. I clearly recall we were near Lexington when something hit us both what had happened. I can't explain most of it. The missing time was the clue that something extraordinary had just happened.

"The hair was there. I didn't care at the time. It did not occur to me about what it could have been and I didn't know about the missing time at the time I looked under the car. I pulled over at the very first gas station to see if major stuff was leaking out. It was gagging just to be near my car. I looked at the clock after I got back in the car and made the discovery. You see it took awhile for the whole thing to sink in. I cannot explain it at all. Of course hair was hanging off my tailpipe wasn't unexpected because I had just hit something big and hairy! Maybe that is woman's logic. I don't know. I just know it didn't matter to me at all. I was three hundred miles from home with the real possibility my car was all jacked up! Actually my car *was* all jacked up! I forgot to mention the oil leak it got in the first letter. I couldn't drive it after that until my husband fixed it. Geez, he was so aggravated with me! I was so thankful to have made it home."

Mrs. Barth said she didn't recall seeing any blood on the car when she got home and she didn't remember if any hair was still hanging from the tailpipe. "I don't think I killed it. I hit it is all. I think it got really pissed off and skunked us! Probably cussed us good for ninety minutes! I'd say it is more like it needed help and time to get it. I think the cat was a snack it had just caught and maybe put down when my car was coming. My daughter saw one in a ball on the side of the road several years ago. My daughter-in-law saw one in a ball when she was a kid. It was hiding on the side of a bicycle trail all balled up! I think they ball up when they want to get on the down low! If you crouched down, tucked your head down and got into the best ball you can with your body, that is precisely what we saw."

Mrs. Barth said she could think of no explanation for the time loss. She offered another description of the thing she hit: "A huge snowball all rolled up...with hair! No limbs at all like a deer or cow would be all askew in death on the highway."

Despite being December, she said it was a mild 60 degrees without a trace of snow on the ground, adding, "I wish it had been a snowball I hit!"

Many things can be learned about phenomena such as these when one learns to ask the right questions. It turns out Mrs. Barth and her entire family have had a long history of brushes with the unexplained, from Bigfoot to UFOs and spectral, or ghostly encounters spanning two different states and several decades. I assured her that I had spoken to many people such as herself - people who seem to have multiple experiences with unknown phenomena. I was one of them myself. As such I could not readily disregard statements about these atypical creatures. Mrs. Barth claims that although it bothers her sometimes she has learned to live with the knowledge that there are ninety unaccounted-for minutes gone from her life. She feels that whatever happened during that period of lost time, she wasn't harmed in any way. She said neither she nor her friend have any plans to undergo hypnosis in an attempt to try and find out what actually happened to them that night.

BOONE COUNTY

According to the *Kentucky Post*, members of the Jones family encountered a shorter-than-usual version of Bigfoot, perhaps a young male, one night in March of 1980. The incident took place in Big Bone Lick, the birthplace of American vertebrate paleontology, where herds of huge mammals once roamed the mineral springs and swamps during the late Pleistocene.

The creature that the Joneses saw was reportedly four or five feet tall, weighing an estimated 300 pounds, with broad shoulders and a flat face. It was bold enough to approach the family's mobile home, shaking the door and causing much alarm to the people inside. When the thing attempted to overturn the trailer it was fired upon by the man of the house - to no effect. It simply ran away on all fours and made its escape by leaping into the nearby Ohio River and swimming north. A police investigation allegedly revealed nothing save for the fact that the area has a history of monster activity. The Jones family claims to have had several more run-ins with the creature on the property. Several articles about sightings of the creature in the area have been written. The following is reprinted from Ron Schaffner's *Creature Chronicles* #2. Summer 1980. It describes an incident in Big Bone, an unincorporated community in southern Boone County, about twenty-five miles southwest of Cincinnati.

Subject: Large black unknown animal sighted on 3/31/80 at 12:30 - 1:00 a.m. and on 4/1/80 at 11:30 p.m.
Witnesses: Jackie Jones and Dave Stulz, 283 AA Ryle Road
Investigators: Ron Schaffner, Earl Jones and John Daily
Police Investigators: Officer Prindle, Officer R. Meyers, Officer J. Whalen and Deputy Sheriff J. Fisk

Jackie, Dave, and son Jason were ready to retire for the night when they suddenly heard an unusual sound coming from the boat dock. They said the noise sounded like a combination of a lion and elephant roar. Jackie turned on the outside light connected to the boat dock when they saw the outline of something moving in the weeds. The object was estimated to be between 2-3 feet wide, around 300 pounds, five foot [sic] in height and seemed to have a flat face. However, no eyes, ears or snout could be seen due to the darkness. The two witnesses also said that this animal tried to jerk their trailer home around, as if trying to push it over. Dave decided to go out and investigate. When the animal advanced toward him, he got scared and shot at the creature with his shotgun. The creature appeared to jump back into the river (the Ohio River backwater) and quietly swam toward the east.

4/1/80 - Dave was talking on the phone with investigator Earl Jones when something was heard outside the trailer. Jackie called for Dave and again he went outside to see what the disturbance was, hoping to get a better look this time. At this point, Jackie began to talk with Jones in a nervous and frightened manner. She was worried about her son possibly being harmed by this creature. Meanwhile, Dave saw the creature jumping over a ditch and again escaping into the water.

Previous encounter - In June of 1979, this same trailer was occupied by Vicki Jones (Jackie's sister). She had an intercom connected to the boat dock and was hearing strange sounds that kept getting louder. Her dog began to howl and seemed scared of something. Then all of a sudden her trailer started shaking. The dishes started to fall off the shelves. Was this the same animal, or something else?

Through local legends and old newspaper clippings, John Daily found out that this creature (or one like it) had been seen in 1950. He was also able to find several articles on a creature that was seen in the area on several occasions over the years. Local residents dubbed it "Satan."

Case Findings/Conclusions - No definite physical evidence was ever found other than the spent shells from Dave's shotgun that were found lodged in a large tree down by the river. So, Dave did fire off a few rounds, as he claimed. Various markings on the ground could not be distinguished as any prints. The Boone County Recovery Team sent divers into the river, but could not find any evidence. Earl did not hear anything unusual while talking with Jackie. We are left with the testimony of the two witnesses, who seemed very sincere and were still frightened as they relayed their encounters to us on separate occasions. Their story never changed. We never mentioned the term "Bigfoot" because that fact was never established. However, the Boone County police officers asked us about the possibility.

A Richwood woman allegedly had a run-in with a Bigfoot creature in the summer of 1994 in the back yard of her home in the Arbor Glen Estates subdivision. She said she was out walking her dog, when he suddenly stopped and began growling at the fence line beyond which was a small creek. The woman looked to see what the dog was barking at and straight in front of her, about fifty feet on the other side of the fence, was a most unusual and frightening figure.
"I distinctly remember the creature," she later said. "He was tall; well over six feet high. He was an off-white color, with shaggy hair that dangled a little bit - maybe three to five inches long in places. The face was a mix between a human and a primate. Not an ape and not a human dressed up."
It stood up from a squatting position and looked at her, revealing a muscular body with a short neck and long arms that reached to mid-thigh. After staring at each other for a few minutes, the witness claimed, the thing turned and ran off into the woods. She said she did the same – fleeing straight back inside her house. The woman recalled that her father had seen a similar creature - also tall and off-white colored - some time earlier near a creek on Shady Lane in Crittenden.

BOYD COUNTY

"I will always remember this because it still sends shivers down my spine," wrote Ashland resident, Dawn C. (full name on file). It was just after midnight one evening back in August of 1994. "My boyfriend and I was [sic] driving to his house from mine and we were on 1-68. This was when 1-68 had no homes built and no street lights as it does now. I was talking to my boyfriend when I noticed he was really quiet. He slowed down and said, 'Did you see that?' and I said, 'See what?' He hit his brakes and when I turned around and looked out the back window I saw a seven to eight-foot-tall shadow looking at us while it was crossing the road. I was terrified and he hit the gas and we were gone. I know what we saw and it was a Bigfoot."
Dawn further described the thing as being entirely covered with hair that was either dark brown or black.
Two more Ashland residents, this time a mother and son, reported seeing an

extremely tall creature with long, stringy hair as it crossed a road one night in 1998. According to the mother, its stride was so immense that the monster crossed the road - a distance of at least twenty feet - in only two steps.

Ashland is an active area for hairy monsters, it seems. Seven years earlier in 1991 a similar creature, also described as having long, stringy hair, chased two witnesses to their car as they were investigating a local bridge that had a reputation for being haunted. The creature ran on all fours but when it stood up, they claimed it was at least sixteen feet tall!

A smaller version of Bigfoot was seen in Boyd County by a local pastor, the Rev. Joshua Sparks, and his five-year-old son one October evening around 8:00 p.m. in 2006.
"My son and I were walking in the woods," Sparks later told me, "off the country road known as Greenfield Road which connects to Shopes Creek and Hurricane Hollow. We had recently discovered some tree breaks and teepee structures in that area. As we walked my son pointed and said, 'Daddy, there's Bigfoot!' I said, 'where?' and he pointed to a location about fifty yards above us on a ridge. There was a Bigfoot creature standing at the top of this ridge. It acknowledged that we were there with a grunt. It then proceeded to break in half a small tree and began hitting a larger tree with a stick. We stood there frozen and not wanting to leave. It then began walking toward us and it let out a loud moan/scream and grunted. I felt then that we had worn out our welcome and I took my son and slowly walked away. We were there maybe five minutes at the most." Sparks described the creature as covered with black hair, upright, at least seven and one-half feet tall, and weighing about 350 to 400 pounds.
"It was dark and my flashlight didn't grant me the ability to see its face," he said. "It did have a distinct odor to it. An outdoor odor."

An alleged Bigfoot print was found in Catlettsburg, also in Boyd County, in late January of 2007 after an unidentified couple heard a disturbance outside their bedroom window the previous night.

BOYLE COUNTY

"I thought I would share a true story with you involving my grandfather and a Bigfoot encounter that happened in the early nineteen-forties and again in the fifties and sixties, Terry (full name on file) told me on Dec. 9, 2009.
"My family is from the Forkland region of western Boyle County near Mitchellburg. This part of the country has thousands of acres of timberland and large hills we call 'knobs.' Even today this part of Kentucky has areas that are not habitable due to rigged terrain. My grandfather died in the late nineteen-seventies having lived into his

eighties and I heard him tell this story many, many times.

"In rural Kentucky in the nineteen-forties work and money were nearly nonexistent and, with him having young children to feed, it was necessary to hunt for wild game or deer for food. One afternoon, while hunting in a valley along the North Rolling Fork in an area called "Scrub Grass," he told of pushing through some wild willows growing along the banks of North Rolling Fork to find an animal across the stream standing on two feet and covered head to toe with black hair. Grandpa said the animal appeared to be young, standing only about three feet in height [with a] muscular build. He said the animal's face wasn't distinguishable due to hair covering it.

"The animal did not appear to be frightened and stood motionless. Grandpa was so taken aback by the sight of this animal [that he] said his first reaction was to shoot. But he doubted his ammo, being more suited for small game, would bring the animal down, and he feared two things: the animal might charge toward him, or there might be more of these things just out of sight in the willow thicket that grew along both sides of the stream.

"So he very slowly backed away from the animal and back into the willows behind him, and then [he] ran, hoping the animal would not follow him. The next morning Grandpa took some men back to the area where he had the encounter to find numerous human-looking footprints of various sizes on a sandbar along the bank of the stream.

"Grandpa knew the forest well and always believed the animals migrated like birds at certain times of the year. He believed these animals sometimes slept in trees and, on numerous hunting trips he told of seeing them swing from treetop to treetop. When food was scarce due to drought he believed missing chickens in the night or torn-off screens to a smokehouse were [caused by] the animals pillaging for food.

"As a child sitting on the front porch with my grandparents on hot fall evenings in the early nineteen-fifties and -sixties, after sundown we would hear wailing sounds deep in the forest and Grandpa would tell Grandma to take us kids inside. The area has many residents now and I moved away long ago, but I would imagine once the sun goes down at certain times of the year these animals could easily slip through the woods undetected by anyone other than maybe a barking dog or two."

"I was walking through my neighborhood, Bluegrass Estates, which is next to a large farm," writes Dakota Poff, describing a sighting that took place near Danville on the afternoon of January 27, 2008. "I looked over and about thirty yards away there was a hairy, black creature about eight foot tall [sic] staring at me with coal-black eyes. It stared at me for about thirty-five seconds then turned and ran away."

BRACKEN COUNTY

A huge, hairy, man-like creature was seen in Bracken County on August 17, 2008. A man I'll call Grant (real name on file), a local deer hunter, claims to have encountered it at 6:30 that morning in the woods of rural Augusta.

"I was squirrel-hunting Sunday morning and was sitting on the hill," he said. "I heard some movements over [on] the other side of the hill and he walked up."

Grant described the beast as eight feet tall, heavily built, and covered in wet, dark reddish-brown hair. The reason he called the thing "he" was because he said he could see its genitals. Grant says the creature didn't see him at first. When it approached to within twenty yards Grant said he held up his rifle and "shot up in the air to scare him. I didn't want to shoot him because I didn't think my .22 could kill him and I didn't want a pissed-off Bigfoot attacking me."

Grant said the creature let out a huge gorilla-like bellow then stared right at him for a few seconds before running away. He said he could add no further details other than that its eyes were covered by hair.

BREATHITT COUNTY

On Sept. 15, 1975, Bigfoot put in an appearance in Breathitt County. The creature was claimed to be around eight feet tall with a slightly human-looking, hair-covered face. It fled into the woods when the anonymous witness stepped outside to investigate. The thing's mournful vocalizations have allegedly been heard by area residents on many occasions over the years and are said to sound "like something from the pits of Hell." Breathitt, like many other Kentucky counties, has a history of reported monster activity.

Over in Hazard, in November 2001, a large, hairy, upright "critter" was seen crossing the road one night in front of startled motorists. Seventeen years earlier, in January 1984, small, barefoot, child-size footprints were discovered crossing a frozen creek in Jackson. No children were reported missing from the area.

The late Michael Paul Henson, well known Kentucky writer and folklorist, wrote in *Tragedy at Devil's Hollow and other Kentucky. Ghost Stories,* (Cockrel Corp. Publishers, 1985) of a bizarre skeleton found at Holley Creek in Breathitt County in 1965, which he was personally able to examine. The remains may or may not have some relation to the subject at hand.

A man named Kenneth White, while constructing cattle stalls under a large, overhanging rock ledge near his home, came upon the perfectly preserved skeletal remains of what he at first took to be an Indian, as it was buried facing East, a well-known Native American custom. When White noticed some atypical aspects of the burial, he asked Henson to help further examine the strange bones, which were covered with a peculiar white powdery substance that disappeared when touched.

Upon reassembling the bones the two were amazed to find that the unusual fellow, in life must have stood at least eight feet nine inches tall. Moreover, the arms were abnormally long with large hands while the feet seemed small by comparison. The skull measured an astounding thirty inches in circumference. But the most unusual aspect of the skeleton was the facial structure, the likes of which neither man had ever before seen. The eye and nose sockets were slits rather than cavities, and the area where the jawbone would have ordinarily been hinged where it met the skull was solid bone. Seemingly, the creature had never been able to open its mouth to eat or speak!

No weapons, tools or clothing were found with the bones, which, according to Henson's account, occupied a position five feet below ground. This led him to surmise that they had been placed there at least three hundred years prior to White's discovery. Strangely, Henson related that the burial site looked like it was very recent, with no sign of dark-colored soil usually associated with the presence of decaying human tissue.

The two assumed the remains were those of an extraordinarily large, deformed Indian. In the same area some twenty years earlier, a local farmer plowed up a sixty-pound, double-edged stone axe, and a twenty-inch flint blade. White later re-buried the peculiar bones and no official examination of them was ever conducted.

Henson died in March 1995 without ever disclosing the exact location of the burial site.

According to author-investigator Mary Green, a lone motorist saw Bigfoot illuminated in his headlights on the night of November 7, 2001 while driving through Hazard. The witness claimed that he saw an eight- to nine-foot-tall "hairy beast" as it crossed the road in front of him at around 7:00 p.m. He described it as a cross between a monkey and a bear with very dark-colored fur. It made sounds like that of a large bear, he said. After he arrived at the spot where the creature had crossed the road, he claimed that he stopped the car and got out to investigate, only to find a line of footprints some twenty inches in length along the roadside.

BRECKINRIDGE COUNTY

Two more late-night motorists got an eyeful of the unknown while driving through Cloverport in Breckenridge County. "Me and my son [sic] were driving down a country road around 11:00 p.m. on 12-21-07," wrote Jim (full name on file). "We had just turned around and was heading back to the city when we both saw something out of the passenger side window. We both said, 'what was that?' at the same time. I stopped the truck and backed up and could see a large object about eighty yards away from the truck. As we backed up, the object continued to look at us. I stopped the truck, rolled down the window and shined a flashlight at the object. It then slowly turned and walked into the woods."

Jim wrote that he and his son drove back to town, got one of his friends, and drove back out to the spot where they had seen the creature. They walked down to the edge of the woods when all of a sudden they heard a growl or roar. They stood frozen as they heard something walk deeper into the woods. Jim described the thing he saw as about six and a half to seven feet tall with its entire body covered in fur. It walked upright like a man and didn't seem to be in any hurry at all.

Yowling sounds in the night have reportedly been heard in the same general area for at least twenty years.

CALLOWAY COUNTY

Another late-night sighting of a Bigfoot crossing the road was reported in 1968 in Murray, Calloway County. The witnesses were Dr. Richard Young and Charles Denton. Two more Calloway County residents reportedly found themselves in the same situation one evening six years later, in 1974, as they drove through the wooded bottomlands.

"My boyfriend and myself were taking a drive after work," an anonymous woman said more than thirty years after the sighting occurred. "I had recently gotten my license and we loved to drive down Rattling Bridge Road. We called it Rattling Bridge Road because it had a wooden bridge, and the slats rattled as you crossed it."

It was late evening, just getting dusk when, seemingly from out of nowhere, a figure crossed the road about 150 yards in front of the young couple. Speechless, they watched as it took a few deliberate strides and was across the road, disappearing into the darkened woods along the creek. The woman recalled that the thing walked upright and was six or seven feet tall, covered with long, unkempt-looking, dark-colored fur. Its shoulders were thick, she said, and it walked with them "hunkered forward a bit."

We will hear almost this same description repeated over and over again from all parts of the state. But we are not done with Calloway County yet.

An eleven-year-old boy vacationing with his family in Hamlin was the next to view the beast, or one like it, in August of 1975. Hamlin sits on the shores of Kentucky Lake in the extreme southwestern part of the state. These mysterious creatures have been encountered all along the shores of this lake and those of the nearby Lake Barkley, as well as in every county that borders their waters.

The boy, now an adult, described his encounter: "My family and I were on vacation in western Kentucky, near Kentucky Lake. For some reason, I was alone. I don't remember what I was doing, but I heard some noise coming from a creek nearby."

He looked out the window and couldn't believe his eyes. There, standing with its back to him, was a huge, hairy creature seven or eight feet tall, covered in dark-brown hair. Curious, at first, as to what it could be, he got up and quietly walked out the back door and down the steps. At this point, he recalled, he realized what he was looking at and panicked. As he hurriedly backed up the steps he stumbled and the back door banged wide open. On hearing this, the creature looked at him and took a step in his direction. Terrified, the boy ran inside, locked the door and laid down on the floor next to the wall so the creature couldn't see him if it looked in the window.

Strangely, his memory ends here. He could not recall any strange sounds being associated with the sighting, or if the creature had approached the house out of curiosity or some more sinister motive. The reason why his memory of the incident ends so abruptly also remains a mystery. It could be overlooked if it happened only once but such is not the case; we will see this disturbing facet of some creature encounters again later on.

CAMPBELL COUNTY

Did Bigfoot visit Alexandria, the county seat of Campbell County, on the night of November 6, 2008? One resident thinks it did. Ryan B. (full name on file) claims that at around 8:30 p.m., as he and his wife were relaxing in front of the television, their dog suddenly ran to the front door, "barking like crazy." His wife got up and they heard a noise outside that sounded like a bird screeching. Ryan hit the mute button so he could hear it better. He immediately got up and walked out the front door onto the porch where he heard "something big" running down the hill about twenty yards away, "crashing sticks and leaves."

Ryan ran back into the house to grab a flashlight, then returned outside and walked to the fence that separated his yard from a deep hollow. He said everything was deathly quiet as he scanned the area with the flashlight.

"I didn't see anything. I'm thinking in my mind that whatever it was is already long gone. I looked around for about thirty seconds then it screamed at me from about fifty yards away. Scared me real bad. The hair on the back of my neck stood up. I've lived in the county my whole life and have never heard anything like this. It sounded like a peacock screaming and I definitely got the feeling that it was warning me off."

It screamed again, deeper and more guttural this time, then ran off deeper into the woods heading toward the Licking River. It sounded like a bull running through the woods, Ryan said. The witness claimed that, although its screech sounded somewhat like a peacock, it definitely was not a bird of any kind.

"It tromped heavily through the woods," he said; "It did not fly."

CARROLL COUNTY

Daniel S. (full name on file) was one of a group of five friends who encountered a Bigfoot on the night of June 1, 2007, on a tobacco farm surrounded by woods on the outskirts of Sanders. He claims that at 11:17 p.m. that evening they were able to observe the beast for nearly ten minutes. "At about 10:45 I was out giving water to my friend's billy goat, while my friends were at a little campfire we had built," he said. "As I was finishing up watering the goat all of a sudden I smelled this foul odor. "

Daniel was familiar with the way the goat smelled and he knew the odor wasn't coming from its pen. He shrugged it off and returned to the campfire, not bothering to mention the smell to the group, but ten minutes later one of the girls in the group complained that she smelled something sour. After a couple of minutes the smell was so overpowering that the entire group was complaining.

"Then immediately we heard what we thought was a coyote until, at the end of the howl, there were three loud grunts," he said.

At this point the girls wanted to go back up to the house.

"As we were getting ready to leave we could hear something in the woods close to us. We were just getting ready to put out the fire when, in the distance, we could see an upright figure," he said.

The group figured it was the father of one of their buddies playing a practical joke and they relaxed a little. They soon realized that it was far too large to be their friend's father. In fact, it was far too large to be any human being. They hurriedly packed up their belongings, keeping a watchful eye on the figure to make sure it wasn't coming any closer, and hurriedly vacated the area.

"As we were leaving I watched the creature cross the field and enter the woods on the other side," Daniel said. He described it as dark-colored and anywhere from six to eight feet tall. The thing that stood out the most to him was the girth of the body, which he said was from three to three and-one-half feet wide. The foul odor, he said, smelled like a mixture of soured milk and mildew.

CARTER COUNTY

Many locations throughout the state are what paranormal experts call "window areas," where multiple seemingly unrelated phenomena tend to overlap. Seemingly anything goes in these locations. Here we have a case where an entire family endured years of terrifying brushes with the unknown, including large, man-like creatures that always seemed to stay just out of sight. The following testimony is from an anonymous man who lived in such a place.

Time: 1980 - 1983
Location: six miles east of Grayson, on US 60 and State Route 207

"I lived in Carter County, Kentucky, in a small community named Rush. I lived in a small hollow with a partially graveled lane that dead-ended at my driveway. This land is hills with pine, oak, and other common eastern Kentucky trees and brush growth. [The] land has strip mines with several ponds scattered through it. There are houses and small family-type farms.

"In 1980 we - my wife and five children - moved to the undeveloped fifty-plus acres that belonged to my wife's father until his death in 1973. We had lived there for about two or three months when I started hearing things that made me a little uncomfortable but not frightened. There were nights [when] the dogs would bark and carry on but would not go after whatever it was they were barking at. And we - the entire family - would even run and hide when 'it' came too close to the house. I asked a couple of the neighbors and they would not discuss it, saying it was just a deer or bear. Yes, there were deer, and a bear was killed within a mile or so of the area but any type of hunter would know that this was very unlikely.

"I hunted and walked in the woods a lot just to enjoy the cool temperatures of the forest and to be out alone. While I was hunting I noticed a few things that wasn't [sic] what I call 'natural' forest happenings. I had not heard of markers of Bigfoot territory, but I saw what I thought was the work of a few local boys out in the woods playing. But as I looked at the three large trees that were leaned on another tree to form a teepee structure without a covering, the question always came to my mind, *Why would anyone want to drag those trees up here and lean them on that tree?* You could see they were not a natural fall or an accident. It was a deliberate structure that was constructed by someone. There were also small trees that were twisted almost in two at from about four to six feet off the ground. These were not caused by the wind but by using two hands to twist, as you would wring out a cloth.

"I never saw any footprints but once, when the dogs were acting up at something in the woods about twenty yards up the hill, I went after it with a 30-.30 rifle. It was about 11:00 at night, in the early winter or late fall. There was a drift of snow on the ground, mostly in spots on the hill. I walked around the hills for over a mile not getting any closer or even able to see what I was after; it stayed about twenty or thirty yards ahead of me. I could never see it but I could hear it walking in the leaves and breaking branches. I decided to just go on to the house.

"The next morning I walked up on the hill to see what kind of tracks I could see. I found my tracks in the snow but I could not find any indication that anything else was walking in front of me or any place around me.

"I have seen eyes that looked blood-red, and another time green, as they were looking at me from the low underbrush at night. While sitting on the porch at night I would hear what at the time I thought sounded a little like an old steam locomotive whistle, but not quite the same. [The sounds] were always a long way off in the hills.

"My wife at the time saw what she described as an old Indian man looking through the window at her. I was not there at the time but she did call the Kentucky State Police. There were no footprints so they said she probably saw her own reflection and I guess [they] just dismissed it. She said she saw it from the mid-chest up. The bottom of the window is at least six feet, six inches off the ground. I am six feet tall and I had to use an eight-inch block just to see over the bottom edge of the window.

"One night we were leaving to go to Ashland. As we were getting into the truck we heard someone on the hill whistling. I called out to see who it was but there was no reply, just more whistling. I told them I had a gun and would shoot if they didn't answer. There was still no answer, so I fired a shot in the general direction and the whistling stopped. But there was no reply. It just started to walk around the hill. I fired another shot in the air but it did not speed up or slow down. I got in the truck and we left.

"I never had a sighting but all these things and a few more such as the throwing of rocks and pieces of wood has [sic] convinced me there is something that is intelligent enough to stay so close and still so undetected is living within our back yards. My son and his girlfriend claimed to have had a visual of it about three or four years ago." (That would be in 1997 or '98).

The witness claimed that he knew of thirty or more people who had seen the thing but he could get none of them to talk about it. Nevertheless, he did say that the children of a family just two blocks down the street from where he lived had been badly frightened one night when they saw a "giant monkey" looking at them through the kitchen-door window. Another local youth claimed that as he and some friends were camping one night, they had heard someone walking around their tent. Before they could look out to see who it was the entire tent - with them inside - was picked up and thrown ten feet through the air.

Another Carter County resident, J.S., (full name on file) claims to have had several sightings of the elusive creatures in 2003 at or near the Carter Caves State Resort National Park, including one that was solid white in color. He described them as nearly ten feet tall and muscular, but "not real massive like the Patterson-Gimlin creature."
He was referring to a short motion picture made in 1967 showing an unidentified subject that filmmakers Roger Patterson and Robert Gimlin purported to be a Bigfoot.

J.S. said the creatures that he saw walked on two legs with a massive stride of at least six feet.

CASEY COUNTY

Picture the scene:
A woman sits in the front room of her quaint country home sewing on a dress she plans to wear to church on the coming Sunday. The back door is open and sunshine pours in. All is quiet in this peaceful setting until a five-year-old boy bursts in through the back screen door, panic-stricken and crying. The door slams as he jumps into the woman's lap and clings tightly to her neck, tears running down his face. " Mommy," he sobs. "Mommy! It's the Hairy Man! It's the Hairy Man! Don't let it get me!"

This is not a scene from some Hollywood Sasquatch movie. The incident allegedly took place on Wilson Ridge in Casey County in May of 1957. For the rest of that hot, long summer the child would not leave his mother's side and would panic, crying and screaming in terror, every time an attempt was made to take him outdoors. He was even too terrified to walk to and from the car without breaking down.

Even as an adult he refuses to speak about the incident to anyone, including his own family. What in the world could he have seen to scare the lad so? Perhaps it was the same "Hairy Man" that scared two other Casey County children four years earlier in Liberty. The children came upon the creature, described as being large and covered with dark-brown hair, which was lighter on the chest area, giving it the appearance of a gray vest, while it was digging in the ground using two sticks as tools.

According to one of the witnesses, who described the incident over fifty years later, the beast was approximately six and a half to seven feet tall and appeared to weigh in excess of 300 pounds. It had hair that was dark brown, coarse and stringy, similar to a goat's. The face was black, and the nose looked like a flattened human nose. It also had two canine teeth that were somewhat larger than a human's. It had no sagital crest (referring to the ridge of bone running lengthways along the midline of the skull, said to be pronounced in some Bigfoot creatures), no noticeable breasts or sexual organs, and no odor that they could detect. The thing's finger- and toenails, he noted, were long, thick, uneven and squared. The youths fled when the monster began to approach them, baring its large, square teeth but making no sounds. This incident reportedly took place only a half-mile from the mysterious Green River, a name that pops up in reports of paranormal activity again and again.

In the 1960s a tall, hairy "thing" was allegedly seen peering into a teenage girl's window in a house on U.S. 127 near Liberty, the Casey County seat. The window reportedly was two stories off the ground. Also in Casey County during the 1960s the vicinity of Goose Creek was said to be the haunt of some fierce "varmint" that no coon dog could tree. In fact, just one whiff of the creature's scent, it was said, would send the bravest dog running in the opposite direction every time.

Goose Creek, a tributary of the Green River, was also the location in which a retired Kentucky State Trooper reportedly heard a nighttime "yowler" in 1965. Another ferocious-sounding yowler was heard in Windsor on February 5, 2008.

On January 12, 2007, at 1:30 a.m., a huge creature described as, "ten feet tall and very hairy" stepped out in front of a passing motorist on Highway 127 in Liberty. According to eyewitness, Michelle C. (full name on file), the creature stood there for a minute then ran back into the woods making "long screeching noises."

Just over a month later, Liberty resident Aaron (full name on file), encountered a similar creature as he was out riding his four-wheeler at 9:30 a.m. on the morning of February 21, 2007.
"I turned [the engine] off to use the bathroom before going down my trail that leads to the holler," said Aaron. "I heard a long yelp, kind of like a turkey-hen makes but a lot more high-pitched, then I heard something take off running. I thought it might be a dog or something, but then what looked like a bear stood up and was about eight to eight and one-half feet tall. It just took off through the field running like it was on fire."
The witness claimed that the beast looked at him before running off on two legs into the woods. He further commented that it had blackish-brown hair and big brown eyes.

The very next month, three Liberty men encountered Bigfoot on the afternoon of May 30, 2007, as they were out riding four-wheelers near the Casey-Russell County line. Joe Lee claims that he, a cousin and a friend were able to observe the creature for at least five minutes. They had stopped beside a creek in the "holler" where they were riding to rest.

"We sat there for ten to twenty minutes, I guess, when we heard something coming down the four-wheeler trail. We thought it was my mom or somebody trying to come and get us so we hid to try to scare her, or whoever was coming," Lee said.

But the intended prank didn't happen as they had planned. They noticed a strong skunk-like smell, and the closer the footsteps came the stronger the odor became. The trio peeked out from the log behind which they were hiding as the footsteps approached and were shocked when "a seven- to eight-foot-tall, hairy, man-like creature walked right in front of our four-wheelers and stopped"

It stared at them for a minute, then went and lay down in the creek. According to Lee, the creature picked up some red clay dirt and started rubbing it all over its body. Then it got up and walked off into the woods.

"I don't know if it was a Bigfoot or not," he stated, "but I know it wasn't a bear or a human."

CHRISTIAN COUNTY

Christian County played host to hairy monsters in the 1970s, an extremely active decade for Kentucky anomalies. On three separate evenings as many as five witnesses observed a six-foot-tall Bigfoot-like creature with broad shoulders and glowing green eyes lurking around some old abandoned houses. In March 1979, an eight-foot version was seen on several different occasions, by motorists traveling along the Pennyrile Parkway. Christian County was named after Col. William Christian, a veteran of the Revolutionary War who was killed by Indians in southern Indiana in 1786.

CLARK COUNTY

No one believed the five boys who said they'd seen a "monster" on Elkon Station Road near the Booneboro River between Winchester and Richmond back in the summer of 1976. "It was a warm, sunny summer day and we had been playing in the woods much of the day," said Donald H. some thirty-four years after the event. "In fact J. (the oldest of the five brothers) had made a path down the hill and had just ridden his bike down the hill, hit some rocks, and flipped over the handlebars. It was also a place where we used to play cowboys and Indians."

"It was getting late in the evening, around 7 or 8 p.m.," Donald continued. "My brother, D., was the last one to leave the woods that day when he came running back screaming that he had just seen a hairy monster. When we all went back there we could see nothing, but there was a strange smell in the air that stunk and we thought that an animal had died and started to rot so we played it off like he didn't see anything. That night he drew a picture of what he saw and it looked just like some of the drawings of Bigfoot that I have seen as of today.

"Anyway, us boys all went down to where he said he seen the thing and we noticed large footprints just noticeable to the eye because it was so dry, but there was a little spring running in the middle of the woods and it was soft ground that the footprints were made in. They looked just like a human footprint but very big. We all tried to get our mother and stepfather to come down and look at them but they just thought we were being kids. Still, to this day my brother swears he saw Bigfoot that day and I do believe him. At the time of the sightings our ages were 12, 9, 8, 6, and 4. As you can see we all were very young and the one who saw it was only six at the time, so you see why no one believed us. I still remember that day like it was yesterday because of the fright in my brother's eyes when he came out of the woods. I still remember seeing the footprints swallowing my bare foot when I placed it inside it."

CLAY COUNTY

Manchester resident David Blanton had no idea that he was about to have a brush with Bigfoot when he and a friend were out four-wheeling just before 1:00 a.m. on June 3, 2007.

"I was riding my four-wheeler with a buddy when we came to the edge of a swamp in Kincaid, which is a vast wilderness five miles west of Manchester," Blanton said. "When I stopped to let my four-wheeler cool off. I heard a terrifying noise out to the left of me. I asked my friend if he heard it too. He was pale as a ghost and had the fear of God in his eyes. I turned my spotlight on, and about sixty to seventy yards out in the swamp was a large, hairy beast with yellow eyes. I am six feet, six inches, and even at that distance I could tell this animal would dwarf me. It slowly walked through the swamp and trees, every now and then stopping briefly for me to see it. It eventually got out of sight traveling up a mountainside."

Blanton described the figure he and his friend saw as eight or nine feet tall and covered with brown hair. It walked with a slight hunch and its arms were very apelike. He said that when he shined the light in the thing's eyes they appeared to be yellow. The creature walked through knee-deep water without making a sound. Its cries were very loud and deep, he said.

CLINTON COUNTY

A six-foot-tall, hairy, dark-colored creature with a black bushy tail was reportedly seen by many citizens in Albany in the fall of 1873. It reportedly had an "ape-human" face and left nine-toed tracks. Other sightings reportedly included the beast's mate and offspring accompanying the creature. The sightings allegedly ceased after a local farmer, one Charles Stern, fired on the thing and apparently wounded it. The monster had reportedly killed livestock in the area and had previously acted entirely unaffected when fired upon.

Though humanoid and hirsute, the presence of a bushy tail leads one to believe that the creature seen in this instance was something other than a typical Sasquatch but where there is one unidentified hominoid there are usually more, and other, more recent Clinton County creature reports do exist.

For instance, another family vacationing near Lake Cumberland allegedly observed a dark figure standing over eight feet tall late one evening in 1998.

"My dad and I were sitting on the patio deck on the front of the cabin when we heard a loud scream too high-pitched to be a bear," a witness later claimed. "My dad looked and saw an approximately eight-and-a-half-foot-tall, dark figure about seventy-five yards away from the cabin. It was really big!"

The witness also recalled a strong smell in conjunction with the figure's appearance. It reappeared on August 4, 1999.

"My eighteen-year-old brother and I had spent a lot of time making a walking path through the woods near our private cabin. Around 2:00 a.m. we decided it would be nice to take a walk on this trail," the woman said. The walk turned into anything but nice as the two soon came upon a tall, hairy creature standing on two legs and shaking a tree.

"It was eight feet tall," she later said, "big and brown, very hairy. It had big eyes. It seemed to be shaking the tree to get something down from it. We froze and stared at the creature for a long time. The Bigfoot calmly turned toward us and began walking. I freaked and ran all the way back to the cabin, leaving my older brother behind."

Her brother later said that he had felt glued to where he was standing. Unable to move, he watched as the thing got to within five feet from him before his paralysis broke and he was able to run away in terror. Luckily for him it did not attempt to follow. Had the creature intended to snatch the boy, he would never have been seen again. "Tree-shaking" is considered by many Bigfoot investigators to be a warning to humans who have wandered into its vicinity. Other accounts of such behavior have been recorded in Kentucky.

CRITTENDEN COUNTY

In August of 1998, a seven-foot-tall, hairy, red-eyed Bigfoot was reportedly seen on several different occasions by residents of Blackburn Church Road in Shady Grove.

"The first time my father and I were going up on a ridge to listen for some turkeys," said one witness, who wishes to remain anonymous. "All of a sudden out of a pine thicket about 900 yards away, we heard something let out this awful noise. At first we were shocked, then scared because we had never heard this sort of noise before. It made this noise two separate times, and we left and headed home. About three months after that took place my friends and me [sic] thought we would drive through the road just to look around. It was about 11:00 p.m. and sort of foggy. We were just driving along when my cousin noticed two red eyes on a bank. I thought it was a raccoon until the thing blinked and walked across the road in front of us about 100 yards up the road.

"The creature walked upright on two legs and stood about six feet, ten inches. We locked the doors and drove off as the creature disappeared into a heavily timbered thicket. A year later, which was on Aug. 10 of '98, my sisters and two of my friends got in a truck and decided to go look for some deer. We ended up going down the same road where we had seen the creature the previous year. The girls were riding in the back just talking to each other when my youngest sister screamed out. I turned around just in time to see the figure of something standing about thirty yards behind the truck. I grabbed the spotlight and swung it around only to find that the thing had disappeared into the woods."

All told, the witness claimed three different encounters with the beast, two of which resulted in actual sightings. The strange sounds were heard about 6:30 in the morning on the fourth day of the 1997 turkey season. The second sighting took place around October of the same year at about 11:00 p.m., and the third sighting happened about 11:10 p.m. on August 9, 1998 near a small bridge.

The creatures are still being seen in the area. On June 28, 2009, Timothy Cox, 42, saw one walking through a pine thicket just two miles from Blackburn Church Road.

"I was blackberry picking in an old Westvaco area just off McConnell Road, " Cox said. "I was picking the berries near a set of three-year-old pines that stood about ten feet tall at the time. Some deer come running [sic] out of the pines about 50 to 70 yards from me to the side. They were running pretty fast." Westvaco Corp. is a packaging products company that owns extensive timberland on the East Coast of the United States.

Cox said he thought it was odd that the deer didn't notice him standing there. He thought they seemed to have been frightened by something.

"I heard something else coming through the trees just a few feet into the trees near where the deer came through. I could see a dark brown-colored thing that was moving the branches apart as it was walking between the rows of pines. This thing was moving at a fairly brisk pace and the branches were popping as it went along," he said.

Cox said he wondered, *what the hell is that?* Whatever it was, it appeared to be approximately eight feet tall. He judged the height by the way it was brushing past branches that were three-quarters of the way to the top of the pine trees.

"I could see an arm and part of its body. It continued down the row of trees. As it got farther away I decided to get the hell out of there and run back to my truck a quarter of a mile away. It scared the hell out of me."

I interviewed Cox on April 6, 2010. He was a straightforward, no-nonsense type of fellow. His sighting took place, he told me, near the Caldwell County line. The creature was walking fast through the trees, grunting as if was annoyed but it seemed unaware of Cox's presence until after he ran from the scene. The wind was blowing toward Cox but he noticed no unusual scents in association with the encounter. Seeing the huge beast scared him thoroughly, he admitted. He did what most people would: he ran away. He was, after all, unarmed save for a small hunting knife. He described the creature as upright, about eight feet tall, with long arms that it used to push branches and limbs out of its way. It had a stocky build and was entirely covered with long brown hair, he recalled.

"It just scared the hell out of me," he repeated. He estimated the creature's weight as 500 to 600 pounds.

According to Cox, both he and his son were surprised while turkey hunting in the area the previous spring when another herd of deer came running frantically out of the forest. He said one of them, a small doe, was so scared that it actually ran into a tree, nearly knocking itself unconscious. Then a terrible wailing roar erupted from the woods, followed by the sound of something very large walking quickly.

Like the deer, the hunters wasted no time in fleeing the area. Cox said the incident scared his son so badly that he was no longer interested in turkey hunting. Cox admitted that the sound scared them both. He'd never heard anything like it before. Later, as he was researching the subject, he came across some alleged Bigfoot recordings from Ohio and stated that they were a dead ringer for the sounds they'd heard. On both occasions he said he had heard the sound of trees and branches cracking and snapping loudly, suggesting that the creature was making no attempt whatever at being stealthy.

Interestingly, Cox said he was first exposed to the Bigfoot phenomenon during a family outing in 1973 when he was six years old. His grandparents, an uncle and Cox were walking along a nature trail on Pineville Mountain in Bell County when his grandfather spotted a figure a couple of hundred yards up the mountain and pointed it out. It was humanoid, covered in dark hair and was standing behind a small tree staring right at them. At first, Cox said, his uncle thought it was a bear, but it had no muzzle and it stood upright with one arm casually draped around the tree just like a man would. Alarmed, the group beat a hasty retreat down the mountain. Despite having been in these entities' presence on three separate occasions and feeling terrified each time, Cox said he believes that the Bigfoot creatures are most likely a form of some unknown, hairy hominid.

CUMBERLAND COUNTY

Back in the 1970s, a man named James Vincent of Hendersonville went out hunting for a large, man-like creature covered with white hair that left behind fifteen-inch footprints and a terrible smell in Black Hollow near Bethpage. The area has a long history of Bigfoot sightings and the creatures are known locally as "Wild Woolly Bullies." The hunt was apparently unsuccessful.

As an aside, the first American oil well was struck in Cumberland County, just three miles north of Burkesville in 1829. It was also the first location in America to elect a female sheriff.

DAVIES COUNTY

Davies County, in the western part of the state, has a long history of monster activity. According to the *Owensboro Messenger Inquirer* in 1978, residents of the 2800 block of Fairview Drive reported that they had witnessed a huge, dark-colored "monster" on several occasions that was apparently observing them from the concealment of the nearby woods. Witnesses claimed it was massive: eight to ten feet tall and four to five feet wide at the shoulders. It usually appeared in the evening hours and was said to smell like rotting corpses. Tracks were found which measured fourteen to sixteen inches long and six or seven inches wide.

Evidently the authorities were unable to offer any further help so a neighborhood posse was formed to rid the area of the gigantic, malodorous menace. The posse consisted of a man named Larry Nelson, his brother and two friends. They trio were well armed. They allegedly came upon the beast by the banks of an old pond where they reportedly fired at it repeatedly with .45 caliber rifles from close range. Miraculously unscathed, the thing ran away into the woods leaving no blood trail at all, only an odd wet spot where the beast had stood.

Several Owensboro motorists allegedly caught the creature in their headlights back in the 1980s. More recently, a seventeen-year-old youth named Josh (full name on file), claimed that he saw Bigfoot in Davies County about 3:20 in the afternoon on July 2, 2006, just outside of Owensboro.

"I was on the northwest end of Bon Harbor Hills where a lot of coal mines used to be and some entrances are still open in places deep in the woods," Josh said. "Me and my dad [sic] were checking out a dam that my uncle was enlarging next to a small pond. My dad had walked back down to a vegetable garden my uncle and his son were growing so he didn't experience it. I could feel a presence looming over me up the ridge about 100 feet away. I stepped into the woods and immediately knew I was out of bounds, literally. I was right next to a teepee type structure that I had read about as being possible Bigfoot boundary markers. I began studying it when WHAM! Out of nowhere this five- to seven-pound rock grazes my ear and knocks the tee-pee over. I was frozen where I stood."

Josh said he looked in the direction from where the rock came from and didn't see anything at first.

"Then I saw about a seven- to nine-foot-tall large shadow jump from behind a big oak tree at the top of the ridge. 'It' took off going down the other side of the ridge and I took off in the other direction back to my vehicle."

A few months prior to the encounter Josh said he was in the same general area when he heard a very loud, blood-chilling scream emanating from a thickly wooded ravine. The scream was followed by a hoard of forest animals fleeing the area.

Kentucky Bigfoot investigator Charlie Raymond interviewed Josh and found him to be credible. He added that the witness claimed to have conducted a search for trace evidence and found some large impressions that he felt were possible footprints of the creature. He informed Raymond of his intentions to acquire photographs of any forthcoming discoveries of footprints or teepee stick constructions.

Interestingly, in the late fall of 2009 I spoke with one woman who claimed that she and her boyfriend had been in the backwoods of the Bon Harbor area in the winter of 2004 and come across something very unusual. Her boyfriend was a county surveyor and his job often put him in spots that were well off the beaten path. On this day, there was snow on the ground and it was very cold. When they arrived they found a huge human-looking footprint impressed deeply into the snow. It looked like a bare human footprint, she said, only it was about two feet long and about eight inches wide. She also remarked that she could clearly see the impressions of huge toenails that had dug into the snow. She didn't know what to think but she said the print scared the hell out of her boyfriend, who insisted that they leave the area immediately.

ESTILL COUNTY

In the summer of 1985 Estill residents began reporting that they had observed a man-like figure prowling through the woods near their homes. Rumors of Bigfoot were running rampant in the area when police searched the woods and apprehended a man, a native of Irvine, who had been reported missing some months previously. According to reports the man was naked except for a covering of mud and foliage. Vines, moss and lichen were found growing in his hair and on his body. Mentally, he was in terrible shape, either refusing to speak or being unable to. He had to be physically subdued and taken to a hospital in Richmond. No further word as to his treatment or progress was reported in the media but the incident serves to illustrate the only instance in which a feral human was actually found to be behind the rumors of Bigfoot of which this author has ever heard. It is almost certain that there are other such cases.

Nearly every mountainous region has tales of old miners that "went crazy" and abandoned civilization to live in the wild, like animals. However, individuals such as these cannot be held responsible for all Bigfoot sightings - even in an area where a feral human was apprehended. Sightings of feral humans are, after all, much more rare than sightings of Bigfoot.

On Bear Mountain in Estill County, 1993, a witness was able to view through binoculars a large man-like creature covered in reddish hair busying itself by beating a rock against the side of a log. Described as being around seven feet tall, with a conical head, apelike face with large, dark eyes, no neck and dark gray skin, the creature was at least two and a half feet wide and covered with short, thick hair everywhere except around its eyes and nose. The thing suddenly stood up, the witness claimed, hunching over with its arms by its knees as if somehow realizing that it was being observed, and faced the witness, waving its head from side to side in a strange manner. It then fled into the woods.

FLEMING COUNTY

In Maysville, Fleming County, Bigfoot reportedly chased a woman around her car at a local shopping center in September of 1980. One month later, according to the *Fleming County Gazette*, a back porch freezer in Fairview was raided by a large, white-haired monster that ran off on two legs when chased, carrying pilfered food items in its hands. A frozen chicken, two loaves of bread and a package of hotdogs appeared to be the motive for the break in.

Trace evidence was reportedly left behind in the form of long white hairs on the freezer, footprints and a trail of frozen goods leading off into the woods. The chicken was found shortly thereafter still frozen - and partially eaten. The witness was sure that no animal could have opened his freezer door, a feat that would require hands. The *Flemingsburg Times Democrat* ran the full story in the Wednesday, October 15, 1980 edition:

BIGFOOT TALES ALARM AND AMUSE COUNTY
By Dean Muse
Has Bigfoot invaded Fleming County, Kentucky? Well, something definitely broke into J.L. Tumey's back porch last Friday night in Fairview. Tumey had just sat down to watch the baseball game on TV at about 8:15 p.m. when he heard a noise on the back porch of the trailer. "At first I thought a dog had gotten onto the back porch but then it knocked something over," said Tumey. "That's when I grabbed my pistol. I ran out the front door and ran out to the back. That is when I saw what looked like a big man running toward the woods. I emptied my pistol at it as it ran."

Tumey said that he ran back into the trailer to get more bullets. When he approached the old stable behind the trailer, the creature ran out and started toward the woods. He fired two more times at it, but didn't hit it. "It was very dark, so I really couldn't tell exactly what it was. It stood up like a man and it was big, but it was so dark, about all I could see was a nig shadow. It made a thumping noise as it ran," he said. Just after this, Mrs. Tumey came home. When her husband told her what had just happened, she called Sheriff G.W. White. He and some of his deputies soon arrived, along with a crowd of people who had heard about it on their police scanners. According to Mrs. Tumey, "About half of Ewing and Fairview showed up with their guns to hunt the creature. It's a wonder somebody didn't get hurt."

People stayed on the scene until about 3:00 a.m. scouring the woods for clues. There was a freezer on the back porch, and pieces of frozen meat were found lying around the porch and in the back yard. Sheriff White found a package near the stable. "I don't know if it was any Bigfoot or not. It looked like a big man. It was dark and I couldn't see very well," Tumey said.

No clues were found that night, but the next day, Johnny Burke and Estill Helphenstine found some unusual tracks. They found some tracks where something had slid down a bank and some more going up the side of another bank. They followed the prints along a gulley deep into the woods. That is when the found some clear prints in the wet sand. The tracks were described as being about 14 inches long and about 6 inches wide. They still were not clear enough to tell whether they were human or animal tracks although the pair said the tracks weren't made by a boot or shoe, but were more like a track left by someone's bare foot.

When the Tumey family started straightening up their back porch they found another clue, some long white hairs left on the doorknob and the freezer. The Sheriff's department sent them off for analysis. Nobody seems to know what it was. Some think it was a man, others think it was an animal, but still others said it was Bigfoot.
Is it for real? Something or somebody did enter Tumey's back porch. Two loaves of bread, a frozen chicken and a package of hotdogs were missing from the freezer. But was the thief a man or a beast? "If it was a man, he must have been awfully hungry to break in while I was in the house," Tumey said. "A regular animal like a bear or dog couldn't have opened up the back door or the freezer and carried those packages."

Some people have said that Bigfoot is nothing more than a product of the imagination and fears. A teen-age girl said she thought it was just something made up by parents to keep their kids from going out and parking. Others have taken it more seriously.

More Fleming county Bigfoot activity was reported from Mays Lick during the summer of 2005. One woman wrote: "In June of 2005 my family had a strange occurrence. My son and a couple of his friends wanted to camp out down in the woods. My husband and one of the other boys' dad went down to check on them before we went to bed. It was a full moon out and they were sitting down there with the boys when my husband saw something move between the trees. He wasn't sure what it was and kept watching. When he seen [sic] it move between the trees again he could see the moonlight between its legs. They got scared and came up out of the woods.
"Of course I didn't believe him so the next day I went down there and found footprints. One was a really good one that we actually poured a mold of. Upon further scouting I found some odd things. There was a bunch of little pieces of tree bark in a circle and it looked and felt like something might have been chewing on it. We found moss rolled back, not tore up [sic] - just rolled back. And we also found tree limbs

stuck in the ground kinda like markers.

"Our friends didn't believe us so one night we got a bunch of us together and went down in the same place my husband first saw it. I had been interested so I did some research on the internet and took a little hand-held recorder and recorded what was supposed to be Bigfoot screams. Around dusky dark my husband started playing the screams on the recorder. He played them a few times and then all of a sudden we heard the god awfulest scream we've ever heard. It was high pitched and drawn out. Everyone was shocked. I don't know what it was but it wasn't too long after that, that a log about the size of a piece of firewood came down out of the woods and landed by my vehicle. After everyone got calmed back down we were standing around the fire when I thought I saw something just outside of the firelight walking toward the creek. I went and got back in my truck and about two minutes later it sounded like it picked up a creek rock and slammed it back down. We all left after that.

"The next weekend it was around midnight when my husband, my son and a couple of friends drove my truck back down there. Without a fire it was really dark. They had a spotlight and my husband's friend was just randomly shining it through the woods when my husband and another person in the vehicle said, 'there it is!' so he brought the light back to the spot where they seen it. My husband instantly started the truck up and his friend told him to shut it off and, when he did, they could hear it running through the woods. They said it was just trashing its way up the hill. But they saw it when he brought the light back down through the woods. It was behind a tree and they said it had red eyes. Another odd thing was that all the grass was laid down flat kinda like in swirls. And there is nothing down there that would lay it down flat. I've seen deer bedding before but this was a large area that was flat by the creek.

"We still go back there sometimes and we haven't seen anything or any signs like we did that year. Everyone thinks we are crazy, which I probably would too if I hadn't experienced it for myself."

She measured the footprint cast at eighteen inches. Both the husband and wife later described the animal to an investigator as about seven feet tall with wide shoulders, red eyes, a cone shaped head, and no neck.

FLOYD COUNTY

An ordained minister and his wife claim they saw Bigfoot in Floyd County in October of 1976. Luke K. (full name on file) says that they observed the creature for about ten minutes that evening between Wheelright and Price. The sighting took place about 11:00 p.m. on Indian Creek near Virgie.

"I am a minister and often called to preach in funerals," Luke stated. "It was October. I remember the weather was beginning to turn cool at night. It happened that I was called on to preach in a funeral in the night service at Marison Funeral Home in Martin. After the service was over my wife and I started back home. We went up Beaver Creek on State Route 1428 as it was a shorter route to where we lived. We went through Price, between Price and Wheelright. There were several miles where there were no houses on the highway side. About three miles beyond Price, as we went along, our lights showed something going at a rather fast walk in the middle of my lane.

"As we got closer we could see this creature real well. It stood seven or more feet tall, was broad-shouldered, and had long, shaggy hair from the top of its head all the way to its feet. I moved over to the left lane and slowed down to about 10 to 12 mph. I tried to see its face but it just looked straight ahead. It acted like nobody was anywhere in the world. My wife and I both saw this creature quite well. It didn't make any noise but my wife rolled down the window on her side of the car to get a better look. She said it smelled real bad. This is the first and only time we ever saw anything like this and for many years we didn't tell anyone for fear they would think we were crazy. We are Christians and I am a minister. I have no reason to lie about a thing like this," he said.

FRANKLIN COUNTY

On the night of June 7, 2007, Frankfort, resident Josh Hardy was driving down a secluded country road near the old Oaks Farm when something uncommon happened. "I was driving down the road and I seen [sic] some deer running down the hill," he later said. "I stopped and let them pass. I started to drive up the hill and a big shadow [was] cast over the road. I didn't think much about it and kept going. I had my windows rolled down and heard a noise. I looked back and saw a huge creature running behind my truck; it covered the whole road in three steps."

Hardy recalled that the creature's height, as is most commonly reported in Kentucky and elsewhere throughout the world, was seven to eight tall and further described it as being covered in black and brown fur.

"It ran like a man but with its head down and out," he said. It took "big, huge steps" as it ran, and he also claimed that a horrible smell was associated with the figure's appearance. Thankfully, he was able to outrun the creature.

Just two days later, on June 9, the same creature, or one just like it, stepped out onto the road in front of another startled passerby. It was 12:39 a.m. and John (full name on file) was driving home from a late-night party at a co-worker's when the sighting took place. He later claimed the animal was a large biped, standing around seven feet tall and completely covered with dark hair. He estimated the creature's weight as being around 350 to 400 pounds. The incident allegedly happened in the Bald Knob area on the north side of Frankfort.

Another Franklin County creature eyewitness, Tony Hall, told of a figure he and a friend saw on March 21, 2008, near the Scott County line. "We were four-wheeling out past Switzer Bridge," he stated. "We were stopped at the bridge, sitting on our wheelers then we smelled something horrible."

The two were startled when "a large creature" suddenly appeared and commenced to walk down the slope of a nearby ridge and into the Elkhorn Creek. "It just walked by like nothing happened," Hall said. He doesn't know if the hair-covered creature saw them or not, but it scared the two so badly they fired up the four-wheelers and sped back in the direction of home. Hall said the thing was tall, human looking and walked with a hunched, or stooped posture.

GRANT COUNTY

In 1964, in Grant County, a seven-foot-tall, dark-colored monster with shiny eyes was seen at a local trash dump just off US 36. The incident sparked a monster hunt craze that had the local farmers crying foul. Two out-of-town teens were accidentally shot and wounded during the fervor. On a single night, local police chased away fourteen carloads of armed monster-hunting teenagers. After officials announced that they planned to hand out citations to all non-locals in the area after dark the monster hunts ceased. Sightings of the creature, on the other hand, did not.

In the spring of 2004 another witness came forward to tell of his glimpse of the unknown as he drove down Interstate 75 just 30 miles south of Cincinnati, Ohio.
"I saw something along Interstate 75 South in Kentucky," he told Bigfoot investigator Stan Courtney, "Maybe 30 to 40 miles south of Cincinnati. I don't recall where exactly along the highway I was at the time, somewhere after three lanes had been reduced to two. And it happened four to five years ago in 1999 or 2000. I don't recall what time of year it was. Maybe autumn. It never occurred to me until recently to report it."
It was late, the witness claimed, between 1:00 and 2:00 a.m., as he was driving back to Winchester on I-64 twenty miles east of Lexington. There were no other cars on the road.
"I sighted what appeared to be a large animal standing in a recess along a road cut, which I wouldn't have seen but for my headlights. There were no streetlights or other sources of light. It stood erect and was covered in dark fur like a bear, which I imagined it must be, but it had no muzzle like a bear. I wondered if it could have been an elk because it was the right height, but I couldn't reconcile an elk with the other body features. It was only in view for three to four seconds and was not moving, only looking directly at my car as I sped by. I passed within fifteen to twenty feet of it. I looked directly at it, and it had an angry expression on its face. It made my hair stand on end."
The witness was later unable to find the exact spot at which he spied the creature, but there has since been much roadwork done. "I'm certain I saw something; [but I'm] just not sure what," he said. "Whatever I saw was six to six and a half feet tall, [with] dark brown to black fur, bipedal posture [and an] angry demeanor." Bizarrely, the witness claimed that the creature was standing with its arms held up at shoulder

height, "as though it were a tree, or striking some pose intended to frighten me, which was very effective. My initial impression was that it struck a human posture. I heard no sound and it did not move."

According to investigator Stan Courtney the witness was particularly impressed with the creature's face, which he described as more humanlike than apelike, looking something like the Cowardly Lion from *The Wizard of Oz*.

GRAVES COUNTY

One Graves County witness, alerted by the sound of breaking limbs one night in Mayfield in 1998, saw a large, hairy, black Bigfoot with small glowing red eyes. Again, the terrified witness fled when the creature started to approach, but then, who can blame him?

"It smelled bad too," his wife later reported. "One evening about dark, my husband was taking tree limbs into the woods behind our house to discard them on an old dozer pile. He heard a noise that he assumed was deer running through the underbrush." About this time, according to his wife, he noticed a foul odor, "like something dead." Looking out through the dense trees and brush he saw a huge, dark-colored, hairy creature approaching.

"It was bigger than him," his wife stated, "and he is six foot tall, 180 pounds." At first he thought it was a bear, she said, despite the red-colored eyes - until he realized that there were no bears in that part of Kentucky. Badly frightened, the man came running out of the woods. He told his wife what he saw and that he wasn't going back to see what it was. "I have never seen my husband that scared before in my life," she said.

The incident allegedly took place in a wooded area containing a gravel pit and a large lake. The animal apparently made no sounds except for the underbrush crushing and snapping beneath its feet. Again, we hear testimony describing the sound of loudly snapping, cracking limbs wherever the creature walks. One might think that such huge beasts would be easy enough to track by simply following the trail of broken trees but such is not the case. Such destruction of local fauna, almost never seen when the area is visited later leads one to theorize that the often-reported tree breaks may be an auditory phenomenon and not a physical one.

Graves County is one of the state's largest counties. Mayfield, the county seat, has a population of just over 10,000.

GRAYSON COUNTY

Another Bigfoot-type creature was seen by a child in Leitchfield in the mid 1970s near Nolin Lake on Interstate 65. "When I was a kid, my grandparents had a little bitty camper at a campsite at Nolin Lake," she later claimed. "One summer, my father took the family (me, my sister and mother) to my grandparents' site for a little vacation. One evening as it was becoming dusk, I remember standing inside the camper looking out the screen door at my father who was cooking at the grill. The campsite sat at the top of a hill in a wooded area. The woods consisted mostly of old growth, deciduous trees, so there weren't really any evergreens or shrub-type trees like cedars that could really block your view. I was looking out the door at my father who was on my left and eventually, out of boredom I guess, I ended up scanning to the right and down the hill into the woods. I remember seeing about midway down the hill, something that caught my eye.

"You know how when you think you see something and in a split second your mind says, 'did I just see what I thought I saw? Well, that's what happened to me. Midway down the hill partially hidden behind a tree was this man thing. I could see his whole head, his right shoulder and part of his leg coming out from behind the tree. It was grayish brown and he was looking right at me. I looked away thinking I had to be imagining it but, when I looked back, it was still there and I had no problem picking him out from the trees. At that point my mother, who was cooking at the stove behind me, said something to me and I turned around to talk to her. When I looked back down the hill, it was gone. I kept looking through all the trees, but I couldn't find him.

"What I saw was big and burly and it didn't make any sounds that I can remember. It had a big, squarish head (kind of blocky with rounded corners) that looked like it sat right on its shoulders. I really don't recall seeing a neck. I could see a massive shoulder and a thick bicep. I could also see its chunky hip and a good portion of its thigh down to about its knee. All the rest was hidden behind the tree."

The witness said she still gets cold chills when she thinks of the strange figure she viewed all those years ago. She said she didn't tell her parents what she saw because she was afraid they wouldn't believe her. The creature, according to her, was much taller than a man, with shaggy, gray-brown hair covering its entire body.

GREENUP COUNTY

The following undated statement was taken by my friend and fellow Bigfoot researcher, Mary Green:

"When I first became a truck driver they put me with a trainer and his name was Bill. I asked him one tine if he had ever seen anything 'out of the way' on the road. I meant a UFO but he started telling me a story about driving the AA Highway (Route 9). It was a moonlit night. He came up over a hill when he saw a freezer box on the side of the road. When he got up to it something looked up, he said. He passed it, went down the road, turned around and went back. The freezer was gone. I asked what he saw. He said it was light tan in color, about seven foot ten to eight feet tall and big. He [said he] never told no one [sic] because they would call him a nut. I asked him why he told me. He said because we were on the AA Highway. I believe him."

So do I. Other Greenup County reports exist. The creature was seen by two witnesses on Turley Avenue in Flatwoods in January of 1996 as they were walking down a gravel road around 11:00 p.m. They observed what looked like a large ball in the middle of the road about 200 yards in front of them. At first they thought it might be a tree stump or large rock. As they continued toward the object one witness began to wonder how such a large object could have ended up in the middle of the road to begin with. When they were within 100 yards away from the object they were startled to see a large, black creature rise up from a crouched position and face them.
Even though it was a clear, cold night with a full moon, the two men were unable to make out any further detail. They watched the thing for about twenty seconds before it turned and walked into the darkness of the woods next to the road. Then the two promptly turned around and fled back in the direction from which they'd come. The thing they saw was black, with very long arms covered with fur that glistened in the moonlight; it appeared to weigh over 500 pounds.
Several old, abandoned mine tunnels are reportedly near the location of the incident and nighttime "yowlers" have also been heard in the area. One of the witnesses claimed that a neighbor told him that he'd seen a huge creature that was at least eight feet tall while he was looking out his kitchen window one night.

Also in Greenup County, near US 23, on Jan. 4, 2001 a nighttime encounter took place with a large eight-foot-tall, 450-pound, hairy beast that made strange grunting noises. A witness said he was so frightened when he saw the thing that he almost soiled himself. "It was walking like a human, kinda, but not exactly. It was very hairy looking and was making some weird grunting noises. I thought about running but I was too scared to run so I stayed." The witness expressed great relief when the figure left. "It was unlike anything I have ever seen before in my life," he stated. Trace evidence was also allegedly left behind in the form of large footprints that were photographed.

At 4:30 a.m. on August 10, 2008 when another such creature frightened Suzy S. (full name on file) of rural Russell. She writes: "I went out for a smoke. The woods were eerily quiet. Usually I whistle at the birds or even mock the new coyote puppies, but this morning there was not a sound to be heard. Not even the crickets. Being silly I decided to make some noises of my own out of shear boredom. I began to mimic deer grunting with a growl attached. I'm not sure how long I was doing this and that's when I heard the loudest crashing noise ever coming from about twenty to thirty yards away.
A high fence stood between Suzy and the woods. She said she could hear what sounded like footsteps crashing loudly onto the forest floor.
"At the same time I could hear tree limbs being snapped like twigs. I was frozen in fear. Whatever I had disturbed was huge and coming straight for me. Then, to the left

of me, I thought I heard a growl. It was even closer than the crashing woods which I turned my attention back to very quickly. I was terrified. My knees buckled. I almost cried in fear. Whatever was moving toward me was coming hard and fast and tearing the woods up as it came. I ran for what I felt was my life. I was so scared it took me forever to even get the courage to peep out the window.

"I did not work the next evening. I decided I needed to get the courage up to look on the other side of the fence, maybe into the woods to see if I could see any evidence of what it could have been. I found two footprints by the fence. They were about eleven to thirteen inches long. Finding these footprints made me very scared and very excited at the same time. I did not stay behind the fence for long. This experience has made me very frightened of the woods," she said.

Suzy said she regrets not taking any photographs of the prints. She said she showed them to a co-worker, who also became frightened.

HANCOCK COUNTY

From Hancock County comes this anonymous, undated account:

Let me begin by saying this is a third-hand account. It was told to me by an uncle who was working as a security guard at the paper mill named [at the time] Willamette Industries, located halfway between the towns of Hawesville and Cloverport. According to my uncle, one of the other guards that he worked with came into the guard shack one night spooked and shaken about something. When my uncle asked him what was wrong the man replied that he thought he had seen Bigfoot while doing his nightly checks around the property. He described having pulled the patrol truck into the park located on the mill's property and getting put to do his checks. Running through the middle of the park is a small creek, and on the northern side of the creek, tucked back into the tree line is a small playground.

The guard described seeing movement and assumed it was teenagers trespassing on the property after hours. As he got closer he realized this was not the case at all. Standing in front of him was a tall, dark, hair-covered figure, its hand on top of the playground equipment, staring back at him. It startled the man and he retreated back to the patrol vehicle and [drove] back to the guard shack, where he described the encounter to my uncle, who told the story to me.

I've been to that park many times in my life and can recall exactly the area [where] the man claimed to see the creature. I no longer live in Kentucky but have no trouble believing that a Sasquatch could reside in that area.

HARLAN COUNTY

In Harlan County in September of 1980 a hairy giant was seen crossing rural Hwy. 1137. The witness claimed it had long, apelike arms, human-looking hands and a large, bulky chest. The head was described as being long and wider at the bottom with a stiff tuft of hair on top. According to the witness, the hair that covered the thing was light colored, long and "nappy."

Bigfoot appeared again in February of 1981, this time in Louellen, near Hwy. 179. The following is an account from a witness:
"In 1981 me and my brother-in-law [sic] were going to work. I saw something ahead of us kneeled down [sic] alongside the road. As we approached it stood up and walked backwards into the center of the road, squatted and looked at us then leaped over the embankment."
The witness described the creature he saw as being about seven feet tall with big legs and a small upper body. It had thin, long hair on its chest and arms, a short neck and short, thick, dark-brown hair on its legs.
"We got within twenty to thirty feet of it, our headlights on bright. The road stays in bad condition there and travel is very slow. About two weeks later another person said he [saw the] same thing running across the road," the witness said.
The creature evidently had been surprised while rummaging through some garbage that someone had dumped beside the road. The witness later spoke to investigator Stan Courtney, who adds that the witness and his brother-in-law, both miners, were on their way to work at about 3:00 a.m., driving the narrow roads of the Appalachians.
"The weather was cool and clear. As they came around a curve the animal was squatting along the road going through some garbage that someone had dumped. He quickly stopped the jeep. They were able to observe the animal for about thirty seconds in the high beam of the headlights. The animal took two or three steps backwards into the center of the road, turned and looked at them. Then it squatted down and leaped twenty to thirty feet off the road and was gone down into the ravine," Courtney said.
He said the witness told him he could see the definition of the creature's muscles as it squatted. The calf muscles were especially huge. The hair was very short on the lower body with somewhat longer and thinner hair on the chest and shoulders.
"The head was round with a short neck. He was unable to see any facial features," Courtney said. "I also spoke with his brother-in-law. He stated that the next year he had seen what he thought was probably the same animal briefly about a mile farther up the road."

Passing motorist Jason Weaver observed a similar creature crossing another Harlan County highway at 1:30 a.m. on the night of July 7, 2007. According to Weaver, as he was driving through the crossing at the foot of Pine Mountain, an apelike creature

darted across the road walking on two legs.
"It got to the edge of the road, then turned around and looked at me and ran off into the weeds," he said.
Weaver claimed the creature, which stood between seven and a half to eight feet tall and weighed around 400 pounds, was covered with rough-looking brown hair and had large eyes with clearly visible whites.

Three months later, in October 2007, the creature surfaced again, this time in Evarts, near Hwy. 38. Four people were four-wheeling in the Big Black Mountain area when they spotted what looked like a large black bear traversing a hillside. When they went to look for tracks they were surprised to find large, human-looking footprints in the fresh mud of the trail. Two of the men were experienced bear hunters from Florida. They agreed that the prints they were looking at were not bear prints at all.

HARDIN COUNTY

A soldier at the Fort Knox Army base in Hardin County reported encountering a tall, dark-haired Bigfoot creature in 1976. It was humanoid but unlike anything the witness had ever seen before.

Just days after his uncle claimed to have had an encounter with a hair-covered, man-like creature near Vine Grove in early July of 2009, David M. (full name on file) saw strange, animalistic eyes that appeared to be glowing in the dark. It was evening and he had stepped outside to see why his dogs were barking. He was able to watch the glowing eyes for several minutes, he later claimed, before they disappeared into the darkness of the night. He felt strongly that the eyes belonged to the creature his uncle had previously seen - whatever that might be.

HART COUNTY

Incredibly, Angela Barth from Bell County isn't the only citizen of the Bluegrass State who claims to have had a close encounter with one of these creatures while driving a vehicle. In his book "*The Locals*" (Hancock House, 2003), my friend Thom Powell wrote:

I was contacted by a rural family from Horse Cave, Kentucky who described to me a curious one-car accident in 2001, which resulted in one human fatality. The residents felt that the fatality resulted from a collision with Bigfoot. The entire family maintained that the public was kept away from the scene of the nighttime collision, but these particular residents lived nearby and were able to approach the scene of the wreck by walking through the woods. From the woods, they observed the authorities burying something beside the road scrubbing the pavement to remove copious amounts of blood and taking extraordinary measures to keep the public away from the scene.

The family had several sightings to relate to me on and around their isolated rural homestead. The wreck that they described was in an area of much prior Bigfoot activity. They called the area of the wreck, just off Highway 218, "Bigfoot Hill." It was easy walking distance from their house. After the wreck and the mysterious burial they heard loud, mournful wails coming from the area for many nights. The residents were therefore very leery of visiting the location, not only out of concern for the fact that the creatures were still around, but for fear of being observed by locals who would wonder what they were after. As I recall, the mayor, who was also the undertaker, lived within sight of the location of the wreck. They sent me a detailed map to the location and I considered relaying it to a local investigator. Instead I convinced the residents to try to investigate the matter more completely by themselves. Perhaps under cover of darkness they could probe the ground for an indication of what type of remains, if any, lay beneath the disturbed earth beside the road at the scene of the wreck. Eventually they were able to do just that, and they phoned me later with the news that the earth appeared to have been once again disturbed, the soil had an intensely putrid smell, but no identifiable remains could be found.

I must say that after following up on plenty of such reports in the past, I was not at all surprised by this news. Par for the course, really. While it was regrettable that the residents didn't get around to probing the ground sooner, such is generally the case. By the time such tantalizing reports reach us, it is generally too late to utilize the information even if it was accurate in the first place. But the credibility of the family was better than most situations: they lived near Mammoth Cave where many unmapped caves provide potential safe haven for any manner of reclusive creature. They were in regular telephone, U.S. mail, and email contact with me. The woman was a reverend and the different members of the family were in complete agreement about the details of the various events that they witnessed. The family reported to me that they began to experience substantial hostility directed at them from unknown sources. Their property was vandalized. Someone tried to run them off the road. Someone tried to run over their son. The landlord wanted to evict them. Finally, they decided to move to another state.

Threats, persecution and even attempted murder by government officials? For accidentally running over a Bigfoot? Why? And what of Mrs. Barth's missing time? Truly these atypical reports seem a mystery that is clearly more science fiction than zoological in nature. Angela Barth says that she hit an object but felt no impact. Instead the car rose "up and over" something. This would seem, to even the most casual reader, an obviously implanted memory as the creatures hair was hanging from the vehicle's undercarriage, which sustained $700 worth of damage. She could not recall the exact point at which the engine had stalled, only trying to start it up again. Obviously, there is something extraordinary about the entire event.

HENDERSON COUNTY

Few places can compare to Henderson County when it comes to hairy monster activity and, indeed, unexplained phenomena in general. We must linger here for a time to truly appreciate the scope of the hairy humanoid situation in this region of the Bluegrass State.

Henderson is truly a magical and mysterious place. I was born and raised there along the banks of the Ohio and Green rivers and while there I've been fortunate enough to witness a variety of astounding sights and experiences relating to the unexplained. This is not, in my opinion, because I am special in some way, but merely because I've lived nearly my entire life in and around the places in which these enigmas tend to manifest themselves. Watershed areas, I've come to understand, are like Bigfoot roadways, which they use mainly under cover of darkness.

I've personally spoken to witnesses of Henderson County monster activity from as far back as 1935 but I'm sure they stretch much further back in time.

In 1971, when I was five years old, my family lived on Collins Road in Reed, at a place we called Booth's Farm. One night, as we all sat watching television my older sister glanced out the kitchen window and to her shock saw a "monster" looking back at her. She screamed and my father, shotgun in hand, rushed out with my mother behind him. He fired two shots at a tall brown figure as it was running down a dirt road that led to the back fields. Dad asked my sister what the thing looked like and she said, "Frankenstein." It became known thereafter as "The Brown Man." The area where we lived, it turned out, is a very active one regarding monster activity with sightings dating back to the 1960s and continuing on to the present.

In 1968 another, or possibly the same, creature was seen there by the previous occupants of the house, a family by the name of Driskell. A search turned up giant, five-toed footprints. We eventually moved after my mother saw a red-colored UFO land behind one of the barns late one evening.

After a brief stay in the city we moved to Spottsville in 1975 where my family endured a terrifying eleven-month ordeal with a group of large, hairy, bipedal monsters with a penchant for causing terror and killing livestock. We spent the next ten years living in the city and longing for the country life. Finally, in 1985, we returned to Reed, moving into a stately old two-storey house on Carlinsburg Road. As luck would have it, the house was haunted inside and out. UFOs routinely buzzed overhead and black panthers roamed the woods beyond the yard. Bigfoot put in a few appearances as well. My former brother-in-law, while driving down Ohio River Road No. 2 in broad daylight, saw what he at first took to be a deer standing alongside the road. Then it stood up on two legs and ran off into the thick brush. It was six or seven feet tall, he said, covered in brown hair and it moved very fast. A similarly described beast, this one with glowing green eyes, approached my four-year-old daughter, her mother, and my sister one evening as they were gathering clothes off the line. The two women were so frightened that they ran off and left the child standing alone by the clothesline. My sister raced back, grabbed her by the arm and ran into the house where they immediately locked all the doors and windows.

One night around midnight a resounding crash shook the entire house. It was so loud that we actually thought a car had crashed into the house. The three dogs that we had didn't bark. We looked out the windows but saw nothing. There was no sign of a vehicle. My father insisted that no one go outside until morning, when we found the garage door ripped off its metal tracks and lying on the garage floor. We never found an explanation for how it got there.

While artifact hunting alone in the bottoms one day I came across a trail of immense footprints crossing a muddy field. The mud was a foot deep so I could make no positive identification of what had made them but the creature walked on two feet and had an extremely long stride that I was completely unable to match.

On another occasion, my stepmother was in the barn checking on one of the dogs when it suddenly began howling in misery. Seconds later something that my stepmother described as "growling and making the weirdest noises" entered the open lower level of the barn beneath where she stood. The sound made the hairs on the back of her neck stand up, she later told me. She could hear whatever the thing was walking around the barn, coming her way. She said she was terrified beyond words, which was totally out of character for her. She was so frightened that she climbed into the pen with the dog and hid her face as the thing approached. She remained in that position, barely daring to breathe, until the thing eventually wandered away. Even though she didn't see it, she said she could hear by its movements that whatever it was walked on two legs. In 1989, after repeated sightings of black panthers, she'd had enough and moved out shortly afterward. Panthers are not supposed to be roaming Kentucky but that doesn't stop huge black, cat-like beasts from being seen there, as well as in many other locations in the U.S. and in the U.K. and Australia, where panthers normally don't belong.

In 1999, while driving down Hwy. 60 one afternoon in Baskett, I happened to look over to a bean field on my left and was surprised to see two large, hairy creatures standing in the beans about ten feet from the top edge of the field. Both were brownish-gray in color and were positioned with their backs toward me. One was squatting down, apparently doing something to the ground or digging around in the beans, which were tall enough to obscure whatever it was doing. Both these creatures were very big, at least six or seven feet tall. Since the highway was full of afternoon traffic coming home from work, I'm sure that other motorists must've seen these things as well. If this is so, it seems that none of them felt particularly inclined to come forward.

It is interesting to note that all these locations are within ten miles of each other and are routinely where all manner of mysterious phenomena are experienced. These places have a few things in common, chiefly being that they are all within a stone's throw of either the Green or Ohio rivers and they are littered with the burial mounds left centuries ago by the Native Americans. Make of that what you will.

Back in the early 1980s, ten-year-old Billy G. (full name on file), while playing alone in the woods in Corydon in Henderson County, was interrupted by a huge apelike creature with long arms as it walked across a nearby field toward him. Its body was muscular and completely covered in dark hair. Billy was so scared that he froze for a few seconds before finally managing to squat down behind some trees until the thing walked past him. He later told me that what struck him most was the immense thickness of the thing's legs; he described them as looking like tree trunks. When it had disappeared into the distance he ran all the way back to his house and never played alone there again.

The Creature of Canoe Creek

Dusk found nine-year-old Roger Curtis and three of his friends at their makeshift clubhouse near the banks of Canoe Creek in Henderson County. It was the autumn of 1990, and they had a fire going. They had gathered some firewood and left it just down the creek where it passes beneath the road near the old Swopes Trailer Park, and they decided that it was about time to go get it. They were a rambunctious group of boys and there was little to trouble them as they made their way back toward the trailer park. After all, they were in the middle of the city of Henderson. What was there to fear?

Nearing the spot where they'd left the wood, which was little more than a forested refuse heap where the residents of the trailer park had dumped their trash for years, the group was surprised to see that the dump site wasn't abandoned as usual. There, standing amid the old chair frames and discarded refrigerators, was a seven- or eight-foot-tall monster. It was bent over at first, Curtis told me during an interview in Aug. of 2007, like it had been rooting through the garbage, but it stood up on its hind legs upon the boys' approach.

According to the witness the thing stood like a man but was covered in thick, reddish-looking hair that was longer and bushier on its head. It was less than fifty feet away; the light was fading fast and they could make out no facial features. The troop stopped in their tracks upon seeing the thing. Then it took off toward the tree line running very swiftly on two legs. When asked if it had made any noise Curtis replied, "Hell yes! That was the scariest part: the noise it made as it ran away. [It was] a high-pitched screaming sound mixed with what sounded like crying. It was a God-awful noise, let me tell you."

At that point the boys ran in the opposite direction, leaving behind the firewood and their campfire without a second thought. They were met mostly with derision when they arrived excited and out of breath at Curtis' house and told their tale, but his uncle Ron was not so quick to dismiss their story. They were obviously upset by something they'd seen and besides, it was well known that people in the area had been hearing strange noises at night. Unexplainable noises. Ron decided to go to the dump himself and check out the area. None of the kids would agree to accompany him, so he went alone.

He later told Curtis that he'd found signs of disturbed soil in several spots, as well as a couple of old refrigerators, which were far too heavy for the kids to have moved, even collectively, which had been rolled away from their original positions. There were no other signs of anything unusual, other than an uncanny silence that had settled about the area.

The youthful witnesses learned pretty quickly not to tell other people about what they'd seen. Laughter invariably rang out in response. Names were called, feelings were hurt and friendships were ruined over the encounter.

Curtis told me he and his friends never went back to the old clubhouse after that, or ventured anywhere else near Canoe Creek. Even today, they still know there's a monster out there.

Ten years earlier and less than two miles north another "beastman" encounter took place along the banks of Canoe Creek. This one also involved children and was even stranger. I first learned of the incident in 2006 during my trip to Hebbardsville to meet a man who claimed to be in possession of what he claimed to be a real Bigfoot tooth to include in my first book, "*Mysterious Kentucky,*" (Whitechapel Press, 2007). Greg Tacket, a longtime family friend, was acting as my guide to the location where two Bigfoot creatures were reportedly seen a couple of years before. When we were, at last, heading east on Hwy. 136, Greg surprised me by saying, "I'm gonna tell ya somethin', Bart, cause I know you'll believe me and not think I'm crazy."

My interest was piqued. I knew that all good Fortean stories began this way -- as confessions.

"One day back in 1980, when I was thirteen years old, me and a buddy of mine were riding a go-cart through the woods along the banks of Canoe Creek behind Woodland Manor. You know where I'm talkin' about? There on Sand Lane?"

I shook my head.

"There was a dirt road we had back there in the woods that wound along the creek, and we was gittin' it down that road [sic] in our go-cart when, all of a sudden, somethin' big and hairy jumped up out of the creek on our right and took off runnin' down the road right in front of us."

Greg shook his head ruefully. "Everyone I ever told about this laughed at me and said I was nuts."

"What did it look like?" I asked.

My guide paused for a second. "It looked like a hairy, humped-back caveman." he said. "It had dark, matted, shaggy hair on its head, shoulders and chest. It thinned out to bare skin on its upper arms and started again at the elbows and went down to its hands. It had a bare midsection, real muscular."

"You got a real good look at it?" I asked. "Yeah. A real good look."

"Did you notice any genitallia?"

"No. The hair started again at the thing's belly and was thick down to the top of its legs, then bare down to the knees. And hairy again from its knees all the way down to its feet."

Greg looked at me trying, no doubt, to gauge my response to this. He could tell that I was taking him seriously.

"I've talked to several people who've seen these things along Canoe Creek. What color was its skin?"

He looked relieved at this. "White." he said. "Like ours."

"Did it run like a man?"

"No." Greg answered. "It ran on all fours, like a gorilla."

I thought for a moment as I drove. "Could it have been someone playing a prank on you? How do you know it wasn't someone in a monkey costume out trying to scare a couple of kids?

"I thought about that a lot. But I know it wasn't. We was goin' over twenty miles an hour in that go-cart, flat out. And this thing was a lot faster than us. No way a man could run that fast on all fours even without a costume. It looked back at us once, crossed the road and shot off like a streak straight into the woods."

"Did it have long, or longer than normal arms?"

"No. It was built just like a strong man, and looked like a man would runnin' down on all fours like that. Only a lot faster."

"How tall do you recollect it was?'

"About five feet tall, I'd say. Taller than the go-cart. That's another thing I thought about a lot. If it was that tall bent down like that it would've been way taller standing up than any man."

"Yes," I said, "Around nine or ten feet tall."

We rode on for a moment in silence. It was Greg who broke it. "There's one more thing," he said. I looked at him and waited. "I know it's gonna sound crazy, but...its head was shaped funny."

"Funny?" I asked. What do you mean?"

He shook his head as if searching for the right words. "Well, you know how a man's head, from the forehead to the back, is more narrow than it is round? This thing's head looked like it grew outward at the sides. The head on top was flat, but the sides just bulged outward past the ears." He put his hands up on either side of his head and cupped his fingers. "Like this, you know what I mean? It had a huge, flat, rounded head. I've never seen or heard of anything like it."

Greg said he and his friend were so shaken up by the sight of the beast that they high-tailed it out of the area and never went back there again. He suffered much ridicule whenever he spoke of the incident and he soon learned to keep his mouth shut about it. He said his friend never talked about it at all.

The Geneva Giant

The Geneva River bottoms in western Henderson County have been the location of sightings of mystery animals for many years, from giant, red, featherless birds to thirty-foot-long aquatic serpents. A deer hunter in this area witnessed an eight-foot-tall creature covered with black frizzy hair walk beneath his tree stand just before dawn one morning in the early 1990s. It walked past him, within a few feet of his location, apparently unaware of his presence. He claimed that it made absolutely no sound as it passed beneath him. Scared to death, he waited until dawn and got the hell out of there. When asked for a description of the thing he replied that it looked like a giant, hairy African American. He refused to hunt in the area after the incident.

Another report from this same area and time period involves a carload of teens out joy-riding late one night. They parked the car next to an isolated area called the Grassy Pond, a large, secluded lake, and got out to stretch their legs. They were standing there talking when a terrible scream came from the other side of the lake, followed by the sound of something huge jumping into the water. They could clearly hear that, whatever it was, it was swimming with overhand strokes like a human swimmer. As it was approaching very rapidly, they were inclined to leave the scene in a very hasty manner.

The Geneva General Store, which sits along Highway 136, was the scene of another sighting of the hirsute giant. In late November 2005, as duck hunting season was in full swing, the store opened at 4:00 a.m. in order to take advantage of the early morning bird-hunting crowd. One of the employees was twenty-two-year-old Kara Fruit, who was used to the routine. But that frosty morning would be anything but routine. On pulling up beside the store her headlights illuminated a very large, hair-covered figure bent over rummaging through the dumpster that sat next to the store. She couldn't believe her eyes.

"It looked like the biggest man I've ever seen," Fruit later said. She stared in amazement as the creature stood up and fled, without looking into the headlights, through the back yards of the neighborhood, in the direction of the river.

"The dogs penned up in the next yard started going crazy," she told me. "That was when I knew that what I saw was real." Panic-stricken, she backed her car up near the front door and waited in the car while she placed a frantic call to her boss, who arrived at the scene a short time later.

"Kara's not the kind to get scared," her boss, who wishes to remain anonymous, later told me, "but when I got to the store she was white as a sheet. She wasn't about to go into the store by herself."

The witness later got a friend, who was six foot five, to stand next to the dumpster for comparison. The man was unable to lean into the dumpster as Kara had observed the creature to do. She estimated that it stood at least two feet taller than her friend. But that's not all.

The general store had suffered a string of three peculiar burglaries in the weeks before the sighting. Strangely, only food was taken. The back door opened near a cooler with sliding glass doors in which were stored several plastic containers filled with sliced sandwich meat of every sort: ham, turkey, bologna, etc. On each occasion the containers were all found completely emptied of their contents. Nothing else was missing. "It was strange," the storeowner later told me. "Whoever it was had complete access to hundreds of dollars worth of cigarettes and other merchandise and all they stole was the lunch-meat."

The first two instances bore no evidence of how the thief had gained entrance into the store, as everything appeared perfectly normal and in its place. The third occasion, however, revealed that a small glass window in the door had been broken. It was supposed that the intruder simply reached in and turned the deadbolt. Oddly, a body was found in an adjacent field in the early 1970s. It was a local man who had apparently died of blunt force trauma to the head. The case still remains unsolved.

Another mysterious, hirsute creature was seen at a remote fishing camp along the Ohio River in Geneva in early July 2009. Eyewitness Bobby Payne was fishing one evening, along with his mother and wife, when an ungodly sound pierced the air. "It sounded like the cry of a young boy in pain," his wife later told me, with a gurgling death rattle at the end. It was so loud that it could be heard above the radio that was blaring loud rock music. The family dog was along for the trip and he whimpered and cowered at their feet. They had heard other strange sounds on previous visits, they told me, sounds that had spooked them and made them leave the location abruptly. One such sound, Payne said, resembled a baby's cries, with growls mixed in.

Interestingly, just a stone's throw from the river camp is the site of an old house that was long rumored to be haunted when it was still standing. The Paynes figured that even though the house had been torn down, perhaps the ghosts still remained and that was what they were hearing. They had no idea that many hairy humanoid reports mention the curious descriptions of vocalizations that sound like human babies crying.

Bobby Payne was about to learn firsthand, however, about the presence of the Geneva Giant. He went to investigate the strange sounds, walking up the riverbank to the camper, accompanied by his dog. Not seeing anything unusual, he moved on toward the trees at the edge of the small clearing. Then an overpowering feeling of dread froze him to the spot. "It was almost like a black cloud went over me," he later told me. "I couldn't move." The dog bolted back in the direction from which they had come. That was when Bobby noticed two glowing eyes situated low among the darkness of the trees. "They were like flames," he said. They flickered in the night as they stared at the frightened man. Bobby felt completely immobilized and could do nothing except sink down on his haunches into a squatting

Bobby Payne as he tells his story to the film-crew of the History Cannel's 'Monster Quest.' (Photo by Tony Gerrard)

Bigfoot in Kentucky -- Page 61

Unexplained 'Teepee' construction at the Geneva river camp site.

position. The eyes were huge, teardrop-shaped, and nearly a foot apart. They seemed to shift color from yellow to orange to red and back again. Then the thing slowly stood up to its full height, around eight feet tall, and walked back into the trees. It never took its eyes off the frightened man as it left. Bobby claimed that he felt a strange compulsion to follow the beast into the woods, but was saved when his wife came running up to him and broke the spell.

A couple of weeks later, as he and another man were in a boat fishing the river very close to that same location one night, Payne spotted a figure standing on the bank among some trees. It was only about sixty or seventy feet away, he claimed, so he turned his powerful spotlight in that direction. He was surprised and frightened by what he saw - a hair-covered humanoid figure standing on two legs. It had long arms and stood around five foot nine or so, he said. Long hair covered the face, obscuring any detail. When the light hit it, the creature stepped behind a tree, then bolted quickly into the darkness and disappeared.

Bobby also claimed to have discovered a strange footprint in a muddy field that summer. He described it as looking like two human hands laid one atop the other and pressed into the mud leaving what appeared to be no less than ten toe impressions. He also claimed to have chased a small black panther the previous summer.

At the time of this writing, the area is still a very active one. I visited the site in July

2009 and found several mysterious objects in the thick woods surrounding Bobby Payne's camp, including a large teepee structure. I took a photograph of the site and later found an anomalous shape on the film that was not there at the time the picture was taken.

All the unexplained activity hasn't kept Payne and his family away, however. On the weekend of February 13 and 14, 2009, Bobby and his wife were at the campsite in the evening enjoying the peace and quiet. A barred owl had arrived a short while earlier, and Bobby amused himself by calling to the bird, and hearing it call back to him. This happened several times when the bird suddenly went quiet. After several more fruitless attempts a frightening shriek suddenly erupted from the darkened woods around them. "It sounded like an ape screaming," He later told me. "Then we heard what sounded like something beating on the ground with its fists." Once again they opted to leave the area as quickly as they could, not returning for two weeks. Then the first daylight sighting of the creature occurred.

The broken and twisted tree that was allegedly damaged by the Geneva Giant.

At around 1:00 p.m. on the afternoon of February 28, I received a call from Payne informing me that he and his wife had just seen the creature near the campsite. According to him, they were walking around the foundation of the old haunted house site when they heard a grunt come from the underbrush about forty yards away. They turned and saw what they described as a seven- to eight-foot-tall manlike creature stand up from behind a tree.

"This thing stood up," Payne said, "grabbed the tree with one hand and started shaking it violently. The whole tree! Then it turned and ran upright into the woods."

Payne's wife told me that she thought she was going to have a heart attack when she saw it. "I've never been so scared in all my life," she said. By the time the thing ran away the couple were running as well - in the direction of the truck. I was at the site less than two hours later, but the creature was nowhere to be seen. I was able to interview the Paynes and photograph the scene, including the tree that the creature allegedly shook. The immediate area of the sighting is comprised of small trees and bushes amid thick underbrush and briars. The investigation of this case is ongoing.

My brother and I had a very frightening experience in Smith Mills, just two miles south of Geneva, back in the 1980s. I wrote the following about the experience in "*Mysterious Kentucky*":

There is a place in Smith Mills, Henderson County, called Burbank's Lake, also known locally as Spook Hill. As you might guess by the name, down through the years this particular spot has garnered a reputation for being haunted. I believe it to be a "window" location as many inexplicable experiences have taken place in this area, including various cryptid sightings such as Bigfoot, water monsters, giant birds and black panthers. UFO activity is not uncommon in this area, and there are many ghost stories associated with Spook Hill as well. Lending to this aura of mystery, no doubt, is the fact that there are two very old cemeteries, long since reclaimed by the forest, at the hilltop.

Also situated there, between the main cemetery and the slave cemetery, are three ancient lakes. One is fairly big and deep and all were rumored for as long as I can remember to contain monster bass. The male members of my family have always been avid fishermen so, one day back in the summer of 1987, we all decided to go and fish there. This was totally against our dad's better judgment. He had lived near the area when he was younger and had been personally warned by Mr. Burbank never to let dark catch him on the property. He never said why. Also, my older half-brother, Harold, had told us a scary story about a time when he and a brother-in-law had went night fishing there in a boat a few years before. He claimed that every time the two tried to land the boat and come ashore the woods would erupt with the sound of breaking branches and heavy footsteps, forcing them to shove back out into the lake.

"It sounded like a herd of elephants was trompin' [sic] around in there," he said. Every attempt to leave the lake was met by this resistance, which frightened them both, and they were forced to spend the entire night huddled in the boat in the middle of the lake. Only when dawn broke were the two "allowed" to leave, which they did in all haste, never to return. This intrigued me to no end, green as I was back then, but the lure of trophy bass enticed us.

We arrived at the lake in the early afternoon and headed through the trees down to the water. We had been able to procure a one-man bass boat with a small trolling motor from a friend. It could just barely hold two people. As there were six of us, four brothers and two friends, this meant that four would be confined to fishing from the banks. We found the place to be absolutely teeming with water moccasins and not one of us had brought a weapon of any type, only fishing poles. Since everyone wanted to fish the other side of the lake we opted to be ferried across one by one rather than walk through the tall grass, trying to avoid a possible snakebite. It took forever for the little motor to chug everyone across the lake. By the time we made it to the other side it was already late afternoon. The sun was making a rapid disappearance behind the trees. We fished awhile without much luck. I remember catching one largemouth that weighed a couple of pounds and then before we knew it, darkness was fast approaching.

My older brother, who had been hogging the bass boat with a family friend, finally sputtered in to shore and began taking everyone back across one at a time. This took around thirty or forty minutes round trip, with five trips to be made.

Complete darkness fell with one of my younger brothers and I remaining on the far side of the lake. We had half a gallon of kerosene and had earlier gathered what wood we could find, which was mostly wet since it had rained a couple of days previously, and used it to build a small fire. We were sitting there bemoaning going through so much trouble for nothing when the sound of breaking branches and heavy footsteps erupted from the woods in front of us. It was a terrifyingly loud commotion and we jumped up in fright. I have never before or since, been so terrified by a sound. Looking back, it was totally unlike me to react in such a manner. Perhaps it was because, at the first limb fracture, we *both* knew immediately what was out there in the darkness of those haunted woods. Worse, the sounds soon began to come from behind us and to our right as well, and they were getting closer. We heard no grunts, no growls, and no breathing Just the heavy footfalls and the terrific explosions of cracking tree limbs all around us. We thought we were both going to die that night, without a doubt, and I still count myself lucky to have made it out of there alive.

We could see nothing, as it was quite dark. There was no moon and heavy cloud cover. When the sounds got quite close I threw some kerosene into the fire, determined to at least see what was about to eat us. The fuel ignited and the fire flared up, illuminating an area of about twenty-five feet in all directions. We saw nothing. The light would only last for a few seconds then it would subside and plunge our surroundings back into utter darkness. When this happened the sounds would start up and approach us again. Over and over I threw fuel into the shrinking fire, washing the woods in sudden firelight. When I did this, the sounds immediately stopped. We never did see a thing. Not even a single eye-shine. The kerosene didn't last too long.

We had been yelling and making a good-sized noise of our own, to no avail. It seemed that only the light was holding our would-be attackers at bay. But the fire was fading fast. Soon it was reduced to a tiny flame at one end of a small, wet branch and the noises were closing in once again. The smaller the light became the closer the ungodly racket approached. I grabbed the burning twig and held it up in front of me as we walked backwards down toward the water's edge. I told my brother to get ready to swim for his life. The noises followed us down to the lake, amazingly, because this area had very few trees! It sounded like invisible branches were being broken by invisible beings. Lucky for us, just as we were about to get wet, we heard the sound of our brother on the boat shouting his approach. We yelled for him to hurry. When he reached us we were in a state of agitation, to say the least. He wanted to know who was next. Well, to put it simply, we found out a one-man boat can actually carry three people in an emergency.

The Spottsville Monster

Mary stood washing dishes at the kitchen sink in the small country farmhouse, her hands working methodically at their chore. It was a Saturday and she was twelve years old, dressed in simple garments and well-worn leather shoes. Her pigtails bounced as she dried and stacked the plates. She was home alone. Midday was approaching and from the window in front of her came the sounds of the peaceful day outside. Birds chirped. A gentle breeze stirred through the branches of the nearby forest and Mary could hear the faint sounds of the rushing river. These were peaceful sounds that belied her family's troubled stay at the farmhouse. Her mother and older brother Herman had gone into town for groceries while she'd elected to stay behind and finish her chores. Neither of them liked the idea, but she insisted that she would be all right. After all, she was almost grown now.

Suddenly the sounds outside ceased and a heavy silence fell. It only lasted a second before a mighty wind hit her in the face and blew the curtains and her pigtails straight out. She gasped and turned away only to see that all the curtains in the house were blowing inward, even the ones in front of closed windows. The back door flew violently inward as well and slammed against the wall. She plainly heard the front door do the same though she could not see it from where she stood. Her face was pale as the wind died down and she stood for a second, staring at the doorway to the living room and hardly daring to breathe. Something was in there, she knew. Something terrible. She could feel it looking at her through the walls and the dawning of that awful realization filled her with utter despair and dread.

She took a fearful step toward the living room doorway. She didn't know why. She didn't want to. She was scared. So scared. Her feet were moving of their own will and she couldn't make them stop. Tears began to spill from her eyes and she clenched her fists as, after a seeming eternity, she stepped into the doorway. She screamed when it came into view. The monster in the living room! It was huge and covered with dark hair. It was so tall that it was bent over nearly double to avoid its head from striking the room's eight-foot ceiling. Its claws were like daggers. Mary screamed again when their eyes met. Through her tears she could see that the monster's eyes glowed an evil red and that, with each deep, ragged breath, blue fire was coming from its nostrils and mouth. She fainted then.

Mary's mother and brother were mildly annoyed at first when they'd arrived home and found every window and door locked. Her annoyance quickly turned to anger and then to fear after Herman beat on the door with no answer. Just before panic set in she told him to break the glass. Once the door was unlocked they rushed inside calling for Mary. At length they found her huddled behind the couch suffering from shock and unable to speak. In the middle of the living room floor, impressed into the linoleum, was the imprint of a gigantic footprint twenty-four inches long. The next day the family abandoned the isolated farmhouse, never to return.

This incident, taken from my book, "*The Inhumanoids! Real Encounters With Beings That Can't Exist*" (CFZ Press, 2010) happened in 1935 in the farmhouse that my own family occupied forty years later. I later learned there was much monster activity during that forty-year span.

"Before the big flood of '37," Herman Snodgrass (Mary's brother) told me back in the late 1980s, "there used to be a little town down there in them bottoms [sic]. It had a little church and even a small one-room schoolhouse. But people didn't stay long. That monster ran most of 'em off."

After the flood only a few houses had remained intact. Hardly anyone had bothered to move back in. The town no longer existed.

Our house was one of the few that weren't destroyed by the flood and people moved in and out at a steady pace during the following years. I'm sure each of them had their own experiences with what would later be called "The Spottsville Monster." I

The Nunnelly farm on Mound Ridge Road, where the author's family endured a terrifying 11-month ordeal in 1975

was able to trace some former occupants back to the early 1960s, all of whom had stories to tell. Ironically, my own parents were warned about the creature by the house's previous tenants. The man of the house said he had fired numerous rounds through the back screen door at a "big, hairy fella" standing outside in the yard.

As for my own family's experiences there, the house on Mound Ridge Road seemed perfect at first. The property contained many types of fruit trees and berry bushes and Dad planned on raising several acres of tobacco come spring. Rose, my mother, looked forward to raising a big vegetable garden. Us six kids could play in the big yard or artifact hunt in the fields along the front and sides of the house.

That first spring started out well despite the steady disappearance of my father's chickens, which was attributed to weasels and such at first. Then my brother Dean and I ages 10 and 9, respectively, began to find the carcasses of dead dogs in the fields when we were out looking for arrowheads. The bodies were all strangely mutilated, being sliced from groin to gullet with all the organs removed including the eyes and tongues. No blood or footprints could be seen around these grisly discoveries, even though most were found in open, cultivated fields. Also strange was the fact that no scavenger would eat the remains. Not even a fly would land on them to lay its eggs. Before the episode was finally over in January 1976 my family would lose a total of over 200 chickens, a goat and a horse and find the remains of eight dogs, a pig, and a goat - all mutilated.

One day my parents heard what sounded like something big drinking water from the small creek just inside the woods out behind the house. By the sound of the loud gulping noises it was making, Dad judged whatever it was to be at least as big as a horse or cow. Soon afterwards we began to hear strange noises coming from the fields and woods outside. Sometimes they would come from close by, sometimes from far away. Our two vicious and highly treasured guard dogs could be heard bumping their heads on the floorboards as they scurried beneath the house in fear of whatever was making the sounds. This caused my father much concern.

As a precaution, when my older brother, Harold, arrived that spring to add on a bedroom and an indoor bathroom to the house, Dad invited him and his family to move their trailer onto the property and set it beside the house. As he was suffering from glaucoma and steadily losing his eyesight, Dad felt that we would be safer with another grown man there who could any intruders if need arose. Harold could also help with raising the tobacco. They moved the trailer in soon after and placed it very close to the house under Dad's direction.

One day a stranger came walking from the far tree line across one of the fields. He was holding a shotgun broken down, and walking toward the house, his other hand raised in a friendly gesture. It took both the adults to finally calm down the dogs when the stranger approached and introduced himself as Roy C. (not his real name), a neighbor who lived less than a half mile up the road. He told my father that he had just been squirrel hunting in some nearby woods and had scared up something big and hairy that ran away on its hind legs. As it was heading in this direction and he hadn't the slightest idea what the animal could be or whether it was dangerous, he said he felt it was his Christian duty to come warn our family about the event. He didn't get a look at the thing's face, Roy said, but it was big and hairy and ran away on two legs like a man. Dad liked Roy immediately and invited him to come back for coffee when he had the chance. The two became great friends and this new acquaintance would play a pivotal role in the drama that was about to unfold.

The first sighting by someone in my own family happened around 8 o'clock one evening when Mom stepped out onto the front porch to call Harold and his wife and their three children over for a late supper. She looked to her left and saw a giant, hairy shadow at least eight feet tall standing in the darkness near an old shed. It was looking at her. She screamed and ran back inside and locked the door. Harold soon rushed over holding his rifle and Dad grabbed the shotgun. Shaking, Mom called the state police. After briefly looking around close to the house and finding nothing the troopers left, most probably laughing at the crazy story they'd just heard. They would be back several more times in the upcoming months as events escalated into an almost nightly visitation by the creature. Eventually, even though it was later learned that sightings of a similar nature were taking place all along the Green River in towns such as Bluff City and Hebbardsville, the police refused to respond to any more monster calls and my family was left to defend ourselves.

Mom saw the thing again at dusk not long after as it ran from a field by our garden and jumped an old fencerow. It chased Dad and one of the dogs out of a tobacco field that he was tending alone one day but it was my brother Dean who had the closest encounter. He was standing in the front yard one day trying to take some garden hoes away from a couple of the younger girls when he heard a tremendous crashing through the trees out back, followed by an unsettling quiet. It was then that Dean said he saw the monster standing in a small gully by an old truck. He described it as being muscular and tall, with a square jaw and small, close-set eyes. It was covered in reddish gray hair, thin and patchy in spots as if it was very old. All of us children saw it one morning while waiting for the school bus. It was standing in a cornfield, towering above the full-grown corn. It seemed to sway slightly from side to side.

By this time the local TV news had heard of the events from the police band radio and decided to send a camera crew and sketch artist out to our house. The artist drew a hairy, man-like animal with no face and a segment about the affair was featured on the evening news. The next day a crew of reporters from the local newspaper descended on our farm to get the scoop. The morning edition of *The Gleaner* dubbed the beast "The Spottsville Monster" and the accompanying article treated the sighting fairly, despite some mistakes, such as calling the monster green in color and misnaming the road on which my family lived. Ironically, this sent the crowds of gun-toting monster hunters descending on Spottsville, searching everywhere for a location that didn't exist. As I recall, not a single one of them ever made it to Mound Ridge Road. Meanwhile, the neighbor from down the road had agreed to try and track the monster down for the safety of my siblings and I. He said he encountered it one day at an old, abandoned house far back in the woods. It was stooping down, he said, looking out the window at him. When he fired it, he said it instantly vanished before his eyes. Shaken, he went home where he dared not mention the incident to anyone, not even his wife. He didn't give up, however, and eventually claimed to have found trace evidence in the form of hair, a claw and a partial footprint left in near-frozen ground. The print, though incomplete, was impressive and showed the clear impression of a large, four-toed foot.

The Spottsville Monster -- illustration by the author, based on witness accounts of the creature. Observed at least since the 1930s, The monster continues to appear to startled residents of Henderson County.

Bigfoot in Kentucky -- Page 69

A partial cast of the footprint of the Spottsville Monster, circa 1975. This photo originally appeared in the local newspaper. The impression, which was later destroyed by authorities, clearly shows a four-toed creature.

When the news coverage began Dad suggested that the reporters talk to the neighbor, which they did. Roy's name appeared in print and he, like my own family, suffered through an embarrassing period of public ridicule. We children were endlessly taunted at school, and the neighbor, who worked at a local fire department, fared much the same.

Strange things were seen and heard for the next several months but the events finally came to a conclusion, for my family at least, when Roy told Dad about a bizarre encounter with the creature he had experienced a couple of weeks prior, followed by a short stay in the hospital. He had been looking for the thing one day, he said, when it started to rain. He was walking a tree line at the time and went into a nearby, long-abandoned old barn to take shelter from the rain. Little did he know the creature was inside. Roy said he stood for a moment at one end of the open-ended barn, when suddenly the feeling that he wasn't alone washed over him and he felt the often-described sensation of the hair rising on the back his neck and arms. He slowly turned around and found himself staring into a huge, hairy midsection. Roy stood six feet, three inches tall but he said he had to look almost straight up to see the creature's face. It was a horrible sight and deeply unsettling, he told me, with a short muzzle, long pointed fangs set into both its upper and lower jaws, black skin, and strange red eyes that chilled and frightened him to his very soul. He reached for the rifle strapped on his shoulder but suddenly found himself unable to move as those terrible eyes froze him in their gaze.

Roy thought that he was surely done for but, despite the beasts' alarming appearance, it spoke to him in a human voice, without moving its mouth, using some sort of mental telepathy. It said, "Don't be afraid... I will not harm you." Then it turned around and ran out the end of the barn that was facing the open, plowed field, now muddy from the rain. It was a few moments before Roy could move again, but at last he was able to shake his head and clear the vision of those red, burning eyes from his mind. When he had composed himself somewhat he walked to the doorway through which the creature had run, hoping to see its tracks in the muddy field. There were none.

Dad, realizing this was no "ordinary" monster, asked Roy if he thought it might come up one night and try to steal one of his children. The man replied that it was not likely, as our family had been there for nearly a year and the thing seemed content with killing animals and merely scaring people. But, he said, if the creature ever did decide to kidnap a child, there would be nothing anyone in this world could do. The child would be gone. Period. For weeks, Dad had kept a five-gallon bucket of kerosene and a mop near the kitchen door in case the creature tried to get in and attack the members of the household. In the event that he could not drive it away with bullets or fire it was his intention to kick the bucket of fuel over and set it ablaze, burning the house to the ground with the whole family inside rather than losing one or more of us to the creature and trying to live with the loss. Better, he reasoned, that we should all die and go to heaven together than trying to live without a single member of the family. All of us had agreed. Soon after the talk with the neighbor we found ourselves once again packing up our belongings and moving back to the safety of the city.

It is interesting to note that the descriptions given of the beast vary from the classic Bigfoot description to one more akin to the "Dogman" phenomenon and seem to indicate the appearance of two unknown humanoids in the same small area at the same time.

I interviewed Roy, our former neighbor and my father's good friend, in February, 2005. What he told me about his further encounters with the Spottsville Monster astounded me. He claimed that he had seen the beast several more times after my family left. Moreover he said he had seen things that went far beyond anything that he had ever dreamed possible. One day, he was walking along an old fence-line next to a field and noticed a strange area that looked like heat waves rising from a hot, summer road. The area was only a few yards wide and to either side everything looked normal. According to Roy, as he was watching, one of the creatures stepped out of this strange wavy area like stepping out a doorway. One second there was nothing, and the next there it was looking right at him! It growled at him and, at the same time, Roy said he could hear, screaming inside his head, the words, "Leave me alone!' Then it turned around, took a step back into the strange-looking "doorway," and disappeared.

After that, Roy said he began watching this area from a distance using binoculars. In all, he claimed to have witnessed several different monsters using this doorway a total of three different times, always appearing or disappearing, seemingly, into thin air. The creatures would then be seen crossing his own property and tripping the sensitive motion detecting security lights in his yard. His last sighting was in August of 2004. When asked if I could see the trace evidence I received another revelation. Soon after the media coverage back in '75, he said, he was visited by the state police and a couple of other men whom he took to be Department of Natural Resources officials. He was shocked when they demanded that he turn over all evidence concerning the Spottsville Monster to them. Moreover, they warned him that if he ever talked to anyone else about the subject, especially the media, he would be arrested without hesitation and thrown into prison on a "made-up charge." He said the men told him he would never see his wife and two young daughters again unless it was through prison bars. In addition, a statement had been prepared for the local paper in his name stating for a fact that what he had seen was nothing more than a large, black bear. Not easily intimidated Roy said he balked at the whole thing at first, reasoning that this was America and his rights were being grossly violated. But his visitors were very persuasive and, in the end, he said he had little choice but to go along with the charade for the sake of his family.

Over the years, Roy said he had tried to get the items back with no luck. One time, he said he and his family came home and found a large freezer bag on the front porch. It held the remains of his plaster cast, smashed into powder. The statement was released to the local paper, which proudly proclaimed the mystery of the Spottsville Monster solved. The hoards of monster hunters melted away leaving behind only the body of a dog, someone's family pet accidentally shot by monster-hunting teens. Everything quieted down and the Spottsville Monster faded into memory. Roy said he never talked publicly of the monster again, and still fears the threats made thirty years ago, as he now owns a successful business and he does not wish to jeopardize it. He blames the inability to speak of his encounters on a heart attack he suffered in 1985, which left him, for a brief time before he was resuscitated, clinically dead. He also claims that his near death experience left him with a certain degree of formerly dormant mental abilities.

As I sat listening to his story it struck me that here was a man who was highly successful and content. He seemed almost embarrassed by the whole situation and genuinely feared the possibility of his name being released to the public again and suffering through the treatment that he endured back in the nineteen-seventies, or worse. Then why was he speaking to me about it at all? I asked.

His reply was simply because it was the truth and people had a right to know the truth regardless of how many choose not to believe it. I agree with him. He also claims to know other people who have seen this creature or creatures but who wish to remain silent due to possible public ridicule.

In 1975, the same year that the Spottsville incidents took place, even more strangeness involving hairy monsters was happening in the heart of the city of Henderson proper.

The following is from a 1997 witness interview:

1. Subject of sighting: Possible Bigfoot

2. Date, time and location of sighting: Summer of 1975-76 -- Afternoon. Pritchett Farm just off Old Henderson Rd., Henderson County.

3. Approx. distance between witness and subject: 100-150 yards

4. Describe in detail animal witnessed: Light brown, hairy being. Large body and

shoulders. Thick neck and big head.

5. Did the animal walk or run on two legs, four legs, or both? Stood on two legs. Seemed to wobble as it stood.

6. Approx. height of animal: 7-8 ft. tall

7. Approx. weight of animal: 350 lbs or more

8. Did you notice any strange smells during the sighting? If yes describe: No, not at this sighting

9. Did the animal seem threatening at any time? No

10. Were you frightened by the encounter? Yes. Very.

11. Did you try to communicate with the animal? No

12. Did the animal try to communicate with you in any way? Yes

13. Describe the animal's skin, or hair, color and texture: Light tan hair. Thinner hair on face.

14. Did the animal act aggressively at any time? No

15. Was the animal frightened of you? No

16. Did the animal leave any physical evidence at the scene such as footprints, hair, etc.? No

17. Do you, or anyone you know, possess any evidence, photographic or otherwise, to support your sighting? No

18. Describe in detail what happened during the sighting and how it ended: A friend and I were riding my motorcycle. We stopped under a tree and my friend started going crazy telling me to "look!" I didn't see anything so I told him to point. I looked where he was pointing and there it stood looking right at us. It made some movement like wobbling. We were both scared so we got back on the bike and left as fast as possible.

19. Has this animal, or others like it, been seen in the area before or since? Yes

20. Do you feel that the animal could be encountered again in the area? Yes

21. Describe, as best you can, the animal's head and face: Seemed to have human-type face. Large head.

22. Describe the animal's limbs, hands and feet: Did not see. Only saw from chest up.

23. Did the sighting take place during the day or night? Day

24. Describe the weather and/or visibility conditions at time of sighting: Excellent

25. Do you feel that the animal you saw was a natural, though unknown, animal, or a supernatural entity? Explain reasons for this belief: Supernatural powers. I had a feeling that it was trying to communicate [telepathically] at that time. [It was] a very bad feeling, very frightening.

Full name of witness: John C. D. (full name on file)
Age: 37
Birth date: 12-23-61
Sex: M
Occupation: Construction

1. Were you suffering from any form of mental illness at time of sighting? No

2. Were you under the influence of any hallucinatory drugs or alcohol at time of sighting? No

3. Have you ever witnessed any unusual animal sightings before or since? If yes explain: Yes. I think I saw this thing in and around my house. I have witnessed a black panther, or very large cat, in area. Also, Just before the sighting, me and my entire family [sic] saw a large, flying orange ball of light in the sky.

4. Have you or any member of your family experienced any type of unexplained phenomena in the past? If yes explain: Yes. My whole family has experiences thought to be caused by this creature such as being watched and some of them think that it doesn't have to be in a visible form to be there.

5. Does the area in which the incident took place, to your knowledge, have a history of unexplained phenomena? Yes

6. What is your religious preference? (optional) Raised Christian

7. Do you have any personal theories about a possible explanation for the phenomena that you observed? If yes explain: No

AFFIDAVIT

I, John C. D., do hereby attest soberly and sincerely that the above document is an honest and truthful account of a strange event to which I have been a witness. All of the descriptions contained therein are accurate and without deception of any type, accidental or deliberate. I give this information freely and without clause, waiving all rights and without regard concerning monetary gains or any other benefits, for the sole reason of sharing this truthful event with others. The aforementioned event did, in actuality, take place and was not the result of any psychopathological delusion or hallucination of any order. I stand by and bear witness to the integrity of the report and the descriptions I have set down in writing therein. I release this information to the author/investigator to use in any way he deems worthy, and to the public in hopes that it will contribute to a greater understanding concerning phenomena of this nature.

Signed: John C. D.
Date: 6-10-97

When I interviewed John about his sightings I was immediately put at ease by his casual, down-to-earth demeanor. We talked for a while then other members of his family began to arrive and join in the conversation. They all had their own stories to tell about creatures that were obviously not of this physical world, but from somewhere else entirely.

The whole affair had begun after the entire family observed a small orange sphere as it cavorted in the skies over the family farm. Of the lot, the sister's experiences were the most unusual. She claimed that there were two creatures that frequented the property. One of them "good," and one of them "bad."

The good one was covered in white hair and the evil one had dark brown hair. On one evening, she claimed, the good creature had actually saved her life after the bad one "walked right through the wall like a ghost" and into her bedroom, intent on doing her harm. The white creature shielded her body with its own while the evil beast fumed and tried to get at her. Eventually it left.

The mother of the family had a frightening look at one of the things as it walked up the driveway toward the house late one evening. She thought it was her husband at first, she told me. It was dark and all she could see was a silhouette. Then, as it got closer, she knew that it wasn't her husband.

It was a tall, hairy monster! And it was wearing an old, beat-up hat and a tattered shirt. As it stood at the door she grabbed the kids and shoved them under the bed. It soon walked off into the night, but the incident frightened them all very badly. I could still see the fear on her face when she recounted the tale. The entire family felt that these things were supernatural in nature, possibly even demonic. They were also convinced that the beasts had the ability to become completely invisible to the human eye.

On January 20, 2006, I interviewed twenty-two-year-old Adam Candler, who claimed that on the evening of July 14, 2005, he was driving down Green River Rd. No. 2, just off T.S. Charner Road in Spottsville, when he noticed a large, dark object stooping down in a roadside ditch. When his vehicle approached to within a few yards the "object" suddenly stood up and ran on two legs into a nearby field. It was seven to eight feet tall, he said, and looked like a man, with slightly longer arms and covered all over with black hair. Due to the passage of time since the sighting took place a subsequent field investigation into the area to look for possible substantiating evidence would most likely yield little, if anything. Chandler stated that two other members of his family and one of his friends have seen this same creature in the same general area.

The Spottsville Monster has been around a long time and is still being seen regularly in the area. It can be argued that the Geneva Giant and the Hebbardsville Hillbilly (later in this chapter) are merely more localized monikers for the same creature, or same type of creature at the very least. In any event, on January 4, 2010, twelve-year-old Samuel P. (full name on file) was walking in his family's fourteen-acre woodlot near Corydon when he heard a series of low, pig-like grunts. As he turned, he saw something big and brown run away on four legs and disappear into the woods. He said he could not see much detail, only the legs, which he described as hair-covered and thin, as the creature fled. He ran home and excitedly told his grandmother, Dora, (not her real name) what had happened. Whether she believed him or not is hard to say, but only a couple of days later he once again ran into the house and told her he'd found a strange footprint in the woods. Dora accompanied Samuel to the place and saw the print for herself. It was strange-looking enough that she got plaster of Paris and made a mold of the impression.

I paid a visit to the family on April 11, 2010, and met both Samuel and Dora. I found them to be very sincere about the whole

Location where the Spottsville Monster was last seen on September 28th, 2010, near the intersection of Baskett Lane (1078-N) and Conley-Thomas Road.

affair. While talking to Samuel, I discovered that only a few days after he'd found the track, he had seen the creature again. This time it was sitting a good distance away with its back turned to him. It was apparently eating something, as every few seconds it brought its left hand, which was humanlike, up to its mouth. According to Samuel, this one was dark-colored, or black, and bigger than a man. Samuel watched the thing for about five minutes, he told me. Once, it acted like it had heard something, cocking its head up and looking around for a few seconds. Having seen enough, Samuel felt it was time to leave. He started backing away, he said, but slipped and made a noise. When he looked back at the creature it had apparently heard him, because it was staring right at him. It had a black face, he stated (whether this was due to skin color or the entire face being covered with hair it was too far away to tell), with a heavy brow ridge and "shiny" eyes. Sam played it cool, walking calmly away as if he hadn't seen the thing. Once out of sight of the creature, he said he ran as fast as he could back home.

Dora said she showed the plaster cast of the track to a local Department of Natural Resources official. She said he told her had no idea what could have made it. I could offer her little more. She felt that it might be a cat print, as the eastern cougar has been steadily making its way back into these parts for the past forty years, but on first glance I told her that it was far too big to be a cat print of any kind. I brought along the only known photograph of a Spottsville Monster cast, taken in 1975, for comparison and the two, save for size, were hardly similar. I photographed the cast and left my phone number with Dora, who promised to call should the creature turn up on their property again.

The Hebbardsville Hillbillies

In 2005, after nearly a year of gathering information and acquiring contacts, I was finally able to investigate rumors that large, hair-covered, bipedal monsters were still being seen in Hebbardsville, just across the mysterious Green River from Reed and Spottsville. I had learned that in the early winter of 2004, two stargazers were parked on Negro Hill on Pleasant Hill Road, overlooking the Green River bottomlands, when they spotted two figures in the field below them pulling up old corn stalks and apparently eating the roots. The creatures were large, apelike and hirsute, one having brown hair and the other white.

Returning to the scene the following morning, signs of the beings' presence, in the form of uprooted corn and tracks, were reportedly found. The creatures were dubbed the Hebbardsville Hillbillies by the locals and the press. I also learned that there was an old abandoned house in the area where something had reportedly constructed a mighty strange bed out of grass and sticks. Although I was warned by a local journalist that a fugitive from justice had been apprehended in this same house a couple of years previously, and it was possible that this man had constructed the makeshift bedding, I was determined to see it personally, if it still existed, and decide for myself the nature of its construction. However, since the source of the information did not reveal the identities of the alleged witnesses, finding any information at all

Negro Hill in Henderson County, a site consider sacred by the Cherokee Indians and a place of recurring Bigfoot activity.

regarding the incident proved to be a daunting task.

As luck would have it, I ran into an old acquaintance of mine, Greg Tackett, a one-time Hebbardsville resident, who claimed to know the story and locations well. He agreed to lead me there at my convenience. I had also been in contact with an old Cherokee gentleman, a Mr. M. F., who claimed to have seen these creatures countless times in the Hebbardsville area since the 1960s and could provide much detail about their appearance and behavior. I decided to try and kill two birds with one stone, so to speak, and both explore the 2004 sighting location and interview M.F. in the same weekend.

Saturday, December 16, 2006, was mild. I had made an appointment to meet Greg and travel to the locations mentioned in the Hillbilly sighting, including the abandoned house where the strange bedding was found. I pulled into his driveway just as he was pulling out. He is a plumber by trade and had received an urgent service call. He apologized and asked if we could postpone the adventure until the following day, which was fine by me. I had scheduled an interview with M.F. for 2 p.m. that Sunday to record his testimony, do a sketch of the creatures he claimed to have witnessed so many times and photograph the tooth and the location where it was found, if possible. I told Greg I would return around 11 a.m. the following day. He promised to be ready. Instead of returning home I decided to go ahead and drive the fifteen or twenty miles to Hebbardsville, and do some reconnoitering of the Pleasant Hill area. Moreover, Greg had informed me that the lady who ran a small country store in Hebbardsville had a copy of the original newspaper article concerning the Hebbardsville Hillbillies. According to him, she had this article displayed on the front counter for many months for everyone to see and had only fairly recently taken it down. He was sure that she would show it to me if asked. I had never been able to read the article. Due to my work schedule and time constraints I had as yet been unable to conduct a microfiche search at the local library.

Twenty minutes later I parked my truck beside the store and walked in. Several people, mostly local farmers, were milling around or eating lunch at the tables in back. A young mother and her two children were standing at the counter behind which two older ladies were busying themselves frying burgers and ringing up purchases. I grabbed a Coke and got in line. When I approached the counter I smiled and ordered a cheeseburger with pickle, onions and mustard. "The burger'll be a few minutes," one of the women said.

"That's all right," I replied. "I've got time."

As she took my money I asked if she was the owner. She replied affirmatively with what sounded like a little suspicion in her voice. I got the feeling that this would not go well for me. Nevertheless, I informed her that I was a local writer, come to investigate the Hillbilly sightings.

"Do you know anything about that?" I asked. "Sure don't." she replied. "Don't know nothin' about that."

"Really? A friend of mine told me you had a write-up from the newspaper. Said you had it taped to this very counter for a long time. That true? Do you have the article?"

"Sure don't." she nervously replied and I could tell immediately that she was lying to me. Usually people love to talk and, more often than not will, if given half a chance. There's no better place in the world than a small town country store if tales are what you're looking for, unless you're an outsider. Though I was born and had spent nearly my entire life in Henderson County, she had never seen me before and viewed me with obvious distrust. I couldn't really blame her. It was just the way of things here.

"Look, all I know is that happened years and years ago on Pleasant Hill Road. And there ain't been nothin' like that goin' on 'round here lately," she said.

I noticed a couple of "good ol' boys" eying me from the back. The next couple of minutes passed uncomfortably and quietly. I took my lunch, thanked her and walked out.

I found Pleasant Hill Road to be hilly and heavily wooded, especially as I drove closer to the river. Bisecting the area was a large swath of land that a local logging/mining company had reduced to pasture by removing the trees and mining for coal, turning great tracts of this virgin wilderness into bleak, treeless meadowland. Despite this, there was still hill after rolling hill of densely forested woodland to be seen with small, gently running creeks snaking their way through. Even the tracts of second growth timber were fairly dense.

I drove to the end of the road and pulled into the parking lot of the old African American church that stood on the ridge overlooking the Green River. I ate my lunch while gazing out the windshield at the lowlands of Ash Flats. I was disappointed at my inability at getting the storeowner to talk to me about the Hillbilly sightings, or even to

The Hebbardsville Hillbilly, illustrated by the author and drawn from witness accounts.

let me see the newspaper article, but I still had high hopes that my luck would improve by the following day. The sun was high and bright and I was loath to go home but I knew that there was little I could do without my guide, other than wander around aimlessly in the woods, so I started the truck and headed out.

Sunday, the 17th was slightly overcast as I got into my four-wheel drive and headed east again. It was already unseasonably warm, with forecasted temps reaching into the 70s. True to his word, Greg was ready and eager for the undertaking and I owe him a huge debt of gratitude for agreeing to help on this venture. We headed out, pointing the truck toward the steadily climbing sun and the Hebbardsville river bottoms. We would have to take the long way around, Greg said, and come up to the hill from below, through the field where the initial sightings had occurred. The old house site, said to be situated back in the woods at the end of Book Lane, was on land owned by the logging/mining company and no trespassers were allowed. If we were caught chances were good that it would not end well for us. Fortunately, we both felt that some risks were worth taking in the quest for answers to mysteries of this nature.

We found the lane and drove on but the dirt road soon turned into a muddy ruin two feet deep, and we realized that the only way to continue was on foot. I stopped the truck in the middle of the road. It was very isolated and there was no chance of passers by spotting the truck from the main road. We were both confidant that we could get in and out without being noticed. A short while later I was standing in the field where the two creatures had been seen feeding on the corn stalk roots. I looked up at the old church, situated high on the wooded ridge above us and took a few pictures. We walked for another hour through the mud but, when we approached the intended spot, there was nothing to see but level ground. The old house that had contained the nest had fallen victim to the area's logging activities. I had arrived months too late to see and photograph the alleged Bigfoot nesting site. Though I was disappointed it was just as well. My camera had inexplicably malfunctioned as we approached an outlying shed and I was unable to take pictures for a time, although nothing unusual was noted by either of us. We made the return trip as rapidly as possible. The day was wearing on and I had other business to attend to in the tiny town of Hebbardsville.

The location at Hebbardsville where witnesses have routinely spotted a creature eating routes and grass. According to witnesses, this creek is a primary route of travel for the monsters.

Bigfoot and Cherokee Hill
(Note: The names of the locations in the following report have been intentionally altered)

A friend of mine who happened to be a local paranormal investigator told me about an old Cherokee man who claimed to have seen the Hebbardsville Bigfoot. My friend helped arrange a phone interview with the witness in November 2006. What my friend had told me proved correct; not only did the man describe repeated, often at will, sightings of groups of the hairy creatures going back to his childhood, he also claimed to be in possession of an actual Bigfoot tooth. Moreover, he said he could describe, in great detail, the physiological features and general behavior of these mysterious "Hillbillies," known to the rest of the world as Bigfoot.

After several more phone interviews a meeting was arranged. Under the promise of strict anonymity, M.F. (not his real initials) agreed to allow me to photograph the alleged Bigfoot tooth for possible identification. M.F. lived only a short drive from the Hebbardsville area, and only twenty minutes from my own doorstep. And so it was that, after my initial investigation of the Pleasant Hill site, I drove Greg back home, turned around and continued on to M.F.'s house. My heart sank at the sight of the closed and locked gate in front of the house. No one was home. M.F. had warned me that he and his wife were taking a trip out of town that particular weekend, but expected to be back home the previous night. Evidently they had not made it. I had

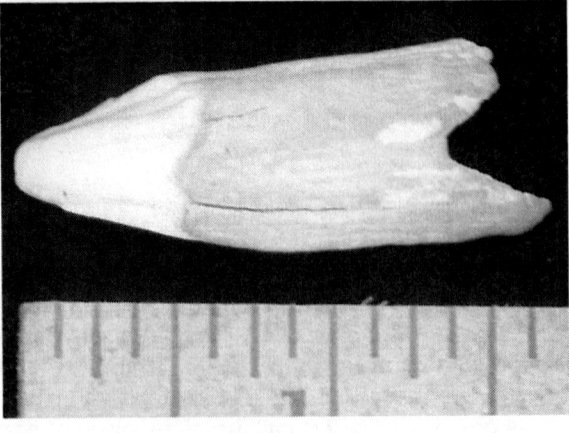

Photos of alleged Bigfoot tooth owned by the chief of the Southern Cherokee Nation, Michael "Manfox" Buley, who came forward publicly about his Bigfoot experiences in 2010.
(Bottom photo by Tony Gerrard)

tried phoning him that morning and his answering machine had picked up. I had hoped, in vain as it turned out, that he would be back in time for our 2 p.m. appointment. I waited a few minutes, then turned around and drove away, feeling somewhat defeated and tired from the morning's excursion.

I arrived back home around 3 p.m. and kicked off my shoes, wincing at the dime-sized blister my boot had left on my right heel. I was sore and tired from all the walking I had done. After reviewing the digital photos of the Pleasant Hill sighting area I decided a short nap would be in order, so I turned on the rotating fan and lay down on the sofa. No sooner had I closed my eyes when the phone rang. It was M.F. He explained that his wife had become ill on their trip, forcing them to stay away an extra night. They had just arrived back home. He was still willing to meet with me, he said, if I didn't mind driving back out to Hebbardsville. I looked at the clock. It was well after 3 p.m., with less than two hours of daylight left. I told him I was on my way.

I found M.F. to be pleasant, down to earth and of obvious intelligence. He immediately pulled the tooth out of his pocket. It resembled a human canine, or eyetooth, but about three times as large. I examined it and noted the obvious authenticity and antiquity of the object, taking several photographs. It was complete with most of the root system still intact. The outer edges were very slightly serrated, almost imperceptibly, which I found most unusual. M.F. had told me during one of our phone conversations that he considered the tooth to be a scared object; for that reason he refused to consent to DNA testing, because that would mean partially destroying the tooth. M.F. refused to allow the tooth out of his possession. As a matter of fact, he said he didn't really care at all about proving the existence of these creatures. They had always been a fact of life to his people. The Cherokee called the creatures the Old People of the Forest, he told me, and their reality caused no controversy except among whites. M.F. said it would be amusing except for the fact that logging and mining were causing the rapid destruction of the Bigfoot's habitat, land considered sacred by the Indians since the beginning of history.

"Can you show me where they lived?" I asked. There was daylight left. He asked me if I cared to take a ride.

M. F.'s story was an interesting one. He had first been exposed to the creatures while growing up in the Spottsville-Reed area, although at least two earlier generations of his family had their own tales of Bigfoot sightings and strange happenings. He remembered his great-grandfather recounting how he had run outside one night after he'd heard some kind of commotion to see one of the "Old People" carrying off two of his full-grown sows, one under each arm, like they were piglets. It swiftly made its escape even though the pigs weighed about 200 pounds each. Around the time of the Spottsville Monster events of 1975, his brother was finding strangely mutilated dead cattle. He lost six head of cattle that year. Literally. All six carcasses were found with their heads torn off and missing. They only found one head, he claimed, and it was stripped to the bone and missing the lower mandible. None of the other meat on the carcasses was consumed or even disturbed by insects. When the family moved across the Green River to Hebbardsville the sightings continued. In fact, he claimed that from the late 1960s until the early to mid-70s, hardly a weekends went by when he and a carload of his friends didn't park near the intersection of Ash Flats and Old Bell roads and observe groups of the creatures, ranging in number from four up to as many as fifteen or more, engaged in eating bitter roots and grass. There were countless sightings, he claimed, by dozens of different individuals.

I asked him what the creatures looked like. He said they had black skin and an average size of eight to ten feet tall, although he had seen one awhile back that was at least a twelve-footer. Their eyes were dark brown with no visible whites. They were bearded, had thin lips, a weak chin and a flat, wide nose like individuals of African descent. They had normal-looking hands of a large size with pale-colored palms, but their feet had a big toe sticking out at an angle away from the other four toes, like an ape's or chimp's. They had extremely long arms that hung down past their knees and could run on all fours an estimated 35 to 40 mph. He said the females also possessed beards, though shorter than the males. They were of more stocky build that the males, had furry breasts, and carried their young beneath them clinging to their bellies. He described the males as being covered with short, straight, usually dark hair, with longer areas of about six inches at the beard, backs of the head and genital areas.

"Pull over here," he said as we approached a medium-sized muddy creek at the Old

M.F. -- Michael "Manfox" Buley, who publicly acknowledged his experiences around Hebbardsville in 2010.

Bell, Ash Flats location. I pulled over and we got out. This was the place, he told me, that he and scores of companions had witnessed the creatures feeding countless times. According to him, they didn't seem to mind being watched unless someone got out of the car. Then they would all rush into the creek and be gone in an instant. They traveled the creeks, he claimed. The water would wash away the tracks and they were excellent swimmers if the water was high.

After photographing the location I asked him if he could take me to the place where he found the tooth. He said nothing for several seconds as he carefully considered the request. I was beginning to think that I had overstepped my bounds, as it were, when he looked up. He would take me there, if I promised never to disclose the location. It was a sacred place, he explained, a burial place of the Cherokee people and home to other powerful legendary beings as well as the "Old People." I agreed and we got back into the truck.

We traveled a short distance from the Ash Flats area and stopped. "Follow me," he said, and started up a thickly forested ridge. Although he was nearly sixty years old, he nimbly ascended the steep terrain. After a short but vigorous trek, we crested another large hill and stopped.

"Look freely." he said. "Take pictures, but nothing else."

I looked around. We stood at the rim of a forested ridge that wound around the area like a circle, forming an impressive natural amphitheater. The bottom of the bowl formation was mostly clear and somehow comfortable-looking. All around me were graves, stacked in layers, some ancient beyond reckoning. Many were marked with stones onto which Cherokee petroglyphs and letters were carved. I had hunted Indian artifacts nearly all my life but had never seen a single stone in Henderson County bearing intact Native American images or writing; now I was surrounded by them.

"This place is called The Great Hill by my people," M.F. said.

Here was buried the bodies of the famous Cherokee chieftain, Double Head, his daughter, Corn Blossom, and countless others. I snapped pictures one after another while the sunlight faded much too swiftly. Daniel Boone, pioneer hero of old, had written of this place.

Twice Boone had been taken prisoner by the Shawnee just across the Green river. Twice his freedom was bartered for and obtained by the friendly Cherokee. Two heavily weathered stones still bore his name and short messages, carved by Boone's own hand during his stay there over 200 years ago. Still other stones were carven with images of cornstalks, deer and sun. Three stones displayed the likenesses of strange faces. No one knew to whom most of the graves belonged. This was the final resting place of the great chiefs of antiquity, whose names were lost forever. Stone circles were present. Raking back the dead leaves revealed a wealth of stone artifacts still lying where their makers had placed them many generations ago.

M.F. said this was also the sacred home of other mythical beings from tribal lore. They were called "The Little People," tiny humanoids standing only two feet tall who could be either friendly or malignant depending on the contents of one's heart.

During heavy rains some of the graves would wash out, he said, and he had needed to rebury some of the bones on occasion. He had found the tooth here in 2004, at the foot of the hill, apparently washed up by the rushing water. No other creature native to the area had teeth like it, he felt sure. The claim was intriguing but not unprecedented. There are many nineteenth and early twentieth century reports of the unearthing of giant human, or humanlike, skeletal remains in the Bluegrass State. Most were said to have been taken from Indian burial grounds, but not all. M. F. said his mother had told him she had witnessed the excavation of one such skeleton in Beals, back in the 1920s. Workmen had unearthed a twelve-foot-tall skeleton while trying to build a bridge over a creek. The remains were said to have been acquired by a private collector.

"The whites don't know about this place," M.F. said. "If they were to find out..."

He didn't need to finish the statement. I knew exactly what would happen if the location were ever made public. Hordes of relict hunters would descend and strip it clean, within a week.

"Can you keep this secret, Bart?" he asked.

I looked squarely into his eyes. "You can trust me." I said.

As the last rays of the sun disappeared and we were left standing in the darkness surrounded by old trees and even older graves, I knew it was time to take my leave. I vowed to return to visit M.F. again soon, for better pictures and more conversation if he'd have me. "Anytime," was his reply. I had made a new friend, it seemed, one who struck me as being perhaps the most knowledgeable person regarding Bigfoot that I had ever met. I had obtained the story and the pictures that I sought, and much more.

I took many photographs of this extraordinary location both out of my own fascination regarding the history of the site and intriguing fact that the giant tooth had been found there. I am indebted to M.F. for the opportunity to do so. With his help I was also able to make a sketch of a Bigfoot's features. I would like to express my sincere gratitude to this man for agreeing to speak with me, sharing some secrets and showing me such an interesting and historically important location.

HENRY COUNTY

Like so many Kentucky counties, Henry County also has a history of hairy monster sightings going back several decades or longer and continuing up to recent times. Two children allegedly saw a Bigfoot there back in the fall of 1978 near their home on Joes Branch Road, between Lockport and Bethlehem. It was just after sunset. A bright moon lit the clear night sky. While they were eating supper the family was disturbed by the sound of their horses raising a commotion in the barn.

"Our house was built into the hillside," one of the children later stated. "The front yard dropped off 200 feet to the road below, then dropped again to a small creek."

The horse barn and chicken coop were situated just across this creek. A three-foot-high hitching post was attached to the barn.

"As we were eating supper, we could hear the horses down at the barn making a lot of noise, kicking the barn and nickering. My parents sent us down to see what was the matter," she said.

The two siblings followed the trail that led down to the road until they came to a point where they could see the barn. "I'll never forget what we saw," one them said. "A very tall, hairy creature was standing by the hitching post to the right of the barn. The hitching post only came to its knees. My brother took off up the hill to the house but I stood there and watched as it walked off."

Other than it being very tall and hirsute the witness could not make out any further details about its appearance, but said that it walked away with "long, graceful strides."

Many years before this incident took place, large rocks that seemed to come from out of nowhere were allegedly thrown at her grandfather. He never could explain the occurrence. The family also heard strange screaming sounds coming from two separate locations outside one night. The sounds made the family's two dogs cower beneath the bed. The screams, which the family felt were two of the Bigfoot creatures calling to each other from a distance, went on for about fifteen minutes.

"Whatever it was," the witness said, "they [must have] met, and all we heard [then] was silence. " In 2000, she said her parents admitted to finding huge, humanlike footprints some eighteen inches long while arrowhead hunting in a location known as Hanse's Bottoms.

The eyewitness waited twenty-two years before reporting the incident, but one year before the discovery of the footprints a similarly described figure reportedly attacked a group of ten deer hunters near Penelton in Henry County.

"Me and my friends [sic] were setting up our hunting camp where we hunt every year," said Richie M. (full name on file). It was about 6 a.m. and just getting daylight. We have been hunting here for years and nothing like this has happened to us before." When they found themselves in need of a rope Richie's cousin volunteered to go back to the vehicle to retrieve it. According to the witness, about half an hour later his cousin came running and screaming back up the hill.

"We all stopped what we were doing and ran to him," Richie said. His terrified cousin told them that he had seen a "big man running at him and growling." The group went down to the area where he claimed he saw the figure and waited. "We sat there for five to ten minutes," he stated, "until we thought he was full of it. Just when we got up [to leave] a rock came flying toward us." He said one of the men shouted, "Come out!" but nothing happened. They got up and walked to where they thought the rock had come from.

"That is where it came at us," Richie said. "It" was a seven- to eight-foot-tall, hairy humanoid creature. The group made a mad dash back to the hunting cabin and locked themselves inside.

"It stayed outside for a long time before it left. It tried to get in one time. Then, after two hours it left. We haven't been back since," he said. Richie claims that the sounds the creature made while it was outside the cabin were "like that of a dog in a fight." No one believed them when they told their tale.

HOPKINS COUNTY

In October of 1990 a Bigfoot was sighted in Hopkins County near Earlington at a place known as the Heckley mines by a father and son who were hunting deer. The son was sitting in his stand, he said, when he became aware of a large brown bush that he hadn't noticed before. Suddenly, to his complete amazement, the "bush" stood up. "It had the shape of a man," he said. "It was a medium brown color and was huge. I was beyond stunned." He said his father observed the creature as well from his own stand not far away. It slowly made its way back into the woods and the two frightened hunters left the area as quickly as possible.

One evening around 9:00 p.m. in November 1995, four campers in White Plains were disturbed by loud, moaning sounds coming from a thickly forested area known as Lonesome Woods. "It was really cold and we had a big fire going," one of the witnesses later stated. "We were all sitting around it to stay warm when all of a sudden this weird moaning sound filled the woods. It sounded kind of like a siren." Whatever it was, it let out a series of three moans that started at a low pitch and built and dropped in volume, in three bursts.

"This scared us because we all grew up in this area and have hunted and camped out here all our lives and have never heard such a cry. We tried to laugh it off but an uneasy feeling lingered throughout the camp for quite a while." He said."

At around 10:30 p.m., one of the group stepped out of the tent to relieve himself - then came running back in and announced that he was leaving immediately. When they asked him what was wrong he admitted that he'd just seen a big, hairy monster drinking from a nearby stream. It stood up and watched him, he said, as he ran away. No sooner had he told his story than the group heard something running through the underbrush at the top of the hill. Shining their light in that direction, they saw a "very large creature running on top of the hill. We couldn't make out a color but it was human-shaped," he said, "with long arms and [it] ran kind of hunched over. It looked to be about eight feet tall." The witnesses claimed that it made an incredibly loud exit as it ran away on two legs over a ridge, loudly snapping and breaking through the limbs and small trees. He described it as sounding like "a truck driving over the branches."

Five years later, in the summer of 2000 near Morton's Gap, a married couple out fishing one night on White City Road were startled by similar noises coming from the nearby trees.

"It was a rustling sound," the husband said, "that became a loud snapping [and] cracking that seemed to come closer. There was a thumping sound as well. This lasted maybe a couple of minutes. We stood there looking in the area expecting someone to come out into the light."

No one came out. His wife was visibly shaken and he tried to reassure her by saying it was probably just a deer. As they recast their lines they heard what sounded like something large run across the road, scattering gravel. Whatever it was, it sounded like it struck the truck three times as it went past. Then the sound of breaking limbs resumed on that side of the woods. From the glow of their lanterns the couple watched the branches of the trees shake and sway in the wake of something monstrously large, so heavy they could feel the thing's feet hitting the ground. They dropped their fishing poles, and the man pulled out his pistol, aimed it in the direction of the sounds, and cocked the hammer as his wife cowered behind him clinging to his belt loops. Now thoroughly unnerved, the couple hurried back to their truck.

Once in the safety of the vehicle, the man said it was a while before they garnered enough courage to go back and gather up their gear. They were doing so when they heard the creature let out a high-pitched, bloodcurdling scream. "When it screamed I did too!" the witness stated. "The sound echoed out into the deep woods. It was unearthly, high-pitched, short, but with a lot of emphasis, as if it meant to hurry us along. It worked! We left there fast!"

It was posed that this might be the same monster that was featured in a 1979 edition of a local newspaper about a three-day flurry of Bigfoot sightings in the Hopkins County area.

The creature, or one like it, returned around midnight on March 28, 2007, when a couple driving west on Rose Creek Road in Nebo spotted what they thought was a dead deer lying beside the road.

"As we approached," said witness, Brad Law, "the animal got up and walked on four feet into the middle of the road, then back across the road nearly swiping my girlfriend's car." They turned to look and saw the beast running across a bean field on two legs. "I know a lot of weird people that make up funny stories," Law said, "but this was the real deal." Law described the thing as six feet tall, completely black in color, with long, furry legs, a big belly, and an ugly face that he found extremely intimidating. "This thing took very large steps," he said.

JACKSON COUNTY

Another Bigfoot was allegedly seen traversing through a hayfield early one morning in Mckee, in December of 2006. "I was standing in my front doorway changing a light bulb," said the eyewitness, "and I heard a popping, cracking sound that I had never heard before. I looked down and both of my cats were running up the sidewalk to me. Maybe a minute later I looked up across the highway behind my mailbox and there was something about seven or eight feet tall just walking by calm as could be. It was huge. Its color was very light white/brown, it's arms was [sic] at its knees and I was not the only one who seen [sic] it that year. Our county sheriff seen [sic] it at his house as well. I know the sheriff very well and I know he would not lie about something like this. He tracked it for about a mile behind his house and found some of its hair on his fence. Many people in the county have seen or heard the things as myself and our sheriff did that winter and, after the sheriff told a few people about it, more and more people started telling about their sightings."

Bigfoot investigator Harold Benny was able to speak with the witness. He said he found her very credible. Benny added the following details to the original account:

"The sighting was at a distance of thirty feet under a street light and lasted six to seven seconds. It was preceded by a series of popping noises that the witness thought might have been caused by the animal clicking its teeth. The animal was heading south, walking in the ditch between the mailbox and a hay field, and left no tracks. The body was muscular and heavy, estimated to be over 500 pounds and covered with neat, white to light brown hair, one to two inches long. The creature's hairless face was brown in color, with a flat nose, thin lips and no visible ears. The appearance was very human. Its arms hung down to its knees and ended in large, hairless hands.

"The witness' aunt noticed an odor in the air that smelled like a dead and rotting animal. Caves dot this area of the Daniel Boone National Forest - London Ranger District. This district is best known for Laurel River Lake, a 5,600-acre reservoir. There is a small pond to the north and a creek directly east. Since the sighting, several witnesses have heard loud howling coming from the area north of the pond. The howls last about ten seconds and are repeated in a series for up to three minutes."

JEFFERSON COUNTY

Jefferson County also has a long history of monster sightings that dates back to the 1940s, including reports of the Pope Lick Monster, often called the "Goat Man." But it is with the apemen of the area that this book is concerned. On October 20, 1967, a fifteen-year-old girl was harassed by a frightening creature as she waited for her school bus on Stone Street Road at 7:30 a.m.

"I caught the school bus every morning to Valley High School," she said in 2009. "The bus went up Stone Street over the small bridge in the direction of Valley Station Road to Valley High on Dixie Highway. [The bridge no longer exists.] In 1967 the little bridge was deemed no longer safe enough to support a vehicle as heavy as a school bus, so the bus was re-routed back through Blevins Gap from Dixie Highway and over Manslick Road to Third Street. Because I was the only student to be picked up in this area, and because there was no place for the bus to turn around, I had to walk about two miles by myself to the intersection of Stone Street Road and Blevins Gap Road to catch the school bus."

One morning in the fall of 1967, as she was walking the familiar route she said she felt "a strange presence." She then heard a very deep, throaty, "metallic-sounding" grunting noise and the sound of something big brushing through the foliage. The area was woods and farmland, and she figured someone's cow or pig had escaped. Nonetheless, she began to walk faster, only to hear that the sounds were not only following her but increasing their pace as well.

"Then I saw it cross the road into the woods adjacent to Blevins Gap, as Blevins Gap goes up the hill and curves around back toward Bearcamp Road. I was running at this point. It started running also. I could hear it keeping up with me," she said.

She described the thing as "black or very dark brown. At first I didn't think it had a head, as it was loping along on what appeared to be four very long legs. Its head was apparently bent down. It was loping, and I could see its powerful big shoulders doing most of the work as it moved along. I was convinced it was a gorilla that had escaped from a circus or something."

She said she ran all the way to a friend's house in Blevins Gap and her friend was shocked to see the terror-stricken look on her face. She said she later described her experience to her uncles, who used to hunt and trap in those woods. They told her it was just "Old Bigfoot." She said she had never heard of Bigfoot at that time, and insisted that it must have been a gorilla.

A nighttime "yowler" was heard many times during the summer of 1971 at Pleasure Ridge Park. In 1977 a couple of stargazers on a late night date by the railroad tracks at Old Taylorsville Rd saw a hairy creature standing about 100 ft. behind their parked vehicle. It was described as resembling the Bigfoot from the movie *Harry and the Hendersons,* only white-colored instead of brown and ferocious looking instead of docile.

"It was close enough for me to look it in the eyes," the witness claimed. "It didn't appear to be bothered by my presence in the least. It was more like it came to get a closer look at me. I didn't wait around to try to make conversation with it. I left. The beast is called the "Sheepman" by the locals, but believe me, there is nothing sheepish about it. Especially up close and personal."

Four months later one of the witnesses claimed to see it again just three miles east of the first sighting.

"There are a lot of stories about this particular creature in town," he said. "But as far as I know, I'm the only person to have seen it twice."

In southern Jefferson County in the summer of 1987, four teens found themselves running for their lives as something big came crashing down through the woods in their direction. The incident was initiated when a disturbing, high-pitched vocalization was heard and one of the youths playfully yelled back. Fortunately, they were able to reach their vehicle and escape.

On Sept. 10, 1998 a couple out jogging in the Jefferson County National Forest encountered a seven-foot-tall, 400-pound creature covered with brown fur which they at first took to be a bear until they saw that it was walking on two legs like a human. They had strayed off the path and were enjoying the scenery when, according to one of the witnesses, "We heard the sound of someone not far [away] breaking up branches. Both of us stopped to listen." Then a loud moaning sound came from among the trees. Their first impression was that someone was hurt in the woods and needed help. The man later admitted that he did not want to go any farther to find out what made the sound. He didn't have to.

A large figure stepped from the woods about 100 yards to their right. At first they thought it was a bear and squatted down to watch. But something wasn't quite right with what they were seeing.

"It was on what I thought were its hind legs," the witness said, "but when it turned the other way I could see that it wasn't a bear." So could his wife. She went into hysterics, screaming in terror as her husband grabbed her hand and began running back to the main road as fast as they could go. They continued running when they reached the road.

"Once we got to the main road we ran all the way back to the off-road parking, got in the car and burned out of there. I knew there was a ranger station about ten minutes away, but we just headed straight home," he said.

The two described the creature as between seven and eight feet tall, covered with brown-colored fur and weighing 400-plus pounds. "We never really saw its face," the man said. "When we were running back to the road I kept glancing back behind us but [I] never seen [sic] or heard anything after that. To this day we talk about it often - but not with other people. I have often wanted to go back but never had the nerve."

Another such creature was allegedly observed at Menallie Lake, near Louisville, at dusk on August 21, 2000. After hearing the now-familiar snapping and crunching of branches and twigs in the underbrush, the witness turned and saw, about fifty feet away, a dark figure as it walked slowly through the woods, "as if looking for something." The witness said he had heard other people in the area talk about the creature, but he thought that they were just telling stories. "I don't believe in Bigfoot," the witness stated, "but after my sighting I don't know what to believe."

JOHNSON COUNTY

Another Bigfoot allegedly approached a country home one day in 1951 in Van Lear and peered in the window. The witness described the thing's face as being covered with copper-colored hair with big, round, brown eyes and thin lips. She couldn't explain why, but she got the feeling that the creature was a female that had somehow lost her young. She felt that it made its home beneath her back yard, in a cave or possibly an abandoned mine. She said she wasn't afraid of the thing and felt sorry for it. She also stated that her mother had seen a similar beast some time earlier at the same location. She waited fifty years to report the sighting.

Most of the reported Bigfoot activity from Johnson County seems to be centered in the small town of Paintsville. Shirley Elkins tells of sighting an unknown, manlike creature on December 22, 1978, on the Lewis Fork of the Big Sandy River.

"We had a major flood here," she said, "and everyone was told to leave town because they said the dam might burst. I ran up to some family's house that had married a kin person [sic]. They kept the radio on all night and gave me a bed next to a wide window. I could see a graveyard nearby, and some dogs began to go nuts barking. Then, with a yelp, they all ran off. I looked out the window and all I could see was fur against the window. It felt like hands [were] shaking the house. Then I saw quite a scary sight: a human-looking creature, as it walked away from the window making grunting sounds. It walked up on the graveyard [sic] and shook a tree, tore up bushes, then disappeared on down the hill. When I told the family they said they hadn't seen anything, but some nights they heard scratching on the side of the house, and their cats and dogs acted scared. They found the garden tore up one summer, and trees shredded. They are dead now, and I don't know who lives there, or if the same thing is still happening."

Two teenaged squirrel hunters in Boonscamp flushed out more than they bargained for in the backwoods in November of 1987.

"I was hunting with a childhood friend," said Scott (full name on file). "I was fourteen or fifteen and he was twelve or thirteen. We had made our way up to some cliff rocks near a gas pipeline right of way that was side-cut below us, and decided to sit down around some oak trees to wait on some squirrels. He went around one side of the cliff and I went around the other. After about thirty minutes I heard leaves rustling and got my gun ready to shoot. The rustling sound got closer and then I seen a squirrel [sic] jump up on the side of a tree. I aimed my gun and was just getting ready to pull the trigger when a limb cracked behind me and the squirrel spooked and ran off. I lowered my gun and said, 'darn it, Gary! You scared off my squirrel.' Then from up above me on the opposite side of the sound Gary said, 'That wasn't me.' He had made his way to the top of the cliff and the sound I heard was at the bottom.

"Being kids and loving to shoot our guns, we both had the same thought; maybe the sound was made by something to shoot at like a squirrel, fox or groundhog. So we ran over toward the noise ready to throw our guns up and shoot. What we saw, instead, left us dumbfounded to this day. It was already running away from us when we got there but it was some type of hairy animal on two legs running down the hill toward the pipeline. It must have been at least six feet to seven feet tall, close to three feet broad across the shoulders, and had huge strides in its run. It covered five yards at a time. In two or three steps it was at the pipeline cut. It took a leap when it got to the pipeline and cleared the other side into the timber. We could hear it running for a long ways away from us crashing through the leaves and brush. Me and Gary [sic] ran all the way home and never really talked about it for a couple of months. I guess we didn't want to believe what we had seen," he said.

Finally, after they were able to talk about it, the two came to the conclusion that it must have been a Bigfoot. Who would believe two teenagers with such a story? Not many. Every time they told someone about their strange encounter they were laughed at and told that they had merely seen a bear or something, so they stopped telling people about it. Scott described the beast as upright, close to 350 pounds, with very broad shoulders and covered with hair. It ran extremely fast with long strides and never made any noise. Nor did it have a odor that he could recall.

"After all these years," he said, " I can say for sure that it wasn't anything I'd seen before or since, and I have spent a lot of time in the woods."

Another Bigfoot encounter took place in 1989, also near Paintsville. "I was on my way home from work," said Vannisa M. (full name on file)."At the time I lived in Greentown, a sort of suburb of Paintsville, next to the river. There was a sharp curve, with an old, dilapidated house only [a few] feet from the road on the right hand side going down Route 40 East toward Thealka. As I rounded the curve I saw this tall creature walking alongside the road to my right. It was covered in white/grayish hair and walked upright, but not straight like a man. It was sort of hunched over a bit. It was heading toward the river. I couldn't believe my eyes, and I drove on home, which was only about a quarter mile on down the road. My good friend lived next door and the next day I told her what I saw. I expected her to say that I was crazy or ask me if I had been drinking, but instead she told me about the time her son and one of his friends had seen the same thing while they were out frog gigging one night. I was astonished."

Vannisa claims her sighting took place about 2:00 a.m. and further describes the figure as between six and seven feet tall with hair about three or four inches long.

Yet another Paintsville encounter took place in the fall of 1999, this time in Flat Gap, near Tolver Branch Road. "I was at Flat Gap with my friend, Clay, in September of 1999," the witness stated. "We were throwing rocks to his dog, Bonnie, when she stopped chasing them and her ears rose. Our hearts started pounding. I looked down the hill about twelve feet away when 'it' jolted across the clearing. Clay said he only saw it at the last second but I saw it all. He thought it was a bear, like most stupid people do, but it ran on two feet like a human. I have studied Bigfoot ever since I could read. I know it was real."

The witness claims that the creature let out a strange "seal-like" yelp as it ran. He added that his family farm, where the sighting took place, has a history of creature activity.

KENTON COUNTY

Hairy, upright monsters have been cavorting around in Kenton County since at least 1959 when passing motorists saw one on a bridge in Covington. Such activity still shows no sign of slowing down, it would seem. At 7:00 p.m. on June 24, 2003, a creature appeared to two sportsmen near a disc golf course. After a challenging but pleasant day of tossing flying discs at targets, the two were walking up from the back of the park when they smelled an odor like a combination of sour meat and wet hair. They dismissed it as a dead animal and continued walking toward the car, which was about forty yards away. They heard a rustling sound in the thick woods and peered into the trees, only to see a nine-foot-tall, dark-colored, hairy creature moving parallel with them through the trees. They both stopped dead in their tracks. One of them whispered, 'What is it?' Then the creature let out a blood-curdling high-pitched shriek that drowned out the sounds of all the local fauna.

"It then started to come toward us in a hunched-over kind of skip. We both took off running for the car with the creature keeping pace behind us," one of the witnesses said. He said they wasted no time in getting out of there. One of them looked back and saw the thing standing slouched over in the road. He said it appeared to be nine feet tall with long, shaggy, dark-brown hair and arms that reached down to its knees. Its hair covered its eyes, they said, and it ran "slouched over with bent knees." The two said they immediately reported the incident to park authorities but were not believed.

A more recent suspected Bigfoot sighting took place on the evening of November 14, 2006, near Fort Thomas. Around 11:30 that evening Chris and his companion, Liz (full names on file) were sitting on their front porch chatting and smoking cigarettes when they were startled by a loud crack that sounded like a large branch breaking. There were dense woods about twenty yards behind the house. The back porch light was on and they could easily see where the woods began, but not past the first line of trees.

"We thought it odd but wrote it off to the natural falling of a limb," Chris later stated. "After that, because the noise had made us aware of the sounds from the trees, we noticed some rustling and we could hear someone moving around. I yelled, 'Hey, whatcha doing back there?' thinking that it was kids trying to spy on us. It continued and then we heard another limb break farther back in the woods, not as loud as the first. I grabbed a flashlight and walked back to the woods with the intention of looking like a tough guy and yelling at whoever was back there. When I reached the woods I stood at the tree line and shined the flashlight in and yelled 'Hey!' It was then that I saw walking away about forty feet in front of me what I thought was a small bear walking on two legs. I got really excited and shouted 'HEY!' to try to get it to turn around, but it didn't. I freaked out and ran back to Liz and we went inside because I wasn't enough of a tough guy to keep smoking cigs outside."

Chris later claimed the thing was about four or five feet tall, with thick hair covering its body. "I couldn't see much else because it was dark," he said.

In a follow-up interview Chris stated, "The hair was either black or brown and looked shaggy but I couldn't determine [its] length. It looked like it covered the entire body. (It made) no sounds. The only sounds we heard were the breaking of the branches and some rustling that sounded like footsteps. As far as the head and body go, it just looked like a bear or a short, stocky person standing up and walking. The stride made it look like it was hobbling a bit. As it was walking away all I could see was the shaggy hair, not really any visible shape to the head. [There was] no smell and no footprints that I could find but I didn't look real hard. There are a bunch of leaves back there which is why we could hear it walking and rustling around. It was definitely weird though. Good luck with the research. I'll be keeping my eyes peeled toward those woods."

A more intimate encounter with one of these hairy creatures came earlier in 2006 just outside of Independence. On June 7, a motorist named Rick (full name on file), and a companion saw a seven-foot-tall, shaggy-looking monster step out from the woods directly into the path of the truck they were driving down Kentucky Route 536 at about 11:30 p.m. Luckily, the truck wasn't traveling at a high rate of speed. According to Rick the creature "walked out of the woods in front of my truck and another truck heading the opposite direction. [It] put its hand on the hood of my truck and [then it] kept walking into the woods on the other side of the road."

Rick was adamant that the thing walked upright like a man, and was not some animal. "My dog was in the truck," he said, "and started acting strange before the creature even walked out."

When asked if he could remember anything further about the encounter he stated, "I was going about 20 mph., accelerating off a turn going uphill. I had to slam on my brakes. I didn't find any prints on my hood, but it did stick its hand out and appeared to look at me but I couldn't make out any features. The truck in the oncoming lane hit its brights and I couldn't see much then. Just a big hairy upright thing crossing the road."

Another Kenton County resident, who wishes to remain anonymous, believes that he was in the presence of the elusive Bigfoot on June 19, 2007, as he was working in his garden in Taylor Mill. It was just about 7:00 p.m. when the incident occurred.

"I was weeding in my garden when I heard someone walking in the woods," he said. "The footsteps were steady, but far apart. They sounded like they were coming from an extremely tall, very heavy human. We don't have any giants here in Taylor Mill that

I know about! And it was definitely someone/something on two feet. I kept hearing the footsteps and stood up to see if I could see who was making them. I could see nothing."

An uneasy feeling came over him, and he admitted he was a bit freaked out by the peculiar sounds coming from whatever was out there. He said he was relieved to realize that the sounds were not coming in his direction. He stood there, he said, and listened as the footsteps faded into the distance.

KNOX COUNTY

This county has a long history of Fortean phenomena of all types. Small wonder that hairy humanoid monster reports can be found here as well. In 1948, Captain Thomas Mantell, a decorated WWII pilot, met his death while chasing an unidentified flying object through the skies over Fort Knox. In October 1976, a soldier reported seeing a hair-covered, man-like monster in the woods just outside the Fort Knox army base.

"I was seventeen years old, in basic training at Fort Knox, and we were spending three days in the woods for bivouac training," he later stated. "Our tents were set up in a circular fashion in a small clearing. It was pre-dawn, about 4:30 a.m." It was cold and threatening to rain that morning, he recalled. After walking about 100 yards through moderate brush to where breakfast was being served, the witness said he was enjoying his break when he realized that he'd left his gloves behind in his tent.

"Fearing punishment by the drill sergeants, I told a buddy that I was going to run back to the tent area to retrieve them. I figured that I would be right back and the drill sergeants would never miss me," he said.

He took off by himself through the dark, silently cursing the fact that flashlights were not allowed for tactical training reasons. As he approached his tent he noticed a figure standing on the other side, bent over at the waist, apparently looking for something in the tall grass some six or eight feet away. Thinking it was another recruit who had lost something, he yelled a greeting at the figure, but there was no response. Puzzled, he repeated the greeting and was met once more by silence. He yelled loudly then, and the dark figure stood up and faced him. The darkness precluded him from seeing any details, but said he immediately "got the creeps." The two stood facing each other then a faint light from a distant truck illuminated the thing for a moment, which was long enough.

"In that second, and from no more than eight feet away," he said, "I observed this creature to have hair which was similar in color and texture to that of an Irish Setter dog, which covered its upper body. Due to the tall grass and the tent between us, I was unable to see its legs. It also had black or very dark eyes and it was humanlike - yet not - and it did not appear to have a distinct neck. It did not make any sound." Now thoroughly alarmed, he slowly began backing away from the tent trying not to alarm the beast. After three steps, he said, he panicked and ran as fast as he could back through the woods toward the rest of the recruits, completely forgetting about his gloves. He suffered the consequences of forgetting them, just as he knew he would, and no one believed him when he tried to tell his story, so he quickly stopped speaking about it.

In 1979 another creature was encountered by four children in a back yard in Flat Lick. "My brother, two cousins and myself ran up on a Bigfoot," one of them later proclaimed. They were in the yard around 5:00 p.m. when they startled the thing, getting as close as five feet away from the beast. "It was walking away from us. It was on its hind legs, walking upright. It was dark brown in color, and it had hair about four or five inches long. It had its arms outstretched about chest level. It slowly walked away from us as if it didn't see us." Stunned, the group watched the creature walk away in that strange fashion. They didn't tell their parents for a long time because they knew they wouldn't be believed. The thing was further described as brown in color, about seven feet tall with a powerful build.

A man-beast made another Knox County appearance on July 14, 1999, to a group of frightened berry pickers. It was about 1:00 a.m. when the alleged encounter took place. It was mid-summer and the group had been picking blackberries all day. They decided to camp at the berry patch to get an early start the next morning. They built a good-sized campfire and everyone went to sleep. Later on, they were awakened by the sound of something large crashing through the woods.

"My cousin was so scared he couldn't move," one of them later claimed. "It sounded like something was running in circles around us, knocking down small trees. Our fire had almost burned out by this time, but I could just make out a large, man-like figure at least seven or eight feet tall. We heard a low, grumbling noise the whole time." They could also smell a rotten stench. This was too much for them, and they quickly got up and ran nearly a mile out of the patch, not even stopping for a breath. The witness said they could hear the thing running behind them as they fled. "This thing, whatever it was, could have caught us at any time. The next morning we returned to find many small trees downed and a new path ripped through the briar patch."

LAUREL COUNTY

"The first time I ever saw a Sasquatch was in 1991," said one London, Ky., resident. "Where I live is pretty rugged terrain, so you would believe anything could be out there. This is how my first sighting occurred: it was about 2:00 p.m. in the middle of April. I was running through our garden with a BB gun just shooting around being a kid when I ran out of the garden and jumped up on this big rock that was on the top of this ravine that led down into this hollow. At the top of this mountain a small drainage ditch ran into it where I was. I jumped up on this rock and said, "Bang!" Well, when I did, I heard a branch break on the right of me."

The witness turned and found that he was only about thirteen feet away from a very strange and frightening animal that stood on two legs. He described it as "about five feet tall with hair that resembled a rabbit in color but was long. It was standing kind of hunched over like a bodybuilder would do when showing his abs. It also had a pointed head but I don't remember seeing a face. It turned and ran through the woods away from me and I turned and ran away from it."

And who could blame him? He said he could hear the thing breaking limbs as it retreated behind him. He ran into the house and grabbed a shotgun, excitedly telling the story to his mother. She could see he was serious so she grabbed her own gun and followed him back outside. "We got back there and I found lots of big branches that had been broken and a lot of slide marks on the hillside. As I walked the little spillway that meets the ravine I found a very discernible footprint on the bank. It was about a size 6 shoe because that is what my mom's shoe size is and we had it there for comparison." Oddly enough, the human-looking footprint only had three toes. The sighting allegedly took place on Highway 229.

A small, gorilla-like creature was seen by a witness and his girlfriend while out four-wheeling down Hwy. 1189 in July 2005. It was standing on all fours and resembled a small gorilla. The witness estimated its height at around four feet at the shoulders, and its weight at about 100 pounds. According to him, the creature's face was white, "like a skull," and flat with no visible ears and no apparent neck. Its hair was reddish-orange, like that of an orangutan. It crawled across a fallen tree as the witness watched, and disappeared. This witness also claimed that he had seen a similar creature previously in the area, which is a remote and very dense stretch of bottomland along the Laurel River.

"I was walking down a trail surrounded by about forty acres of woods near a pond and small stream," said London resident, David G. (full name on file). It was just after 3:30 a.m. on the morning of May 24, 2008. "I heard leaves crunching behind me and turned around - and did not see a thing. I walked a little further and smelled the worst smell I have ever smelled. It smelled like I was in a swamp. I heard the leaves crunching again beside me. I looked and saw it. It was probably fifteen or twenty feet away. It stared at me for about thirty seconds and I ran toward the house, which is about a quarter mile down the trail. I haven't went back [sic] since." What David claimed he saw was a huge, ten-foot-tall, hair-covered creature. It had long arms, a large head and flat face, a big body and was covered with black hair except for its head, which was covered in brown hair.

LAWRENCE COUNTY

Another Kentucky resident got a glimpse of Bigfoot in November 1992 while he was hunting early one morning four miles from Blaine on Route 11. "I was deer hunting, watching a clearing between two thickets," he later said. "It was between 7:30 and

8:00 in the morning. The temperature was below freezing and there was a thin layer of snow on the ground. The thickets were cedar thickets. I was sitting on an old road, in the head of the hollow, about a hundred yards from the trail crossing the clearing. The clearing was about fifty or sixty yards across." While he was sitting there quietly he heard, from the top of the thicket to his left, the crashing of brush and limbs breaking very loudly. They sounded like large limbs. "It lasted maybe ten seconds or so. About five minutes later, I heard the same noise, maybe fifty or seventy-five feet down the hill in the direction of the clearing. Brush and limbs [were] thrashing, breaking, and hitting together. Then about five minutes later, the same noise [came from] closer down the hill. The last time, it happened about twenty yards into the thicket from the clearing. Then, out of the thicket stepped something, walking on two legs, black from head to toe, with its arms swinging by its sides. I couldn't see its face. It walked across the clearing in probably no more than five or six seconds. I was too scared to move, but I took my gun and eased out of there, too busy watching the clearing to really look for tracks, but the grass was so thick I couldn't have seen any anyway."

The witness said he got in the truck and waited for his hunting partner, worried that something might have happened to him. "I walked partway back into the area and met him coming out. He asked if I had seen a large pile of feces in the road through the clearing on my way out. I had walked down that road about thirty minutes earlier and it wasn't there then. He said it was in the area where I saw this thing cross. He described the feces as loose, with grass and long, black hairs in it. I then told him what I saw and he said he was sure it was a bear and my imagination added to it. He never did believe me and no one else has either. But it's true," he said.

My good friend and Bigfoot investigator Tony Gerrard believed him. And so do I. Gerrard was able to contact the witness and found him to be credible. He was also able to add, "The sighting occurred at about 100 yards distance. The witness could have gotten a much better look through his rifle's scope, but he related that he was so shocked that he didn't think of it. He described the height as larger than human-sized, "but not unusually bigger." The arms reached "maybe a little below the hip." The gait was described as "long steps, walking fast, very much like a human." No vocalizations were heard."

In 2004, also near Blaine, a husband and wife were out ginseng hunting early one summer morning when they began hearing the sounds of snapping trees and brush in the woods surrounding them. The husband looked up to see a large hair-covered creature watching them from the trees. It was later described as being covered in long, reddish-brown hair with a man-like face, large, dark eyes and huge shoulders about four feet broad. It stood six or seven feet tall, they claimed, and had a muscular build. It smelled like a cross between a skunk and a wet dog.

The man described the creature's head as being somewhat pointed toward the back. Its face looked like a bearded man's with hair thinner around the eyes and forehead. It had a wide mouth with thick, dark lips. The area has history of creature sightings. The couple claimed that two of their dogs had come up missing earlier in the year.

Their bodies were later found ripped apart with organs missing. In 2004 something threw a large, football-sized rock at the husband, as he was deer hunting behind his house.

Another man told him that while driving south on Route 201 he saw a large, hairy creature run across the road on two legs and he refused to hunt in the area after that. One week later the wife claimed that around dusk the dogs started going crazy. She stepped into the back yard and saw a different, lighter-colored creature standing about seventy-five feet away. Moreover, the husband claimed that four years earlier, while hunting in the company of his father and brother, the group heard what sounded like two Chinese men talking from one hill to another, then the sound of a large tree falling. They quickly left the area. Trace evidence in the form of many trees twisted in two about six feet from the ground was later found in abundance.

Lawrence County also played host to Bigfoot in the late 1980s, this time in Louisa, when a seven-foot-tall white creature reportedly approached a car driven by terrified coon hunters late one night on Route 23. According to the hunters, the monster had long hair and walked in a peculiar manner - with its arms sticking out in front of it, somewhat like Frankenstein's monster. The witnesses said they fled the scene before it got too close.

LEE COUNTY

Three witnesses were terrified by a monster one night in Beattyville, back in 1957. Phylis (full name on file) was a passenger in an old truck struggling through the rain and mud of White Ash Hill. Her grandmother was in the front seat and her uncle was driving. It was about 11:00 pm. and Phylis would end up waiting nearly fifty years to report what she saw that night.

"The road was dirt and mud in those days," she later said. "It was raining and muddy. My uncle was having a hard time getting up the hill to where we intended to leave the truck and travel on foot, as usual, to the top of the hill [to their home]. Something very large and frightening would run back and forth across [the road] in front of our truck and throw branches from the holly thicket on one side of the road. This continued for twenty or thirty minutes until my uncle finally managed to back down the hill. Upon checking the next morning the road was a muddy mess but you could certainly tell that something had gotten mad and stomped around. Broken branches were everywhere."

Phylis described the frightening creature as being "Large [and)]dark-colored. [I would] guess it was nine to ten feet tall and very angry. [It was] hard to see more. I was a child and very frightened. My uncle and grandmother refused to tell anyone. They thought they would not be believed!"

LETCHER COUNTY

The rain beat down on the tin roof of the little guard shack located in the mountains of Kentucky near Whitesburg. It was just about midnight on September 1, 2003 when an intruder approached the shack. Inside sat the security guard who had just returned from making his rounds and was doing some paperwork. He was just relaxing despite the damp, just listening to it rain.

"That's when I heard a loud crunching sound beside the shack," he later said. "So I stood up and watched the shadow from under the sides of the shack. It was moving toward the door. A few seconds later it was trying to open the door by pulling on it. That's when I yelled, 'What do you want?' That was when I heard the most terrifying sound ever, like a screaming howl. And it then began to pull harder on the door."

The anonymous witness said he felt pure dread come over him, such as he had never felt before in his life. "So I got a poker and put it in the coal stove that was our heat source for the shack. It got red glowing hot. I then told whatever it was what I had and [what I] was going to do with it if it opened the door. After a few minutes it got quieter and I watched its shadow move from under the door."

After several minutes had passed with no activity the man made the decision to get to the safety of his car as fast as possible. "I threw open the door of the guard shack so that the light from inside would show a little outside, and made a run for my car. I got in, locked the doors, started it up, put it in drive and got on the C.B. radio to inform the other guards of what I had just encountered. I stayed the rest of the night in my car. The next morning when my relief showed up I informed him of what I had encountered and I looked for footprints, but the heavy rain made it difficult to find any that would be useful. But I know what it was without a doubt. It was a Sasquatch!"

The man claimed he later learned that several other security guards refused to work at the site due to strange happenings there. The area consists of strip mines, mountains and woods.

Three campers were surprised by something uncanny about 1:00 a.m. on the morning of June 4, 2006, as they were enjoying the outdoors in Ermine. Dustin (full name on file), along with two of his buddies, Neil and Aaron, were on the mountain camping out for the night. "All of a sudden we heard something running down a big long field of grass. We all heard it so we run down closer [sic] to see what the hell it was. Then after we got closer to it we seen [sic] it walking down the road. It was running like no man could run. It also was screeching and making a lot of banging noises in the distance."

He said he reported the sighting to the police that night, describing the thing as, "a big brownish black creature that was very large in size. It was probably seven to eight feet tall."

LEWIS COUNTY

Lewis County played host to a creature described as being five or six feet tall, stocky and covered in black hair back on May 20, 1969. It was observed by three people who were taking a walk that sunny afternoon. "I was about five or six, taking a walk with my older brother and sister," one witness later stated. "Near our house was an abandoned house. As we were about to pass it we saw a black figure on the porch. My brother and sister ran and I followed them as fast as I could. Our dad went back after we got home to check things out but saw nothing. Around this time there were some strange sounds heard at night that Dad called a wildcat. Also, we raised a garden and we found that something was picking corn, taking it to the end of the garden and shucking it to eat. My second-oldest brother told me that, when he was a boy, he saw what he called a gorilla looking in the window one night. This would have been in the 1940s or '50s."

A gigantic man-like figure covered with shaggy, reddish-brown hair was reportedly sighted by a school-bus driver in Vanceburg on two separate occasions back in the late 1970s. On the second occasion he described the beast that he'd seen as a "big thing with matted, patchy red-brown hair like it had been burned." Both sightings allegedly took place on or near Vanceburg Hill.

Another such creature was observed near Concord on May 21, 2008. It was about 4:00 p.m. when Jimmy O. (real name on file) was out digging yellow root on Route 57. "I walked up a hill to avoid crossing a deep hollow," he stated. " As I got to the top and started down the other side I could see a field. When I got close to the field I could smell a strong odor. I walked to the field and saw what I thought was a bear, but when it stood up and started to walk to the other side, I knew it was no bear. I have seen a lot of bears before."
Jimmy said he yelled loudly, and the figure stopped, turned its head and looked at him. Then it made a high-pitched sound, turned and walked away very quickly. "As I came to the other side of the field it made grunting sounds," Jimmy claimed. "I saw it for maybe twenty seconds more. It walked into a grove of cedars and disappeared." Jimmy described the thing as seven to eight feet tall, with long reddish-colored hair covering its body. It had big shoulders and long arms that reached to its knees. He estimated that it must have weighed 400 to 500 pounds. He also recalled that it walked with big strides and he saw two human-looking footprints that it left behind. Moreover, he claimed that he had seen the same type of creature in the area when he was a child.

On May 20, 2007 another Kentucky couple caught a glimpse of the unknown while returning home from a friend's house in Olive Hill. "Me and my wife [sic] were driving along Route 59, about two miles from Route 1662," the witness later said, "when a tall creature walked out in front of our car. My wife screamed, 'Bear! Bear!' I told her it was no bear. It stood on its hind legs. The creature stood in the road for about forty or forty-five seconds then walked across the road to the field to the right. I got out and got my spot light and gave it to the wife. I followed the creature to the creek, where it walked up a real steep hill [and] I couldn't follow anymore. All night we heard strange growls and squeals. The dogs barked all night." The witness described the creature as seven to eight feet tall, brownish-red in color, weighing 400 to 500 pounds, with long arms and broad shoulders.

Another hairy humanoid was seen in Lewis County in the spring of 2008. The witness claimed that he and his children had been getting glimpses of the thing at their home on Firebrick Road near South Portsmouth for the prior three or four months. He described the beast as seven to eight feet tall, with no neck and covered in grayish-black hair. A horrible smell, a cross between a skunk and rotten meat, was associated with the beast, and the horses and dogs were badly frightened when it was in the area. It always walked on two legs and the witness felt sure that the creature was responsible for his missing livestock.

LINCOLN COUNTY

An 11-year-old child saw Bigfoot in Broughtontown just before dusk one evening in September of 1974. She had gone out to a wooded area at the base of a nearby hill to bury a bird that she'd found injured in the wild and which had later died. Accompanied by her two dogs, she crossed the gravel road in front of the house, walked across the creek and into the woods.
"I had finished burying the bird," she later said, "when my poodle dog, Cotton, started whimpering. At that time I heard the crunching of leaves. I assumed it was the other dog, Jack, walking to me but he came out in front of me and was also whimpering with his tail tucked between his legs. I had never known any of the dogs to behave in this manner. They were looking to the left of me, where the crunching sounds were coming from." She looked in the direction of the sounds and claims that she will never forget what she saw.
"When I looked up the thing stopped moving. It was probably about fifteen to twenty feet away from me. I saw a huge, long-haired thing. At first I thought it may have been a bear, but it was standing on two legs and, as my gaze travelled up from about its knees, I saw long, really hairy arms that couldn't have been a bear's."
She said she never saw what the rest of the thing looked like. Completely unnerved, she "ran like the devil" back toward the house. She only paused for a second in the middle of the creek, she said, to allow the dogs to catch up. The next spring, mysterious footprints were found going up a steep hill in the area.

Another similar creature was seen by a local deer hunter at about 8:00 a.m. one morning in November of 2001 in Crab Orchard. "I was out hunting, and I was looking at the edge of the woods," he said. "Some crows started to make some noise and I heard something coming through the woods. Then I saw something big and black near the edge of the woods. It grunted and made some other noises that I can't describe." He said he thought it was a bear at first, until the creature stood up. "It had a stick and threw it at something in a tree. I got scared as it walked standing up. I thought if it came any closer I would shoot it." Luckily the thing, which was standing about fifty yards away, turned and walked noisily back into the woods. He described the creature that he saw as eight feet tall when it stood up, covered with black fur.

"It held and threw that stick like a man," he said. He returned to the area a half-hour later but could find no evidence that anything had been there. He also recalled that, as a child, he had found a large human-looking footprint in the soft mud behind his school in this same area.

LIVINGSTON COUNTY

A smaller version of Bigfoot, perhaps a juvenile, was seen in a wooded area of Livingston County back in October, 1969. A passing motorist spotted the diminutive creature while driving home from a friend's house around 11:30 p.m. that night. "I observed a dull white-colored creature walking upright on two legs," he later said. "The thing was approximately four feet tall and completely covered with light-colored, almost white hair. I was within twenty-five feet of it and its head and face was [sic] almost humanlike. It walked upright and held its front legs, or arms, out in front. It crossed the road in front of my truck and continued into the woods."

The witness claimed to have spoken to a neighbor who saw the beast on three different occasions on her farm. The peculiar posture exhibited by the creature, walking with its arms held out in front of it, is another bizarre Bigfoot trait that has been reported before.

LOGAN COUNTY

An ape-man was seen one mile north of Hwy. 78 near Russelville in Logan County, in 1972 by a deer hunter named Philip M. Wilkins. He described it as seven to eight tall, weighing approximately 500 lbs., with a short neck and arms that hung nearly to its knees.

"What I saw still creates goose bumps on my arms," he said. " I cannot detail the fear I experienced getting back to my Jeep. There is no mistake in what I saw."

The creature put in another appearance in 1991, this time near Lewisburg, one mile from the Muhlenberg County line. A father and his son had arrived home about 9:00 one evening only to hear loud "roaring sounds" coming from the woods on their property. The son ran inside and grabbed a shotgun. On entering the woods, he encountered a large, hairy, man-like animal of some sort. It fled when the gun-toting witness gave chase, allegedly breaking branches off trees up to a height of eight feet.

Another such creature was observed crouching behind a telephone pole near Lewisburg by three witnesses on June 8, 2009. It was between 9:30 and 10:00 p.m. Eyewitness Colby A. (full name on file) said he and two friends observed the creature from the safety of his vehicle for about five minutes. "When we went to leave we turned around and saw [another] creature behind us," Colby said. The trio took off down the rural road, driving about 35 mph "It was still up there with us," Colby said. He claims that he and his friends had seen the thing a couple of times and, "It is not scared of us at all." He describes it as being about seven feet tall, with very wide shoulders, and weighing about 500 pounds. Colby said it had a patch of white hair on its chest and had a distinct smell, something like a cross between a rotting animal and a skunk.

"We've had rocks thrown at us a couple of times," he said, "and we have heard a whistling sound every time we have heard the creature or smelled the odor." He also claims to have found something that looked like a huge nest that was, "too big to be from anything around here." In addition, Colby said he took pictures of a large handprint on the back of his vehicle that he thinks may have been made by the creature.

LYON COUNTY

"I was driving home from a night out at the lake with my friends," said an anonymous witness. "It was sort of misty out and I couldn't see very far in front of my car." It was about 10:30 p.m. on the night of May 1, 2000 on a deserted back road in Eddyville. "I saw a large creature walking across a trail in front of the car. I came so close to it and I almost hit it. It turned and looked at me and lunged at the car. I just put the car in reverse and sped away from the area as fast as I possibly could. In the distance as I was driving away I heard a low growling sound. I couldn't really see the face but it almost looked humanlike from what I could see. It was rather tall and hairy. [It had] large hands with some fairly long claws. The face was humanlike and the body almost apelike. It was like a huge beast. I don't really know what it was," he said.

A Grand Rivers angler describes an event that happened one morning in July, 1999: "I went to the edge of a small bay on Lake Barkley near Davenport Bay to do some fishing. I cast a lure into the water when movement across the bay caught my eye. I looked up and saw a figure in the bushes stand up and run up the hill. I was familiar with every animal native to the LBL (Land Between the Lakes) and this was something I've never seen before. It ran upright on two legs with the arms swinging at the sides.

It ran like a human. I watched as it disappeared over the hill. A minute or so after it disappeared I realized my lure was still floating in the water. I'd forgotten all about it! I tried to make my way around to the other bank where I'd seen the figure but the brush was too thick. Over the rest of the summer I returned to the same spot several times but never saw it again."

The witness, Brad O. (full name on file), estimated the creature's height at about six feet. "It was covered from head to foot with brown fur," he said. "There was short hair on the head. The fur didn't look shaggy or unkempt; it looked smooth and shiny. I could see the muscles moving under the fur. I didn't see the face. I only saw the backside. What was strangest of all was that it had what can only be described as an hourglass figure (wide shoulders and hips and a slender waist.) The legs and arms were long, but not overly muscular." The appearance of the creature led the witness to conclude it may have been a young female.

Another Grand Rivers resident, this time a deer hunter, claims that he saw a creature resembling Bigfoot at 8:00 in the morning on November 26, 2007 in the Jenny Ridge Graveyard. "My father and I were going hunting at LBL and I had already harvested a deer," Tristan (full name on file) stated, "so I figured I would just stay in the truck. My dad went into the woods after we ate breakfast and I dozed off. I woke up after about thirty minutes with my stomach hurting. I sat up and rubbed my eyes. I looked out the windshield at the graveyard ahead of me and there it was. I thought, 'thank God it's walking away from me.' I lay back down for a couple of minutes, in shock from what I just saw. A moment later I sat back up again and it was gone. I was glad that it had disappeared." Tristan described the object of his uneasiness as being about seven feet tall and covered in shaggy, dark-colored hair. It walked slowly, he said, on two legs like a man.

MADISON COUNTY

Bigfoot appeared in Berea in the early 1970s. "It was about 1972 or '73 in Berea, Kentucky," said a witness who wished to remain anonymous. "I must have been fifteen or so. My brother, a friend of mine, and I were sleeping out in our tent made of plastic tossed over one of those umbrella-type clothes lines. The plan was to sneak out later to walk up town to meet with our girlfriends. It was probably about 2 a.m. when I came out of the tent. Our house was built into a hillside and over looked the college-owned cornfield and out across the county, which, at that time was not very developed. I was standing with my back to the field looking up the hill at the stars while waiting for the others to get up. I got impatient and had turned around toward the tent to tell them to hurry when I saw what I first thought was my neighbor standing at the corner of the house next to the pine tree that grew there. Problem was this thing looked to be about seven or eight feet tall, as it's head was into the branches. My mind was racing, trying to grasp what I was seeing. Why was my neighbor wearing white? How did he know we were out here tonight? Why was he standing so still and how the hell did he get so tall? We, meaning "it" and I, stared at each other for several seconds. Then the thing turned and pushed off against the tree and bolted down over the bank and into the woods toward the cornfield. I was impressed with the speed, the lack of noise it made while running and the fact that the tree, which was pretty big, actually swayed when it pushed off from it. About that time my friend came out of the tent and I told him about what I had just seen. I don't remember if he acted like he believed me or not.

"My brother was more inclined to believe my story because he and my sister had often heard what we called 'the cruncher' while sleeping out on the screened-in back porch, which is about fifteen feet off the ground on the back of the house. Back before we had air conditioning we three kids would sleep on the porch during the summer to get the cooler night air. We had a small mutt dog that would sleep with us. Many times we would be woke up [sic] to the sounds of, at least to our young imaginations, an animal munching on animal bones. We were scared to death but would look over the edge trying to see what ever it was. We never did see anything because the woods were so thick and we were so far up. We knew we weren't crazy because the dog would sit there stock still and give one of those low, throaty growls that would make a person freeze if you heard it in the dark. We tried a couple times to get the dog to go outside and chase the thing. We never saw a dog resist so hard. She acted like we were trying to shove her into a fire or something. After that dog died we got another that reacted the very same way and was only about half as smart as the little mutt dog.

The witness remembers that the thing was covered with off white to tan-colored hair that was thinner on its face and abdomen. He could not recall any facial details but did remember that its arms appeared to be longer than that of a human.

"My brother and sister can verify 'the cruncher,' he said. "We also built a playhouse in the back yard which we only slept in one time and that was on Halloween with several other kids. We once went into the cornfield and picked so much corn that we had to leave it piled up in the thicket with the idea to get the rest the next day. Problem was, the next morning it was gone, every last ear. [There was] way too much for a raccoon or even a family of raccoons to have hauled off. I should add that this was what we called 'field corn,' which became rock hard when ripe and was used to feed cows and pigs. If you caught it at the right time it was pretty good to eat, otherwise it would crack your teeth. It finally hit me a few years later that 'the cruncher' was probably eating the field corn, and not munching on bones.

After a while, the area started to get built up and we heard less and less of the noise. There was an article in the local paper about the time all this was happening about a family that lived farther out, but not that far from us. There was some unusual stuff happening around their home. They were finding what they thought were big nests of leaves around their property and had caught glimpses of something on occasion passing their windows. I still have the article somewhere. It was in the local paper, the *Berea Citizen.* I wanted to contact the family but never did; I was afraid of being called a nut. I've only told a few people about this. It still raises the hair on the back of my neck to tell it and, as I just discovered, to write it down. This is the only event of my life that is unexplained."

Our next Madison County stop is at Flint Road, Waco, Ky., in September of 1983. It was late afternoon on a beautiful fall day and Bigfoot was about to appear to a twelve-year old boy. "This incident occurred in the later part of 1983 (September I believe) just outside of Richmond, in Waco," said the witness, now thirty years old. "I was out riding my bike when I decided to go visit a friend. He lived about a quarter mile off the main highway at the end of a gravel road. His house was the only one on the road and was completely surrounded by thick woods. After arriving, I walked to the door and realized nobody was home. As I returned to my bike I heard a loud crash from the side of the house. I quickly looked and saw a large, black figure tearing a huge limb from a tree. The figure was at least seven or eight feet tall and covered in thick black hair. I couldn't guess the weight, but it was big. The figure was standing upright and was looking right at me. It was no bear. I quickly jumped on my bike and peddled like hell toward the main road.

"The ride back to the main road seemed to take forever and the entire distance back I could hear branches breaking and what appeared to be heavy footsteps running alongside me. I was terrified. I thought for sure I was about to be attacked. Then I hit the main road and it stopped. I kept riding, but couldn't help but wonder why whatever it was stopped chasing me once I hit the road. I don't know what it was, but I do know if it were a bear it wouldn't have stopped, and it was fast because it was able to catch a terrified kid peddling his butt off.

"I had another encounter, this time with witnesses, in the same area when I was nineteen."

The man later spoke to an investigator and told him that the creature he saw was about fifty yards away. The sighting only lasted a few seconds but he was able to add that the thing appeared to be slightly pigeon-toed. It stood and moved upright and had a thick, muscular body covered with shiny white fur.

Another such creature, this one covered with thick, reddish-colored hair, was seen in the Bear Mountain area in the summer of 1993. "It was in July ninety-three," said the man. "I was hiking up on Bear Mountain near my family's home in eastern Kentucky I had my pair of binoculars I had just bought and wanted to try them out on a high view. As I rounded the cliff, I was looking down this hollow that leads into a briar thicket. I had been hearing this odd tapping noise all the while, and saw this dark brownish figure near a log close to the thicket some 250 yards away, more or less. At first I thought it a rare sighting of a black bear, but when I looked at it through the binoculars, I couldn't believe what I saw. It was sitting on a log with its back to me. It had a rock in its hand, beating on this log's side. It had a back that was at least two and a half feet across and covered in short, thick reddish-brown hair. It looked like a giant hair-covered man with no neck.

"With the bins (binoculars) I could see in good detail, so there was no mistake. The hands looked human, four fingers and a thumb, the skin a dark grayish color. The head was conical, like a lowland gorilla. Suddenly this thing must have smelled or sensed me, because it stood up and looked in my direction. It had a bulged forehead near the eyebrow, large round dark eyes, and a flared gorilla-like nose. The jaw was slightly long, but did not protrude at the mouth. The nose and eyes areas were free of hair, the skin [was] a dark gray. The nose, mouth, and chin were covered in hair. The creature was huge! I later looked at a tree it was standing near and it had to be near seven feet tall. It stared up the mountain at me, and made a peculiar motion with its head, waving it from side to side, and [it] seemed to hunch over a bit with its arms dangling at it's knees. It then turned and dashed off through the thicket. I never saw it again. Needless to say, I got the hell out of there."

A dark-colored humanoid creature that stood ten feet tall and had glowing red eyes allegedly scared a group of eight Boonsborough youths in July of 2006. The eight were night fishing in a local creek at about 1:30 a.m. when they heard something large coming up the creek in their direction, "breathing really hard and loud." Travis D. (full name on file) stated that, within seconds after the group had heard the sounds, a terrible odor that "smelled worse than a dead skunk" had permeated the area and they decided to flee. According to Travis, they soon regained their courage and returned to the area and found a very large, unmistakably human footprint in the mud. They shined one of their flashlights at a nearby small bridge and observed the huge figure standing beneath the structure. Once again, for good this time, they decided to leave the area. The incident, I am sure, curtailed any further nighttime fishing trips in the area.

MAGOFFIN COUNTY

Salyersville, the county seat, also has a history of hairy humanoid sightings stretching back several generations. As we have seen, this is no surprise when it comes to Bluegrass counties. The only real wonder is that sightings of this nature get reported at all. An apelike creature was allegedly observed there back in the fall of 1972 by a resident out squirrel hunting near Hwy. 1081. He said he was sitting quietly, surrounded by woods and hills, listening for squirrels when the sighting occurred. It was early morning and the leaves had not yet fallen from the trees. He didn't hear it coming, he later told an investigator, but saw it moving away from him at a distance of about seventy yards. It was walking casually away on two legs, and paused once to look around before continuing on. It was about seven feet tall, covered in reddish-colored hair, very muscular with strong-looking legs. He said it looked like it could have weighed up to 500 pounds. He didn't shoot the beast, he claimed, because he didn't know what it was.

Many Kentucky old timers, when confronted in the woods by an unknown creature of any type, often shot first and figured out its identity afterwards. After the thing was well away, the witness said he approached the area through which it had walked and found several large, human-looking footprints impressed into the ground about an inch deep. His own boots made hardly any marks at all. His father, he claimed, saw a similar beast in the area in 1969.

MARSHALL COUNTY

A Marshall County mail carrier claimed she saw Bigfoot in the spring of 1990 while she was attempting to deliver a package to a residence on Cole Cemetery Road in Benton. It was early afternoon on a pleasant day. She was 30 years old and eight months pregnant.

"In April 1990, I was attempting to make a residential delivery," she said. "While walking up the gravel drive I noticed a flock of birds flying overhead coming from the direction of a thick grouping of trees in the back of a field to my left. They were chattering loudly and flying wildly in what seemed to be a race. As they got closer I noticed that there were different species flying together – blue jays, cardinals, blackbirds, finches, etc. This struck me as odd. When I reached the steps to the porch I heard the thunder of hooves hitting the ground and turned and saw many horses that were in the field come running from the edge of the forest toward the house. They where whinnying and making a lot of commotion. Before I could really think anything about it, I saw several deer leaping from the thick trees and running through the fields away from the same spot, and behind the horses. My first thought then was that there was a fire. I hurried to the door and knocked very hard and repeatedly, while scanning the sky for any signs of smoke. No one answered. Having delivered there before I thought the occupant might be around back in the barn, so I left the porch and turned to walk in that direction." According to her, that's when she heard the most terrifying sound that she'd ever heard in her life. "I knew it could not have been human or from any known animal in this area," she stated.

The sound had come from a thick group of trees and echoed over the fields. "It was a mixture of a deep lion's growl that heightened into a scream containing the same low, deep, loud rhythm. I stood stunned, half scared and half curious," she said.

From the area where the sound had come from she said she could see a large figure shaking the trees. "It was something very tall," she recalled, "very large in width and very strong-looking, as some of the smaller pine trees about ten to fifteen feet in height were being shaken back and forth vigorously and violently. The figure itself was not totally visible but hidden mostly behind the shadows of the larger trees behind and around it. It was dark in color, dark brown or black, with a thick furry outline. It looked to have stood well over seven feet in height. It began moving along the edge of the trees toward the house, just keeping inside the safety of the shadows. The horses in the pasture were on the far right-hand side now, rising up and hitting the fence with their hooves. This was too much excitement for me, and I turned to run to my truck. That hideous sound came through the air again, but this time it was much closer than before. I quickly made it into the truck, started the engine and left very rapidly, halfway expecting the engine to be flooded or the battery dead, like in some lame horror movie."

She said the event left her shaken but it was her duty to return the next day and reattempt the delivery. Upon reaching the house, she briefly explained to the occupant what had occurred the day before, expecting him to laugh at her story. "To my surprise, he agreed that there had been some strange sounds coming from [the woods] lately, and that his horses were frequently spooked by something in the area. He also stated that a friend of his had took his hunting dog back there a few weeks prior to this incident and that the dog took out after something, disappeared from sight, [then] let out curdling yelping sounds and went quiet. He said his buddy found what was left of the dog. Its head was not to be found, and that there had been a foul odor around the area at the time."

She said the man told her the culprit was probably a bobcat and cautioned her not to go into the woods by herself, which she said she was hardly likely to do, after hearing that frightening sound and seeing the terrified animals.

The sighting only lasted from twenty to thirty seconds, she later said, with the mysterious figure remaining about 100 feet away in the shadows, just out of full view. She couldn't see any facial features but she felt that the creature, whatever it was, was staring at her. As she stared at the thing she said she got goose bumps, the hair on the back of her neck stood up, and her legs trembled with fear. According to her, the animal was "eight feet to nine feet tall, at least," and was from three to four feet wide. It was covered with dark-colored hair that was darker than the tree trunks. It moved slowly and deliberately, cautiously taking a few steps and then pausing, and then a few more steps before pausing again. The witness claimed that she watched the beast take about eight to ten steps in this fashion before she left the area. Land Between the Lakes is located about twenty miles from the site of the encounter.

MARTIN COUNTY

Bigfoot made an appearance in Martin County one summer afternoon in 1950 deep in the mountains of Warfield. After the witness had seen the creature she was told not to tell anyone about it because they would surely think that she was crazy. It took 53 years for her to overcome the fear of public ridicule and tell her story.

"In 1950 when I was twelve years old, I lived in a little hamlet called Beauty, located in eastern Kentucky along the border of the Tug River. We children played in the mountains almost all summer long. We had heard of a rock cliff back up on the hill that had a cave in it and we decided to go looking for this cliff with the cave. Being kids, we didn't keep track of how far we climbed or what ridges we went on, but finally we reached this cliff. We were standing at the base looking up through the shadows of the trees when I noticed there was someone standing up on the rock about ten feet up, looking back at us. He was, I judged, about six feet tall and muscular. His arms were longer than a human's. His legs [were] about like a human.

He had hair much like a chimp's hair grows on its arms and legs, not fuzzy hair like a bear. His chest seemed to be pretty hairless. [It was] very hairy around the genital area so one could not tell if he was male or female. I didn't see any breasts so I judged it to be male.

"He was holding a heavy stick in his hand as he stood there looking down at us. I could not see his facial features. I would say that he was an intelligent being from the way he behaved. He stood looking at us for about fifteen seconds then he stepped back out of our sight and was gone. It was not until I was an adult that I realized what I had seen. I believe that this being knew that we were children. I believe he allowed us to see him because we did not present him any danger. Of course we yelled and tore up the bushes running back off that hill! I told my grandma that we had seen a gorilla and she told me people would think I was crazy so I kept it to myself." The sighting occurred in the early afternoon with good visibility.

At about 3 a.m. on May 24, 2006, in Inez, four campers were able to observe a gigantic, hair-covered creature for over ten minutes.

"Me and a few of my male companions [sic] were gathered around a campfire. One of my friends had passed out due to drinking and we had carried him inside the tent," one of the witnesses said. "Several hours later, we heard groaning sounds coming from the direction of the tent. We thought nothing of it. Little did we know that something had been watching us. The groaning went on for hours until we finally checked our drunk [sic] friend. He was silent and the groaning continued. I peered behind the tent in the direction I thought the sounds were coming from, and there was, about fifteen feet from us, what appeared to be an apelike creature sleeping, It was rolling around as if it were trying to find a spot to get comfortable. I was quiet for several minutes and then I called to one of my friends to check this out. He came to see what the fuss was about and when he saw the creature he screamed in fear. The creature raised its head, looking startled. It rose from the ground it appeared to be about seven or eight feet tall."

The monster took off in a hurry, according to the witness. He said it had brownish hair that appeared to be about two or three inches thick around its body.

Two more Martin County campers were surprised on the night of February 17, 2006. "My wife and I were camping in the woods," said J.T. (full name on file). "As we were falling asleep I heard a rustling noise outside the tent. I wanted to go outside to check to see if we had put our food away, so as not to attract bears. As I went outside I turned my flashlight on so I could see what I was doing. When I did this I saw something step into the woods." the witness, badly frightened, dropped his flashlight and ran back to the tent, leaving the hot dog buns and cheese where they lay on the table. As he climbed back into the tent he looked back to see the creature as it fled into the woods, screeching and grunting. According to him, the creature was at least seven to seven and a half feet tall, "grotesquely hairy" and possibly wet.

The very next month, on March 11, 2007 a seven- or eight-foot-tall, hair-covered creature with long teeth reportedly frightened two children as they waited for the school bus in Milo. " My sister and I were waiting for the bus," said Jared Waller, "when something started throwing rocks at us." He figured it was some of his friends playing a prank until they heard a growling noise coming from some nearby trees. Bravely, Jared went to see what it was, then spied the huge "monster" that he said struck at him, causing him to flee in panic.

MASON COUNTY

A rather well publicized Mason County Bigfoot account appeared in the October 12, 1980 edition of the *Chicago Sun-Times*. It concerned Charles Fulton and his family, who claimed that, while watching television on the night of October 4, they heard a commotion out on the front porch apparently involving one of Fulton's roosters. When he looked out, sure enough, there was the rooster in the hand of a seven-foot-tall, 400-pound manlike creature with long white hair and (by some accounts) glowing pink eyes. When the thing realized it had been spotted, it threw the rooster against the side of the house and headed around behind the building.

Fulton said he grabbed a .22 pistol and promptly gave chase, despite the bizarre appearance of the intruder. He later told investigators that he fired on the creature twice to no effect as the monster made its escape in a "slow-motion" kind of run, exhibiting large strides but, strangely, moving at low speed. Fulton said he felt sure that he could catch up to it but, even more strangely, the faster he ran the farther away the creature appeared. "It was like a dream," he said. The *Chicago Sun-Times* ran the following article about the encounter in the Sunday, October 12, 1980 edition:

One Look at Bigfoot is Enough

Maysville, Kentucky (UPI) -- Anna Mae Sanders, still awed by the sight of Bigfoot, says she doesn't want another look at the 7-foot creature covered with long, white hair. She is certain she saw it last weekend outside the home of her son-in-law in rural Mason County.

"I just hope that thing doesn't come back," said Saunders, 60. "I never saw anything like it in my life. It just looked like a big, white fuzzy thing standing there on the porch. I never saw its face; it was above the 7-foot high door," she added.

Saunders' son-in-law, Charles Fulton, said the creature had one of his roosters when he opened the door, but either dropped it or threw it as it jumped off the porch. He described the so-called Bigfoot as having long white hair with glowing animal-like eyes.

Fulton, 39, went outside and saw it standing between the house and an outbuilding.

He fired two shots with a .22 caliber pistol but they seemed to have no effect. "It loped off at a slow-motion kind of gallop," he said. Fulton and his family were at their rural home in a heavily wooded area watching television Saturday night when one of the children came into the living room and said someone was turning the back door knob.

Thinking the child was joking, Fulton made him sit and watch television. "A few minutes later, something like to have tore my front door off," Fulton said. He said he did not tell authorities about the sighting because he feared no one would believe him.

Saunders and the three children said they also saw the creature from inside the house. Fulton discounted the possibility that the creature was a bear because of its upright position, and said it definitely was not a man in a costume.

Sanders, who lives in a mobile home near the Fulton home said, "I'm scared to death to stay by myself now. Whenever I go back to the trailer, I look in all directions." She said there had been similar sightings recently in Aberdeen, Ohio, just across the Ohio River from Mason County.

When later contacted by two Bigfoot investigators Fulton further added that the thing's hair was long, like a horse's mane. He stated that the thing was man-like, "except those eyes were like that of an animal." He said it was a strange experience for him, especially the way the thing ran with long, slow strides, "like in slow-motion." He said he felt like he should have been easily able to catch up to it, but the faster he ran the farther the distance between himself and the creature became. "[It was] almost like a dream," he said, "the kind of dream like when a wild animal is chasing you and you can't seem to run away."
The rooster escaped with no serious injuries.

On October 10, a woman claimed that she'd been chased to her car by a hairy man-like creature as she was leaving the Central Shopping Center in Maysville. The creature put in another appearance in Maysville a couple of weeks later, on November 5. According to a report on file with the Maysville Police Department, around 4:00 or 5:00 a.m. that morning a truck driver named N. Clay was hauling a load of steel just west of Maysville on U.S. Route 68 when he saw what he at first thought was a hitchhiker. On slowing down he was shocked to see a six- to seven-foot tall, apelike creature with white hair.
The police stated that they believed Clay was serious about what he reported.

In 2007, Jeremiah H. (full name on file) claimed that he'd had a couple of different run-ins with a Bigfoot-type creature in Maysville in late 2002 and early 2003. Both incidents involved multiple witness sightings of the strange creature.

"The first encounter I had," Jeremiah stated, "I left my house around 10:30 p.m. to go pick up a friend from his house in Germantown. I was traveling north with three other friends on the Clyde T. Barbour Highway. I had turned left onto KY 435 and drove to my friend's house in Germantown. I picked him up and decided to go the same way that I had went [sic] to pick him up. There [were] three people in the backseat and someone in the front of my car. We had turned the car around a right turn traveling at around 20 mph. As I turned the corner there is a two-story farmhouse on my right and on the same side about thirty feet to the side of the house was a very small garden with tall weeds on the side of the road. On the other side is a drop anywhere from ten to fifteen feet.

"As I drove, I caught a glimpse of what appeared to be a large dog on the side of the road, so I slowed the car to let it run across the road without hitting it. I turned on my brights to scare it from its position as I slowed to around 5 to 8 mph. It moved slightly as someone in the backseat had asked, 'What is that?' I then replied. 'I think it might be a dog.'

"The eyes glowed red from the high beams. This so-called dog had blackish fur on the shoulder area. As I pulled closer, I stopped the car, put it in reverse and turned the car to face the animal. My lights now fully caught the animal still hiding in the weeds, which were around three feet in height. I pushed the horn and it stood on two legs at a height of around six to seven feet tall. All of my friends started screaming and asking. 'What the hell is that? As everyone in the car was screaming I had already put the car into drive and peeled the tires to get away. One of my friends then turned in his seat looking through the back window as I looked through the rear-view mirror [and saw] in the moonlight this animal run into the field toward the forest.

"The second encounter was on the Clyde T. Barbour Highway, going southbound toward home. Me and my brother [sic] were making our way home from Aberdeen, Ohio. I was driving and it was a clear night with the moon out bright, I was driving around 55-60 mph up the highway hill. I had just passed KY 435 and the same spot from the last encounter when I scanned the highway in a daze and looked up at the hill where they had used dynamite when they were building the highway to blow the hillside out for the pavement. I looked up the hillside at the limestone and caught a glimpse of a rather tall animal with blackish fur running with my car. I pointed at the beast, which apparently had been running on two legs and asked my brother, "What is that?" As we moved on, still watching the animal, it jumped from the hill and landed in some trees and disappeared." Jeremiah described the creature as being tall - around seven feet. "It stood, walked, and ran on two legs, with [its] arms reaching its pelvis. It had black fur and red eyes in the bright headlights. [It had a] large body, possibly three and one-half feet wide, with stringy hair [that was] longer on the shoulders that looked like it was wet."

Another Mason County creature sighting happened on August 16, 2008. Two Dover, squirrel hunters were in the woods at 7:30 a.m. that morning when they heard a twig snap behind them. Thinking it was a squirrel attempting to outflank them, one of the witnesses, George A. (full name on file), said they turned "and there he was. He was around twenty-five yards away. He acted as if he was looking for something." George described the creature was eight feet tall, really muscular, with "a lot of hair."

MCCREARY COUNTY

Dog Slaughter, McCreary County, Cumberland Falls State Park - Daniel Boone National Forest- 1984: As told by witness, Mr. W. (full name on file):

The year was probably 1984. Me and a buddy [sic] decided to go camping for a night or two on the Cumberland River in the Daniel Boone National Forest. It was in August and it was very hot that day. This place is called Dog Slaughter and it is very secluded. It is quite a ways below the Cumberland Falls State Park and the only way to get to it is to backpack in or canoe. It is really rough terrain and it is rough going. I'm just guessing, but we estimated [it was] at least three miles or so to the nearest main road and then you have to travel a ways to get to where there are people.

We had been going backpacking there for about five years or so and it is really beautiful country. The fishing is real good, too. A year or two before, I stopped and asked a park ranger or game warden if we could pack a gun in there and he said he wouldn't be back in that place without one. Anyway, we got in there that afternoon just before dark. We wasn't [sic] going to stay that long so we didn't take a lot of food. We had a lantern, tent and fishing poles. My buddy also brought a portable Coleman stove, which he almost left behind because it was so rough carrying it in there, much less trying to pack it out.

We got to our camping spot and dark was coming fast, though the sun was still up. It doesn't take it long to get dark back in those mountains. As we walked upon this sand bar we were looking around and that's when we found huge footprints in the sand and they looked like somebody had walked around the sand bar barefooted. But these tracks were really big. We followed them and they walked right into the river and across a little cove and then up a huge logjam. There was just the one set of prints. What was really odd was where the tracks started, there was a brand-new, shiny, fish stringer still tied up with about eight really nice white perch on it. Somebody had walked all the way into this rough place and caught these nice fish and just left them there to rot; they had already started to decompose. This was really strange, but we never really gave it much more thought.

We set the tent up in front of this huge boulder, next to the river. My buddy got the stove going and we started cooking some beans and pork shoulder. We lit the lantern when it got dark and we didn't bother with building a fire. We was going to wait until the next day to gather firewood because this place is full of copperhead snakes, and we didn't want to get bit gathering wood after dark with no light. After we ate, we talked for a while and then got in the tent to sleep. We were so tired, and we were going to get up early and fish. The crickets and frogs were really making quite a racket on that riverbank until they all stopped and it got really quiet. That's when we heard something jump off the big rock behind our tent. When it hit the ground it grunted. Then we heard a twig or stick break. That's when this thing started growling, coming toward us. The growl was so big and loud it filled that whole river bottom up with its growl.

    I looked at my buddy and said, 'Do you hear that?' By then we were both getting worried. It was between us and the way out. No matter, we still couldn't have gotten out of there because we were so far back in the mountains, and the way out was all uphill now. He said, 'What are we going to do?' I told him that I wasn't going to stay in this tent with whatever it was coming toward us. I didn't have a gun, just a hunting knife and hatchet. But, thankfully, my friend had brought his .22 rifle. So he stuck it out of the tent door and shot off about five rounds. I guess this scared it back, because it didn't come on into camp. It just stayed out in the woods growling until just about daylight.

    We never did see what it was. But after reality set in and we realized where we were at, [sic] I was starting to get worried. I had already made up my mind to jump in the river and take my chances there. That's the only time in my life I've had the hair stand up on my neck from fear.

    There are black bear in there, but if this had been a bear we would have never kept it out of camp because of the pork shoulder we were cooking. Besides I've heard and saw [sic] bears before out in the wild and this was no bear. It sounded big and mean and it meant business. When daylight finally did arrive we thought we saw something big and black walking on the rocks way up the river, but by then we were both so sleepy we couldn't make out what it was. It didn't look like it walked on four legs, but we couldn't be sure. We didn't stay another night, not really because we were scared, but because we were so tired and didn't really want to go to sleep and have it come back, and besides, a bad storm was coming and we barely made it out of there before it hit.

    I don't know to this day what it was we heard or what those footprints were, but we talk about it still every time we get together. I've been going camping on the Cumberland River for years and that's the first time anything like that has happened back in that wild place. Though a couple of time before this, when we would go back in there, we would notice this strange smell on a rock that stuck out over a little stream that run out of the mountains into the river. The rock is covered with moss and is a nice rock to lie on and relax. The last couple of times, though, this rock smells like a monkey's cage, like something that really smells bad has been lying on it.

    I never could figure out those footprints, because anybody that knows Cumberland River at all knows it's not safe to walk around with boots on much less barefooted because of the copperheads; they're thick in that place. I wear a size ten shoe and the footprints made two of mine. The Cumberland River is a great place for varmints to hide. I never will forget it as long as I live!

    Again, it is that which we cannot see that scares us the most. I conducted several telephone interviews with Mr. W. and we spoke of the incidents at length. He sounded very sincere and credible and he still wondered, after more than twenty years, about the source of the terrifying vocalizations and gigantic footprints they had seen that day on the Cumberland River. Whatever it was had scared the two men half to death. It was the only time in his life, Mr. W. told me, that he had felt such fear of something he could not see. They didn't want to see it; they just wished it would go away. If it had continued on into camp he said he was more than ready to throw himself into the river in order to escape. He related to me how his friend was an extremely rough and tumble sort who was not afraid of anything and always in fights and scuffles. Fearless, was how Mr. W. described him, until that night.

   The large, black figure they had seen during their retreat the following morning looked as if it walked on two legs like a man, and they wasted no time in fleeing the scene. That was one fishing trip, he told me, that neither of them would ever forget. The name of the area in which the event took place, Dog Slaughter, might hold a clue as to the history of Bigfoot activity there, as it is widely reported that these creatures possess an extreme dislike for dogs.

   More recently, in the same county in 2003, Pine Knot was the scene of another nighttime sighting by a motorist driving down Hwy. 92, between McCreary and Whitley counties. According to the witness, around 8:45 p.m. on the night of February 20, he saw in his headlights what he at first took to be a deer approaching the road. Fearing it might run out in front of his vehicle, the man slowed down and, on closer inspection of the animal, he is surprised to see a seven-foot-tall, gray-colored Bigfoot with large, red eyes. He said the creature began to act in a threatening manner.

"The thing ranted around like it was angry or something," the witness stated, "I floored the vehicle." He later described the creature as being of medium build with an "athletically muscular frame, large, domed head with hairy face."

   Nighttime "yowler" activity has also been reported from the Parker's Lake area in 2003 and 2004.

MCCRACKEN COUNTY

From the Newark, Ohio, *Daily Advocate* comes this curious nineteenth-century account of a "wild man," which was allegedly trapped and captured in Paducah.

Newark Advocate - 1883

"A KENTUCKY WILD MAN

A Man Covered with Thick Hair Who Refuses Bread, but Voraciously Eats Meat and Relishes Fruit

Among the passengers the other night bound for New York from the West on the day express was a wild man, who occupied a seat in smoking car No. 158. He was accompanied by James Harvey and Raymond Boyd, his captors, both of whom belong in Paducah County, Kentucky. They had three second-class tickets to New York, which privileges them to three seats in the smoking car of any first-class train. They were on their way to Bridgeport, Conn., to make arrangements with P. T. Barnum to exhibit their prize in conjunction with his circus. When the day express arrived at the Broad Street station, James Harvey ran down the platform into the restaurant and purchased a box of sardines and some sandwiches for the wild man's supper. His companion remained in the smoker in charge of the wild man. He was dressed in citizen's dress, and wore big, cloth shoes. His hair reaches nearly to his waist and falls over his shoulders, completely covering his back; his beard is long and thick, while his eyebrows are much heavier than those of an ordinary human being. There is nothing imbecile about the wild man's manners or actions. He cannot talk, and seldom makes any sound whatever except a low howl like a leopard. His actions are as much those of the hyena in the zoological garden as it is possible for anything in human form to be. Raymond Boyd, who seemed to have perfect control over the wild man, said his body was covered with coarse, brown hair as thick as the hair on a horse's hide. The palms of his hand look like the paws of a bear, and his fingernails, which were over an inch long, resembled the claws of an eagle.

He was first seen in Paducah County thirteen years ago, and was known as "Mum, the Hermit," because whenever anyone accosted him all he would say was, "Mum's the word." He lived in an old pine hut in the woods for about five years, and was seldom seen by anyone. Finally he abandoned the hut and took up his abode in a cave under a ledge of rocks known as "Lizard Rock." A little over six years ago two or three citizens of Paducah County, while out hunting, saw him run into his cave without a stitch of clothing on him. He was seen several times after that wearing no clothing. Three years ago it was discovered that a thick coat of hair had grown all over his body. Boyd and Harvey built a man-trap for him over three weeks ago, and placed a big piece of freshly killed beef in it. They watched the trap for three days before he entered it. He was not afraid of any bird or beast of prey, but ran terrified away from any human being that approached him. It took two days to accustom the man beast to their presence. The tinkle of a small dinner bell they used had a great influence over him. He watched the bell intently but would not touch it.

Some time ago a farmer missed a calf and two sheep, which had strayed off. They were tracked to "Mum's Cave." There all trace of them was lost, and it is supposed that he devoured them. In his cave, which he had occupied for the last seven or eight years, Boyd and Harvey found the skeletons of small animals and the skins of over fifty snakes. Some of the skins belonged to the most venomous species of reptiles. The floor of the cave was alive with red and green lizards and hundreds of toads hopped about. The wild man ate the box of sardines voraciously, and the two sandwiches which were handed him were greedily pulled apart. He ate the ham and threw the bread away. Whenever a train passed on the opposite track he crouched down in the corner of the seat terror stricken. After the train passed he would put his hand to his ear and listen with a look of animal cunning stealing out of his restless eyes, like a panther about to spring on his prey. Every time the engineer blew his whistle the wild man would grab the back of the seat with both hands and hold on until the whistle ceased blowing. Boyd had a little tin music box which he manipulated with a crank. The one tune of "Empty is the Cradle" was ground again and again to the great satisfaction of the ex-hermit, who sat and looked at it silently but would not touch it.

When Conductor Harry Smith took out his glistening nickel-plated punch to cancel the tickets the wild man watched the punch intently until he heard it snap. Then he got down in the corner of the seat fairly shivering with fear, and set up a low howl supposing, evidently, that Conductor Smith was about to wing him. Boyd and Harvey said that there was a story to the effect that the wild man had originally come from North Carolina, and that during the war he had been a sharp-shooter on Bald Mountain, and that shortly after the war he had murdered a whole family of settlers in the mountain and had fled. Both Boyd and Harvey appear like shrewd fellows, and expect to make a fortune out of their prize. Their great anxiety and fear is that the authorities will interfere with them, and claim that the man is simply a lunatic, and place him in some institution. They had the snakeskins in a box in the baggage car, together with some other curiosities found in the cave. Boyd said that the wild man will not touch anything but fruit and meat, which he eats ravenously, and much the same as a wild beast. Cigar smoke bothered him a great deal and he kept driving it away from him with his clawy hands. When the train arrived in Jersey City the men took a carriage, and said they were going to take the New Haven night boat from the foot of Puck Slip and avoid a daylight crowd in New York. In case they cannot make satisfactory terms with Barnum, or some other prominent circus man, they intend exhibiting their prize themselves as soon as they can extensively advertise him beginning in New York City sometime in May. In the meantime they are going to keep him in some secluded place on Long Island."

MCLEAN COUNTY

On July 12, 2006, Bigfoot appeared three miles southeast of Beech Grove, on Hwy. 136. "I was on my way to work," the witness said. "It was approx, 4:30 a.m. I was riding my motorcycle. I have an extra-bright headlight on my motorcycle and, as I approached an area with a sawmill, I noticed something squatting beside the road. I slowed and passed this thing and was no more than four feet away." The witness could scarcely believe what he was seeing. "I looked right into its eyes and face. The hair was about two and a half to three inches long, black and shiny. I know it was not any animal I had ever seen before. No Bear. No Dog. Nothing. The height if this thing, had it stood up, would've been at least six and a half feet tall. I continue to ask myself, *Did I just see what I thought I saw?* I was too shook up to stop and double check." To this day, he claimed, he wishes he had stopped and verified what he saw. He said he still looks for it whenever he is out night riding in the area.

MENIFEE COUNTY

It might appear that these Bigfoot creatures are attracted to the headlights of cars, motorcycles, and four-wheelers. Over and over we read of their harassment of such vehicles. This behavioral trait would seem completely at odds with a species of clever "apes" who wished above all else to remain undiscovered.

Another frightening incident involving a Bigfoot-type monster and a four-wheeler occurred in 1998 in the Daniel Boone National Forest near the Menifee-Morgan county line. According to the witness, he and a girlfriend were out riding after dark one evening in October. He was familiar with the horse trail they were on, and had parked near a small pond when a "tremendous roar" came from the tree line about forty yards behind them. "I was instantly terrified," he said, "as this was a sound I had never heard. It was loud and near." His girlfriend screamed in fear and he immediately started up the ATV and headed back down the trail toward a privately owned, dirt logging road. Having reached the logging road with no sign of pursuit by whatever it was that had made the noise, he sped up only a little - until he noticed a dark figure running through the trees alongside the road to his left.

"This thing was running on two legs. It looked like a very tall and large human form. I looked directly at it for a few seconds, turned back to look at the road, then turned and looked in its direction once more to discover it was still there keeping pace with us." He said he looked down at his speedometer. It read 22 mph. As he approached a slight curve and had to slow down a bit he looked around again, but the creature had disappeared. One second it was there and the next there was no trace of it anywhere. The two were unnerved by the encounter, to say the least.

METCALF COUNTY

Smallfoot, The Mysterious Creatures of Summershade
Summershade is a small town nestled amid the hills and hollows of what lowlanders like myself would call "Hill Country." It is located in Metcalf County and the scenery there is strikingly beautiful and much different from the marshy lowlands of western Kentucky. Mountains, valleys and stone-bottomed creeks dominate a landscape covered with seemingly endless expanses of thick, virgin forest. Within these forests, and scattered upon the sides of the stony mountains and creek banks, there can be found entrances to countless caves that open into murky caverns containing passages leading deep underground, connecting to the largest known cave system in the world,

nearby Mammoth caves. Who can say where all these tunnels lead and what might be found within them? Perhaps even an unknown species or two might live in such immense subterranean networks and utilize them as convenient and highly effective escape routes when needed.

In 1995, my brother, Robert, moved to Summershade. His property consisted of roughly seventy-five acres on two parallel ridges covered with thick growths of pine and fir. A small, rocky stream ran near the house, separating it from the barn and completing the picturesque scene. All was well for a few months. Then Robert noticed that some of his chickens were starting to disappear. He could find no trace of them, nor any spoor left behind by any nocturnal visitors to his hen house. The chickens were just gone. He thought little of it, even though our family had found out the hard way back in Spottsville some twenty years earlier what a steady disappearance of barnyard fowl might mean. Chickens were, after all, usually the primary targets of any and all roaming predators, being easy prey, especially when cooped. None of the larger livestock seemed bothered and nothing else on the property was disturbed. Nonetheless, as the weeks went by, the chickens continued to vanish and he remained bewildered as to why. It was not until after two family friends, Tim S. And Chris W., (real names on file) had come for a lengthy visit that the unidentified chicken thieves were finally seen.

When Tim and Chris announced that they intended to stay for several weeks, Robert offered them the use of a good-sized camper to sleep in. They took the camper about 100 yards from the house and parked it beside a heavily wooded area so as not to disturb anyone or be more bother than was necessary. When they retired of an evening, they would drive to a dirt access road and walk a few steps to the camper. Later, the bedraggled pair told my brother that several times, as they returned to the camper, their headlights had illuminated what appeared to be "little, hairy creatures." These things were two or three feet tall, they claimed, and were covered from head to toe with dark brown hair. They shied away when the light hit them and ran swiftly out of view, alternating between bipedal and quadrupedal locomotion. Moreover, they appeared to travel in groups of from two to four individuals.

One night, as the two were readying for sleep, they heard a strange noise, a "chattering" sound, coming from the darkness outside. They peered out very quietly, and were alarmed to see a considerable group of these creatures in the woods just outside the camper's door. Worse yet, they seemed to be stealthily approaching the camper, darting from tree to tree. Despite this, every so often one or two of them would let out another "monkey-like" grunt. Chris immediately grabbed the handgun Robert had given them for protection. He would've started shooting to frighten away, Chris said, if Tim hadn't stopped him. He feared that such an act might anger the creatures, maybe even enough to make them swarm the camper. Then what? They certainly couldn't shoot them all. They noted that the diminutive critters were covered in dirt and dried mud, as if they were freshly returned from a digging endeavor on one of the many nearby creek banks. The two youths were relieved when they decided to step outside with their flashlights and again the creatures made a swift retreat from the lights. Even so, neither could sleep a wink after the episode. They hadn't wanted to say anything to Robert about it at first. But now things were getting serious.

The adults of the household could tell that both the boys were telling the truth and did not disbelieve their story. They had absolutely no reason to make up such a tale. Besides, Robert himself had seen a somewhat similar creature up close and in broad daylight, back in Spottsville when he was ten years old. That one had been around ten feet tall! Surely, if that was, indeed, what they were dealing with now, the three-foot variety couldn't be all that scary, especially not with an array of firearms available. Nearly the entire family hunted and were adept at handling firearms. How much trouble could some little, furry creatures be? Robert completely failed to take into account the overwhelming advantages that even smaller animals may afford themselves by traveling in groups. But he would become rudely awakened to this fact one evening not long after.

As it happened, one night Robert and the two boys, now accompanied by Chris' father, James, found themselves outside after dark, trying to locate one of the horses that had escaped. All four were armed with handguns of varying calibers. It was best not to take any unwarranted chances. No telling what could be hiding in the nearby caves. The two adults carried powerful flashlights in addition to their weapons. As they searched a forested area near where the camper had sat, the group became aware that they were not alone in the woods. They could see small, dark figures moving swiftly and noiselessly through the trees around them. The two boys pointed wildly at the things in silent vindication. The men shined their lights to and fro and drew their weapons. The boys followed suit. Whenever the light beams would hit one of the beings, it immediately shrank back into the night and out of sight, running at first on its hind legs before dropping down to all four, then rising once again. They exhibited no eye-shine, the group noted, and these, too, appeared to be covered in mud. Robert also related how, when standing, the creatures' front legs looked somewhat longer than the back ones.

The worst of it, he later told me, apart from seeing the weird little boogers in the first place, was that they were intent on advancing toward the group of humans, maneuvering their way in on all sides in an apparent attempt to surround them. Where before, they had made chattering noises, this time, the creatures were operating in complete silence. What these things had in mind as an end result, fortunately, was never discovered for, when one of the things became bold enough to approach within a few inches of James, the alarmed quartet opted for a hasty departure from the area.

James later told me that one of the creatures had rushed in from behind him and ran straight up into a tree without slowing down at all. The force of the movement was such that he could feel the wind on his neck. They all considered themselves lucky that they had somehow managed to make it back to the safety of the house without firing a single shot.

I subsequently interviewed each of the witnesses and they all agreed on every detail and each strongly attested to the fact that they weren't particularly interested in going outside after sundown because of it. I walked much of the area in question but could find no evidence in the form of physical traces of the reported creatures, nor any apparent signs of digging on any of the nearby creek banks. By the time I was able to make it to the site things had quieted down, it seemed. In the ensuing months Robert informed me that every single chicken that he owned had disappeared.

Business and personal reasons kept me from returning to that part of the state for many months. Then, in May 1998, another sighting took place. This one by Robert's son, D.J., and one of his friends, a neighbor from down the road. My mother had recently returned from Yuma, Arizona, and had decided to move a trailer onto the property next to Robert's house. She had purchased three dairy cows to put out to graze with the horses.

The two youths were busy entertaining themselves in the back yard on the day in question, when they noticed that one of the cows had separated from the other two and was running around in the field. On closer inspection they saw that it was being chased by one of the strange, hairy creatures. This one was slightly larger than the ones previously seen by his father - around four or five feet tall. It also looked quite dirty, they told me, and it displayed the same curious ambulatory gait as the other witnesses had described. The only reason the thing didn't catch the cow, the boys claimed, was because it had accidentally run into an old barbed wire fence and stumbled to the ground. After this the creature seemed to give up the chase entirely.

The boys said they found a footprint that had been left behind by this thing but a subsequent thunderstorm obliterated all traces of it. They described it as looking like the print of a man, except for the toes, which appeared to be split-hoofed.

The fact that one of these unknown creatures was confidant enough in its abilities to single handedly attempt to bring down a full-grown heifer says much about the animals' apparently aggressive natures. Not to mention the fact that a pack of them had tried to surround four armed people. The pattern here seems to suggest a mostly nocturnal animal. That they were covered in dirt or mud in every sighting appears to give credence to the supposition that they might utilize, on a regular basis, the intricate and extensive cave systems that exist in the area. They would almost certainly be omnivorous, taking full advantage of every available food source. Could these mysterious creatures actually live in the area, yet still remain unknown to modern science? I believe the answer is yes.

South Central Kentucky, like the rest of the state, is no stranger to reports of hirsute, apelike humanoids both small and large. Sober witnesses have been describing such things, from all parts of the state for generations. According to Loren Coleman's *Mysterious America,* in nearby Monroe County there exists a location called "Monkey Cave Hollow." The name was given by early settlers and referred to the strange tribe of "monkeys" that inhabited the area, living in caves and foraging for roots and berries. According to Coleman, these critters were hunted to their apparent extinction, with the last of them reportedly shot and killed around the turn of the twentieth century. I humbly submit the strong possibility that at least some of them got away.

The region seems to be a favored haunt of these mysterious "monkey." Bordered on three sides by the state's largest lakes; Barren River Lake, Dale Hollow and Lake Cumberland, the land between and around these bodies of water remains largely unspoiled. At the time of this writing I have been to the area several times and gazed upon its many picturesque mountains, valleys, forests, rivers and streams. There are more than enough resources to adequately sustain and conceal large numbers of secretive creatures such as these. I've explored some of the region's streambeds and forests and marveled at the natural beauty to be found there. In some of the caves one can put his ear to the ground and listen to the swift water running through the darkness far below. Much of this region's wilderness areas are so remote that very few, if any, people frequent them. I have no doubt that scores of the area's caves eventually interface with the aforementioned Mammoth Cave system in nearby Edmonton County, which remains an enigma in itself and still holds many secrets that have yet to see the light of day. One of them, I'm certain, must be the existence of small, monkey-like, nocturnal humanoids.

MONTGOMERY COUNTY

Another Bluegrass Bigfoot appeared in Montgomery County on January 30, 2007 and was once again seen by two passing motorists driving down a lonely back road in Mount Sterling. "It was about 6:30 p.m. and we were just coming home from the store," said Blaine W (full name on file). As Blaine and his wife drove down Paris Pike Road, a small, country lane, they noticed a tall figure walking down the roadside ahead, which they at first took to be a hitchhiker. "We usually don't pick up hitchhikers," he said, "but we thought this could be one of our neighbors." Blaine began to slow the car down to a crawl while his wife started to roll down her window. Then the headlights hit the thing fully. It turned to face them and the sight of it froze all thoughts of neighborly kindness in an instant. There, standing before them, was a frightening, two-legged, man-like beast covered with coarse, black hair. Worse still, it was seven feet tall, and had eyes that glowed red in the headlights.

"We did not know what to do," said Blaine, "so we sat there for a few seconds in disbelief. We honked the horn and he took off on two legs. Even when he was gone you could still smell his horrible stench." The witness claimed that, as it ran away, it had made a loud grunt, "like a deer in mating season, only louder."

NELSON COUNTY

The information in the following account was taken from a story published in the Nov.

2, 1978 edition of the *Kentucky Standard*. It recounted an incident in Bardstown in October 1965 in which a family came into contact with a mysterious being called "The Wortlechort."

The hills and hollows of Nelson County, where this strange encounter took place, are normally peaceful spots where farmers plant tobacco and corn against the ridges, and cattle graze the gentle slopes rising from the creek beds. Raccoon hunters pick their way through the woods and step lightly over fences. The crisp autumn nights are usually filled with nothing more fearsome than a screech owl's, sharp cry or the occasional bark of a fox. It was on such a night in October 1965 that two young brothers saw something that they've never forgotten.

Neither of them will deny that it happened. One says he doesn't talk about the incident to may people anymore. "They just laugh and call you crazy," he said, "but our eyes didn't fool us."

That evening, their parents were attending a fall school festival. Before they left, they instructed the boys to go to their grandmother's farm and look for a cow that was expecting a calf. They needed to check on the animal and bring her back to the barn. One of the brothers described what happened next:

"It was not quite dark, and we'd taken the pickup truck to the back field as far as we could drive," he said.

When the terrain got too rough for them to drive any farther, they left the truck and headed up a fencerow to a clump of trees where the cattle usually bedded at night.

"As we moved up the fencerow, we spotted something in sort of a hunched position. There were a lot of bushes growing around the field and we couldn't see too well. We didn't think it was a cow, but we didn't know what else it could be," he said.

When they were about 100 feet from the object their dog started barking uncontrollably, and then backed off, refusing to follow the brothers any farther. At this point they were no more than fifty feet from whatever it was. All of a sudden, the creature rose up in two legs and began running away from the startled boys. The boys gave chase, only to have their quarry stop under an arch formed by two trees and face them. Its brown, hair-covered body appeared to be seven or eight feet tall. Speechless, the boys aimed their flashlight at it and caught the glowing red reflection from its eyes.

"We couldn't have watched it for more than a few seconds, then we both ran off, scared to death," said one of the brothers, now an adult. "I turned once to see if it was chasing us, and I saw the creature put its hand on the fence post and just flip it over into the next field."

The next day, when their father went out to the field to check out their wild story, he found a path trampled through a field of uncut oats in the exact spot where the boys claimed the monster had jumped the fence. They never saw the creature again, although that doesn't mean it wasn't lingering nearby. Later that year, their mother and sisters heard an unusual noise in the barn that they couldn't explain.

That summer, another unexplained incident happened to the family. In a certain corner of the garden, something would eat the corn as fast as it came on the stalk. In

1965, few people had ever heard of Bigfoot, but several years later, when one of boys was in college, he ran across an account of Bigfoot sightings in the Pacific Northwest. "I've never doubted that's what we saw that night," he said. "We didn't know what a Bigfoot was, so we called it a 'Whortlechort.' I read everything I can about them [Bigfoot] now, and almost every account that I've read seems to match up with ours." Through his reading he has also learned that Bigfoot are believed to be vegetarians and to be very shy of people and domestic animals.

"I don't think I'm scared of it, but I never go up in that field at night without thinking an awful lot abut what I saw. I believe God created the world through evolution, and maybe what I saw is the missing link between man and apes," he said.

Bigfoot returned to Nelson County, this time on Nelsonville Road in Boston, Ky., in the late fall of 1978. Only one of the three witnesses to the event came forward, and this only after thirty years had passed.

"Myself and two buddies were bow hunting [in] a tract of land we had used for quite a few years," He stated. "This is about a 500-acre patch of hardwoods that borders the Kentucky Turnpike. We always camped in an old abandoned barn right off Nelsonville Road, just a few miles out of Boston. It was a cool November afternoon and we had decided to do some scouting. We had walked a set of railroad tracks about a mile back into the middle of the area we always hunted."

"We made our way off the tracks and were slowly working through the woods. The area is mainly gentle rolling hills and bottoms. We were spread out about 100 yards apart and had just topped a small ridge. About 200 yards down in the next bottom something caught my eye. I noticed something black moving quickly through the woods, and it was out of sight in a matter of seconds. I thought it was pretty odd, as there were no bears in this area of the state back then, and we had never noticed any farm dogs or other livestock this far back in the woods.

"When we met on the tracks to head back to camp I asked my buddies if they had noticed anything strange while scouting and neither of them had seen anything. I casually mentioned what I had seen and left it at that. Later that evening, back at the barn, we had finished supper and had turned in to our sleeping bags to call it a night. It was cool and clear and the local farmyard dogs were carrying on pretty good and the katydids were really putting up a fuss. As the area was really loaded with fox and everything seemed to be pretty active I decided to try and call one up from inside the barn."

He pulled the cellophane off a pack of cigarettes, squeezed it between my thumbs, and started a series of calls, sounding like a rabbit in distress.

"This tactic had worked well for us in the past. This evening it worked a little too well. After about five minutes of me screaming on the call the local dogs were really worked up good and sounding off like crazy. What happened next I'll never forget until the day they lay me in the ground. From way off in the distance a low moan started up that grew into a load mournful roar that sent shivers down my spine. We all sat up in silence for a few seconds and noticed that not a single dog or katydid was making so much as a peep. The woods had become dead silent," he said.

Not believing what they'd just heard, he let out one more blast of calls from the makeshift varmint call. Again it started up low and grew into a spine-chilling roar.

"This time it really put the fear of the Lord in us all. My buddies were begging me to stop and it really didn't take too much convincing. The hair on the back of my neck and arms was standing straight up and goose bumps had come up all over me. I put the cellophane away and got as deep down in my bag as I could. None of us said another word and sleep was nearly impossible. We all three lay in that barn dead silent till morning light," he said.

Needless to say, none of the party felt like heading out to go deer hunting in the early morning darkness. They got up, packed up their gear, and headed out of there as fast as they could.

"I was seventeen or eighteen years old at the time and had spent nearly all of this time in the woods and on the water and [I] had never, ever, heard anything like what we did that night," said the witness, now 48. He claimed that, years later, he heard an alleged Bigfoot audio recording made in Columbiana County, Ohio, that sent chills down his spine because it sounded exactly like what he had heard in response to his "varmint call" on that long-ago hunting trip. Similar vocalizations were also reported to have been heard in Bardstown in the summer of 2006.

OHIO COUNTY

Another hirsute hominoid appeared in rural Ohio County in the Panther Creek bottoms between Whitesville and Pellville, twenty miles southeast of Owensboro. It was late afternoon in September of 1976.

"I had gone to the back of our farm to get a part off an old junk car," the witness stated. "My German shepherd, Prince, was with me. This old car had been pushed off the path and it was all grown up around it with briars and such, so the easiest way to get to the part I needed was to climb over the top of it."

As he was busy removing the part he needed, he heard rustling in the leaves nearby but thought nothing of it, assuming it was his dog or a rabbit or possibly some other small animal. At length he retrieved the part, a windshield-wiper motor. He was climbing back over the car when he heard the rustling noises again.

"I looked to my left. About twenty feet away, behind a small cedar tree, was something big, black, and hairy." The witness said he didn't stick around to get a better look, but he noticed that the thing was standing on two legs behind the tree, watching him through the branches. "I remember that the hair was black or a dark color, with lighter patches that could have been mud or dirt. The arms were at its sides but I don't recall the details. I left as quickly as possible, calling for the dog as I ran. He had always been very protective of the whole family, so I thought he would protect me if this thing came after me." He was wrong. Prince, tail tucked firmly between his legs, bolted past the man like he was standing still. "Up until then, I didn't think he was scared of anything," his master said.

The witness stated that he heard no vocalizations from the creature and did not smell anything unusual during the encounter. He said he did not believe that he'd seen a bear. "I was scared to death," he said, "so I didn't get a good look. I will regret that for the rest of my life."

Or maybe not. In some cases, it might be better to follow the dog Prince's example and just run away.

Chad Askins was accompanied by one of his friends when he parked his vehicle near a creek bed on an old, abandoned farm in Ohio County just about dusk one evening in 1988. They were there to relax for a bit and sip a cold one or two before heading back to their homes after a long day of hunting. They were parked facing the creek bank, which sloped upwards a few feet in front of them before dropping down the other side into the creek bed, which was not in view. They had only been there a few minutes when a large, dark shape rose up from the other side of the bank, as if whatever it was had been stooping down in the creek. Askins saw the thing immediately as it rose to its full height and observed that although it was roughly human in shape, it was of tremendous size and covered with dark-colored hair.

Both witnesses could hardly believe their eyes as the thing took two long, slow strides to the right, then stopped and turned in their direction. Instead of turning its head, which seemed to be mounted directly onto the thing's shoulders with no visible neck, Askins said it turned its entire body from the waist up. The sun was just setting behind the monster, which turned it into little more than a stark silhouette, but they could see that it had extremely broad shoulders and was very thick through the middle. They could not see any facial features nor could they see the creature's lower extremities, which were blocked from view by the slope of the creek bank in front of them, but they stated that it had a human-shaped head with long hair and thick, muscular arms. Chad felt sure that it must have been over ten feet tall. It just stood there calmly, he said, completely unafraid as it watched the two men in the descending darkness. The feeling of calm was not mutual, however, and the pair wasted no time in exiting the area.

I asked Chad why the encounter had such a frightening effect on them, since the creature had made no threatening moves. He replied that, to him, the scariest thing was the monster's sheer size and the fact that it looked immensely powerful, like it could break a man completely in two with no great effort. There was also the fact that it seemed entirely unafraid of them, making not a single move to flee their presence as most wild animals would.

Further questioning left me with the strong impression that he knew very little about the Bigfoot phenomenon other than the fact that he was convinced that this was the identity of the animal they saw. When asked to compare what he saw to the subject of the famous Patterson-Gimlin film of the late 1960s Askins said he was entirely unaware that such a film even existed, and seemed anxious to view the footage if he could. This witness struck me as being completely honest and intelligent and his sincerity while recounting the event was obvious.

OWEN COUNTY

On September 17, 1994, Frankfort, resident Mathew Hall saw something that he could not explain. It was about 1:30 a.m. and he and a friend were driving down a lonely road, taking a shortcut to their destination. It had been raining and the road was slippery. When they came across a section of road that was covered in water they pulled over by a large tree. To their surprise, their headlights illuminated a large, hair-covered figure walking through the woods.

"We looked at it and it kept walking," Hall said. "It looked human but walked with a hunch. It was seven to eight feet tall."

They drove slowly down the road a little farther, still looking at the creature, and were alarmed when it turned and looked back at them. "It looked at us, then we took off," he said. "When we took off it ran out into the road and stared at us as we drove away." Hall said the thing walked with a slight hunch. The hair covering its body was a dark color. He also claimed that they had both noticed a terrible smell when they pulled over just before seeing the monster. Hall estimated that the entire encounter lasted some three or four minutes.

The Kentucky River borders the entire western boundary of Owen County. Eagle Creek, said to be the world's longest creek, meanders through this area. And, if eyewitness testimony is to be believed, so does Bigfoot. On December 14, 2009, Johnny Jones was out rabbit hunting with his nephew in Glencoe. "My nephew went to round up two dogs that would not come back. He was blowing the dog whistle. I was standing by my truck messing with the CD player. I looked up to see a hairy creature walking away from me on two legs. I shot my gun and he ran off," Jones said.

He described the figure as being about six feet tall, and covered in reddish-brown hair. "I could see his underskin," he stated. "It was dark, maybe black." Jones reportedly took pictures of a footprint left by the creature, and said a local game warden had made a mold of the same print.

PERRY COUNTY

Bigfoot appeared in the mountains of eastern Kentucky about ten miles north of Hazard in the summer of 1977. Around 11:30 p.m. on that clear July night in Chavies, two local boys got the shock of their young lives. "I was young, about twelve or thirteen," one witness later said. "I had gone to spend a few weeks with my uncle and cousins. They lived in a secluded area. Only our family lived in this holler and the houses were fairly spread apart. Well, my uncle worked [the] night shift in a mine down the road so that left me and me cousins and aunt at home nights alone."

The area where they lived was heavily wooded, very dense and overgrown. That night, "My cousin and his mom and me [sic] were the only ones up and we were watching TV. Just about thirty feet from the back door there was a corral with my cousin's pony in it. We were watching TV when all of a sudden the pony went absolutely crazy. We all jumped up to see what was going on. Just by the way it was carrying on we thought [there] was a bobcat in there with it, which isn't unusual to find around there."

He said the two boys knew it was up to them to run whatever varmint was scaring the horse off the property. "Me and my cousin [sic] both grabbed frog gigs and thought we would just go out and it would run off," he said. "Feeling real confident we went out and, when we rounded the porch and could see [what was there] we both just about messed our pants. It wasn't a bobcat. It was big and it was on the other side of the corral headed away like it heard us and was leaving. I swear this to be a true statement. It stepped over a four-rail fence as I would [over] one of those things you put in a doorway to keep a child out. All I ever saw of it was its back; it never looked around at us. It stepped over the fence and in a mere moment it crossed the dirt road and leaped across the creek and up the side of the hill."

But the creature wasn't done for that evening, as the witness was to find out. "I had another cousin who lived around the bend in the direction it went whose dog disappeared that night. It was chained up and the chain was ripped out of the doghouse, so whatever it was took the dog chain and all. No way that dog did it, and a person wouldn't have had the brute strength to do that. It was a strong setup."

The witness described the creature he and his cousin saw that night as, "Seven to nine feet tall, and as wide as two men standing shoulder to shoulder." He said they heard no strange sounds, nor smelled any strange odors during the encounter, however, "[We] sure saw something, and it wasn't a bear. My family was raised in the woods and we are all good woodsmen. Even at that age we had spent all our lives hunting, fishing and exploring those hills, and this was something very unique. I thought about someone playing a trick on us but everyone knew that if you did something like that you could easily be shot. I have no doubt that it was a real animal."

Carlen Dixon claims to have heard the cries of these creatures in southeast Kentucky in 1986. He is but one among what must surely be many thousands of Kentuckians who could make the same claim.

"A friend and I were walking up the Coal Harbor hill at approximately 2:00 a.m.," he states. "No drugs or alcohol had been consumed by either of us. We were walking on the road up the hill when we both heard a 'scream,' for lack of a better word. It definitely was not human, but [it] sounded like no animal I had ever heard. It was simultaneously high-pitched and growling; it was very strange. It first seemed to originate from a pretty good distance away. This was mountainous country, and we were near to the crest of the hill. The sound seemed to come from the valley below. When we first heard it we both froze and looked at each other. After the 'scream' ended we both asked 'What the hell was that?' and we started to move a little faster up the hill. After twenty to thirty seconds we heard the sound a second time, only now it lasted longer - about six to seven seconds - and sounded much closer."

At this point Dixon said they ran up the hill and back to his friend's home as fast as they could. "My friend, who still lives in the area, says that he has heard the sound on two different occasions since then," he said. Dixon states that he had never heard the sound again until he listened to a purported Bigfoot audio recording from Ohio. He said the sounds matched exactly. "And a WAV file [Waveform Audio File of sound bites] is as close to that sound as I care to get again," he said.

Dixon also claims to have spoken with a person who saw a large, hairy creature as he was traveling one night in the area. The figure was standing on a slope near a guardrail and, when the vehicle's headlights hit it, it had crouched down as if trying to hide. He said the witness told him the thing's shoulders were "massive."

Monicka P. (full name on file) and two of her friends saw Bigfoot on June 28, 2007 during their stay at Buckhorn Lake Sate Resort Park in Perry County. It was just after 4:00 p.m. and her friends stepped out onto the balcony of their cottage.

"We were standing on the balcony looking into the woods trying to spot some deer," Monicka said. "Then we heard strange gurgling sounds and smelled a weird smell." The trio was nonplussed as to what could be responsible. Then, "Tony [one of the group] spotted some creature running through the forest to his left," Monicka said. The figure stepped into a clearing and everyone had a chance to observe it. "It was about seven feet tall, with matted, brown hair," she stated. "It did not even look at us. It just kept on walking and disappeared into the forest." She said the sighting only lasted about ten seconds.

Liza H. (full name on file) claims that she observed another such creature on January 13, 2010. "I was on my way to Hazard. It was around 9 o'clock in the morning," she said. " I was traveling up Hall Rogers Parkway between Hyden and Hazard when, in a field to my right, I noticed a large animal next to the wood line. I originally thought it might be a bear since we have had so many sightings of bears here in the past few years, but as I got closer it stood up like a man would. That's when I slowed down to take a closer look. It was about six and a half or seven foot [sic] tall. It was a mass of very dark hair. It covered its whole body. It had very broad shoulders and its head almost looked too small for its body. It took a few steps and then seemed to jog into the woods. When it moved it was in a sort of slumped posture and its arms hung to its side almost to its knees. I have to say it spooked me a little. I have never seen anything like it and really don't know what to make of it."

I spoke to Liza and found her to be very sensible and honest. She claimed that she had seen the thing at a distance of about 300 yards, so she was unable to make out any finer details.

PIKE COUNTY

In the early 1990s two youths out adventuring in a place known as Kimper, near

Pikeville in rural Pike County, came across a line of very large, humanlike footprints in the snow. Mystifyingly, the tracks simply stopped after a short distance.

In mid-October of 1994 no fewer than eight raccoon hunters encountered a Bigfoot creature on an old abandoned mining road in the Appalachian foothills near Virgie, less than ten miles northeast of the Jefferson National Forest.

"We were raccoon hunting," one member of the group, a Mr. R. Mullins, reported. "We had turned our dogs out and let them get a head start on us. We gave them a half-hour or so to let them get far enough ahead of us then [we] got in the truck and started down the road. You can only drive about ten miles in a truck until the road becomes too narrow to pass." The group rode in the truck, three in front and five in the back, until they reached the point where they had to stop. Then, "We called the dogs but got no response, so we waited. About thirty to forty-five minutes later, the dogs came running back to the truck with their tails tucked between their legs like something had scared them to death." He said they didn't think much of it, at first, figuring the hounds had been spooked by a bobcat or a similar animal. They loaded the dogs into the truck and started back down the mountain. They had only made it a couple of hundred feet when the driver slammed on the brakes. Luckily, they weren't going fast, as the area was rumored to conceal some old mine shafts.

"I was in the [bed] of the truck not knowing what was going on," said Mullins. "I looked into the back glass and saw the three in the front of the truck pointing ahead of us." All five men then stood up and looked. "What we saw was huge, standing about seven and a half to eight feet tall. The color was hard to tell with the shadows but I would say it was either black or dark brown. After about ten seconds, the driver put the truck in reverse and we backed up fifty feet or so. We all got out and asked one another if we had all saw it [sic]. We all did." He said they weren't all sure exactly what they had seen. Some said it was a bear, others said it was Bigfoot.

Mullins said he eyed his cousin, who had told him earlier in the year about the night he had seen a hairy, manlike creature in the woods of Christian County. He said that the lady who was with him had "gone crazy" at the sight of the thing in the headlights, screaming and crying and carrying on. He said two other members of the group were especially nervous. They had claimed for years that they had been chased down off the mountain one night by something they couldn't identify. Whatever it was, there was more than one of them and from the sound of it.

"After about ten minutes of talking about it," Mullins said, "we got back into the truck and drove back to where it had stood. We got out and walked up to where we saw it. There was a waterhole on each side of the road but in the center was mud, and in the mud was a very large footprint. [It was] not a bear track. It looked like a huge human footprint about fifteen to sixteen inches long. It had a very large big toe and only three small toes. We looked in awe at this track until we heard sticks breaking." This scared them, Mullins stated, so they jumped back into the truck and peeled out of there in a hurry. Bravely, the group decided to return a short while later, but the monster was long gone. He said they found the track had been obliterated by the vehicle's tires.

Members of the group have returned to the spot a number of times in hopes of seeing the thing again but so far, it hasn't showed. "I never would have thought that I would see something like this," Mullins said. "I know that it wasn't a bear and it wasn't anything modern science knows about. I would never have given any thought to a story like this being true. But after seeing something firsthand that I have no answer for, I believe now."

Slightly more than a year later, at 8:00 p.m. on December 24, 1995, another such creature was seen by passing motorists as they drove through Elkhorn City.

"Before my grandmother died we used to visit her every Christmas Eve," said Andrew, (full name on file). "She lived in western Virginia and we lived in eastern Kentucky. We would always drive through the Elkhorn City/Grundy, Virginia, area to get to her house. One night, on the way to her house, we were just passing through Elkhorn City when we were stopped at a traffic light." It was at this moment that something very strange happened. Andrew, then just nine years old, said he still recalls the event vividly. "A Bigfoot crossed the road from the left, which was nothing but a rocky hill," he said. "It ran across the road to the right, where it jumped a guardrail down an embankment. My parents, obviously frightened, told me it was just a monkey and not to worry about it. I didn't bother them with it any more, but I always remembered what I saw that night. It was six to seven feet tall, slightly hunched, [with] very shaggy dark-brown hair. As it passed the car, its arms hung low, seemingly to its knees, and they swung very far back and forth, like a bowler."

Pike County, the easternmost county in Kentucky, is also the state's largest county consisting of 789 square miles, and is historically noted for the famous Hatfield-McCoy feud that raged there from 1860 to 1891.

POWELL COUNTY

In Powell County in Aug. of 1978, a ten-year-old vacationer running an errand noticed a strong, disagreeable odor while walking down a dirt road in National Bridge State Park, part of the area known as the Daniel Boone National Forest. He then noticed a huge five- toed footprint in the middle of the road. Looking along the path he saw what he had first mistook for a small tree suddenly walk quickly away. He described this "tree" as very tall and covered with dark, greasy-looking, shiny hair. It had very long arms that swung as it walked away on two legs like a man.

The boy ran back to camp and led his father and his uncle to the location where they observed the giant track and found that it was twenty inches long. Later that night, the family was awakened in their tents by a loud noise that sounded like a large boulder rolling down the hill and plunging into a nearby lake. The next morning more large footprints were found around the camp as well as an overturned picnic table. Talk at the nearby lodge centered on an RV which had allegedly been overturned during the previous night with the sleeping owners still inside.

More recently in Powell County comes another report of a Bigfoot near water. Early on the morning of April 20, 2004, a lone traveler, walking home on Hwy. 15 along the banks of the Red River near Stanton, got quite a surprise. It was about 2:30 a.m. when he paused to rest and noticed an awful smell that he later said was "hard to describe." He said he sat there for but a moment when, "I heard a big splash in the river. I looked around and saw a big shape in the water. At first I thought it was a bear, but then it stood up. It looked like it was fishing. I don't know how deep the water was but it looked like it was standing about four feet out of the water, and had long shaggy hair."

Bigfoot investigator Tony Gerrard later spoke to the witness, who told him that he smelled a bad odor before he heard the splashing. "It stank really horrible; then I heard a splash," the witness said. He was about sixty feet from the creature, which was moving around and splashing in the river. The witness told Gerrard he thought it might have been fishing. "It was a clear night. I could see the body shape; it was pretty broad across the shoulders. It was big! It had a long head, not really pointed, but sort of cone-shaped. It didn't look like it had much of a neck. The hair looked kind of long, about like a Irish Setter."

The witness said he could not see any facial features. He estimated the height to be at least six or seven feet. The hair was dark in color. The witness hurried down the road, but since the road parallels the river at this point, he had the creature in view for several minutes. "Once it stopped and kind of looked around, then it went back to what it was doing," he said.

Another Powell County Bigfoot encounter happened on Sunday, November 5, 2006, in Powell County, near Red River Gorge. Mena (full name on file) and her fiance were outside their home when they began to feel like they were being watched. It was an uncomfortable feeling but they didn't let it worry them too much. "Then, that night when we went to sleep, we thought we heard raccoons playing with the foil we left out," she claimed. "When we peeked our heads out nothing was there and the foil was all intact, so we went back to sleep. I couldn't sleep so I stayed awake. A few minutes later I heard a man's footsteps, or what I thought was a man's footsteps, messing around in the leaves."

Her fiancée woke up then, as he had heard it as well, but when he looked outside he saw nothing, she said. "A couple hours later we woke up and started cooking breakfast. It was still very dark - around 3 a.m. When my fiance was stirring up the fire he saw two eyes peer out of the brush. They were red. When he went to look at it again they were gone. He also smelled a rancid ferret-like smell. We figured we had enough moonlight to start packing, and we were both really freaked out so we packed up in the moonlight and started down the path. We both felt like we were being followed. We got halfway to the parking area and we heard someone walking below us except it was a really good drop and [there were] no paths below and it was 4 a.m. and we were the only ones camping so we figured, Oh, good. People. We were relieved until we started getting to the parking area, and all of a sudden I heard something jump behind me, running. I walked faster and then right next to me above the bushes something was charging or trying to scare us, so at that time we pretty much ran and it chased us the whole way. It seemed like it was trying to run up the hill to cut us off. We got to the parking lot and it stopped."

Mena claimed that the creature made strange growling sounds as it chased them on what sounded like two legs - then four - but, other than the red eyes they never saw the animal involved.

Bigfoot investigator Charlie Raymond was able to contact the witnesses, who assured him that the creature's eyes were at a distance of about chest level from the ground. Both witnesses were pretty shaken up. There was a full moon that night although the skies were heavily clouded. When asked about the smell, Mena's fiancée replied, "At one point Mena went to sleep and I was rounding up for the evening when I smelt something very odd. I grew up around the woods, and I know what various animals and the woods are supposed to smell like. This was not one of them. It did smell similar to a ferret, but for me to be able to smell a ferret it would have to be really close to smell as strong as I did. I immediately jumped up as soon as I smelled it, and there was nothing there. If it was another animal, the amount of smell that I smelt, the animal would have to be very close, and I seen [sic] nothing. When we did go to bed we left our tinfoil that we had cooked in, in the fire pit. Once we had quieted down in bed we heard footsteps leading up to the camp. [Then we heard something] messing around with the tinfoil. Then the footsteps were walking around the tent and [we] even heard something brush up against the tent. We were too terrified to look. After whatever it was had left, I looked out, and of course nothing was there. We also heard footsteps on the way out, but not voices. I thought to myself, *Great! There are humans out here, too.* So [that made me] feel better. The footsteps seemed to be about 200 feet up the path from us. We could hear so well because it was absolutely silent, really weird for 5 o'clock in the morning. Usually birds are up at this time. We got to the place where we heard the steps, and something came up from the gorge running past Mena, scaring the hell out of her. We both ran. When we got back to the car we realized [that even though we heard] footsteps, we did not see anyone at all, and any campers that would be out there would be in the sack, not out in the middle of the woods by themselves."

Three more campers were reportedly harassed by strange, nocturnal creatures that emitted piercing screams in this same area in October of 2008.

PULASKI COUNTY

"My great-grandmother grew up on a small farm in Somerset in the 1920s," said Frederick J. (full name on file). "The farm, of course, was full of animals. Most were chickens. They would sell the eggs to the local people in the area. One night, after it was good and dark, my great-grandmother and her family were settling down for the evening and getting ready for bed, when they heard a huge commotion out by one of their chicken coops. Fearing that a dog or some other animal was trying to attack the chickens, her father ran out to the chicken house in order to frighten off whatever animal was there. When he arrived at the coop, he found it to be overturned, lying on its side, and he witnessed a very large manlike animal running away. The next morning, the family went out to investigate the damage, and they found huge footprints in the mud. The prints were too large to be a bear's and too human-looking to be any other animal's print. Another sighting of the animal was never made but, sometimes late at night, strange screaming sounds were heard coming from the woods outside."

What was it that terrified an entire family over the course of seven days from July 10 through 17 in 2007 while they were vacationing in Burnside? Could it have been a juvenile Bigfoot, or something else entirely?

"We were on a family vacation at Lake Cumberland Resort off Roberts Bend Road," Said Jennifer W. (full name on file). "On Tuesday the 10th, my sister-in-law and I were enjoying a rainy night out on the back lower patio of our cabin. We were just out there talking. It was about 2:00 a.m. when we heard something very large drop from a tree, hit the ground, and then stumble. We were so scared we went in the cabin and locked the doors. The next morning we went out to the upper deck of our cabin to look down on the area where we heard the sound the night before. We observed a large area, I would say about six feet wide by at least ten feet long, where all the brush had been laid down.

On Wednesday the 11th, at around 10 p.m., my family and I were driving up KY-751 and my husband and I saw an animal on the side of the road going into the woods. It was on all fours and crawling. It looked right at us. On Thursday the 12th, we experienced the most frightening thing I have ever been through. My sister-in-law, my nephew, his best friend and myself were all out on the back lower patio of our cabin. We were laughing, talking and generally just having a good time but we could not get over the feeling that we were being watched by something. We decided to go in the cabin. We went to the upper level into the kitchen. It was about 1:30 a.m. and out of nowhere we heard this deep, angry scream from the wooded area behind our cabin. We all stood there silent, looking at each other. At the same time we all said, 'Did you hear that?' When we realized that what we heard was heard by everyone, we ran to all the doors, made sure they were all locked, then turned on every available outside light on that cabin. We were all so shocked and afraid to even move. I then went downstairs to lie in bed with my daughter.

"At around 3:00 a.m. I left my daughter's room to go to the bathroom and, while I was in there, I heard this loud thump on the side of the cabin. I just froze. It was like it knew where I was inside that cabin. The next morning my sister-in-law went back out on the upper deck to try and observe anything that might explain what we went through the night before. In the distance we could hear this dog barking crazily and something hitting a tree. Later that day I went to the side yard of the cabin and found a dead squirrel and a bird with no head. Needless to say, we were so afraid we were ready to cut our vacation short a day because we just felt so uncomfortable. We could not get over the feeling of being watched.

"We ended up leaving the next morning but we didn't sleep at all that night. The animal my husband and I saw on Wednesday the 11th was about four feet long and it had long black fur. The legs were not that of a dog; they were shorter, and the neck was also shorter. It had a small head and looked directly at us with yellow-orange eyes. All I can say is that the sound I heard was like nothing I have ever heard before and [I] hope to never hear [it] again. It will be with me forever."

ROCKCASTLE COUNTY

A Livingston resident claimed that he and his brother had a frightening encounter with an unknown humanoid entity back in the fall of 1986. "Me and my brother were out in the woods of southern Rockcastle County deer-hunting and drinking some beer," Douglas (full name on file) said. "We were on our way back to the truck when we spotted a large figure up ahead of us on the side of some cliffs. My brother, James, said, 'That feller looks like he's gonna jump off that cliff.' So we walked a little closer to him and seen [sic] that it wasn't a man, but more of an ape. After we watched the creature from about forty to fifty yards away, the creature suddenly leaped off the cliff onto a nearby large tree. Then James said, 'Let's get the hell out of here before that thing gets ahold of us!' We got the hell out of there."

The witness stated that the creature was from seven and a half to eight feet tall with long, stringy, light-brown hair. He estimated its weight to be around 400 pounds. The sighting took place next to the Rockcastle River.

A more recent Rockcastle County encounter took place on June 17, 2007 in Mount Vernon. "I was driving home from work and I was on Scaffoldcane Road when I first saw it," said James O. (full name on file), who happened to be on the right stretch of the lonely road at the right time to see something truly amazing. "It was standing in the middle of this big curve and looking down into this Spur area."

The creature, which James described as seven feet tall, with arms that hung down to its knees, seemed to look at the car, then at the woods behind it, while moving its hands as if it was watching, or waiting, for something in particular. "It growled at my car as I brightened the lights," James claimed, "then it threw a rock at my car. I honked my horn." This seemed to frighten the thing somewhat, according to James, and it ran into the woods on the other side of the road. He further claimed that the creature's eyes were human-sized, but red in color, and that it had a silvery mane streaked with black.

Ten days later the creature appeared again, this time to two youths lighting firecrackers out by the old rock quarry in Mount Vernon. One of them later wrote: "My friend, Jeremy, and I were at the old rock quarry near Mount Vernon, lighting firecrackers when I told him I felt like something was watching us. We shrugged it off at first, saying it was probably nothing. After about ten minutes I felt it again. It was a cold feeling and the hair on my neck stood up, so we decided to leave. As we started to leave I saw a creature standing about 100 yards away on a dirt mound at the base of the southern cliff. It looked to be around six feet tall from that distance, so I presume it was at least seven to eight feet tall. It had very light brown hair all over the portion of its body that I could see." Startled, the two ran all the way home - a distance of over a mile.

ROWAN COUNTY

A family of eight allegedly encountered a bizarre and frightening creature that seemed to come straight from a nightmare on the night of July 8, 1972. The Miller family was returning home to West Virginia after visiting a relative in Owensboro, Ky., for the Fourth of July weekend. It was just about 12:30 a.m. The 455 cubic inch V8 motor of the 1966 Oldsmobile was purring along down the eastbound lane of Route 64 just two miles from Morehead when a back tire suddenly blew out.

"There was eight family members in the car," Stanley Miller, one of the children, recalled in 2008, "me, my dad, Roy J. Miller; my mother, Doris Ann Miller; my older brothers, Roy J. Miller, Jr. and Robert Huston Miller; my sisters, Brenda and Dana, and my cousin Mike Parker - and our collie, Laddie." Roy Sr. pulled over to the side of the road and made everyone get out of the vehicle so he and his eldest sons could jack up the car and fix the flat tire.

While his father and brothers were working, Stanley and his cousin, Mike, sat on the guardrail overlooking an old farm field. The dog, Laddie, was looking at the field as well. Only a few moments had passed when Laddie started whining. He suddenly jumped up, dashed back into the car and lay down on the rear floorboard, whimpering in fear. "At this time me and my cousin [sic] were looking across that old farm field and I noticed this tall, dark shadow way across the field," Stanley said. "Then we both noticed that the tall shadow had moved, and was moving across the filed coming toward us. Coming right across! It was moving very slowly but it was getting closer. We both got afraid and told my mother. At first my mother was joking with us about it, but when she saw that we were really afraid she started watching it, and she saw that it was moving slow, coming toward us. Then she got afraid."

By this time his father and brothers had stopped their labor and were also watching the dark shadow as it approached. "We were all just kids back then," Stanley said, "and we all started screaming and crying for my dad and older brothers to hurry up and fix the tire. My mother was screaming at my dad to hurry up and go." As the monster got closer, Stanley said it started "screeching out loud," which served to magnify the fright that the group was feeling by this time.

They could now see that it was manlike and had arms and legs. Worse, it was truly gigantic, standing between ten and fifteen feet tall! "By this time we had all jumped back into the car and [were] screaming at my dad to go. I remember my sisters crying and screaming at him to hurry up. By the time my dad jacked the car back down on its wheels that creature, that monster of a thing, was just down the embankment from us. It had done crossing that large field, and was coming up the embankment straight at us, screeching loudly. It had kind of long, misty hair and its eyes lit up an orange-red color. It had wicked, evil eyes and was walking and screeching. My brother, Roy Jr., was shining the flashlight on it as it was on the embankment. We all seen it. [sic] It had its arms out kind of crooked."

Finally, in what seemed like just in the nick of time Roy Sr. jumped back Into the car, gunned the engine, and sped off into the night, leaving the "monster" far behind them in the darkness. The family made it home to Gauley Bridge, West Virginia, safe and sound, but with a fright that they will never forget.

Mountains, valleys and forests. Perfect stomping grounds for the elusive Bigfoot, it would seem. Another Morehead sighting unfolded late one night in May of 2006 before the startled eyes of four passing motorists. "We were in a SUV driving the connector in Morehead, Kentucky," said Matt U. (full name on file), "when we saw something that looked like a man standing upright, covered in black, shaggy hair on the right-hand side of the road. We stopped for a moment to take a look at the creature when something startled it, and it darted for the woods behind it."

He described the figure as tall, around seven feet, covered in black, shaggy hair "that strung on him," and very muscular, with thick legs. The creature was standing only about twelve feet from the vehicle and remained motionless for about ten seconds before fleeing. The witness was able further able to recall that the beast had a conical-shaped head with a gorilla-like face and arms that hung just below its knees.

Rowan County resident and Bigfoot eyewitness Taylor M. (full name on file) claimed that he and three co-workers at the Cave Run Lake Marina saw Bigfoot at about 9:30 p.m. on the night of July 9, 2006. Taylor said that he was just about to get off work when he went out to the dock to gas up a jet ski. He said he looked up and noticed a "really big, hairy figure" over by the shoreline. It appeared to be drinking water from the lake. Taylor went and got his boss and a couple of co-workers, who returned with him and saw the beast. When they turned a spotlight on it, Taylor said it let out a "really loud and distinctive scream," before standing up and running into the woods. He later described the creature as very tall, around eight feet, and hairy-looking, like an ape.

In this same area lies part of the Daniel Boone National Forest, which was an active location for the creatures as late as June 14, 2008, when a Bigfoot investigator from West Virginia allegedly had a close range sighting through night vision goggles. The family that reported the sightings claimed the area had a history of creature activity including nighttime sightings and incidents of unexplained rock throwing, at least one of which had caused physical injury.

RUSSELL COUNTY

In the late 1960s a Russell County resident on his way to work allegedly observed a large, hirsute, apelike creature as it crossed Hwy. 196 near Jabez. Ed (full name on file) later claimed that for ten years, from 1973 to 1983, something would stalk him and his friends every time they walked a certain hill between their cabin and the Thomas Branch of Lake Cumberland. Whatever it was walked on two legs and would stop every time he stopped, and continue on every time he did, shadowing his every step. It always stayed out of sight, never once revealing itself, but Ed said he could hear it plainly. He was twelve years old when this started, and has spent his life since then wondering what it could have been that haunted that particular hill. I think we can safely venture a guess.

SCOTT COUNTY

Four passing motorists, members of the same family, observed Bigfoot one night in September 1985, as they were driving home at around 10:00 p.m. The figure was later described as about eight or nine feet tall, hairy, and manlike. "The arms were longer than any man's that I'd ever seen," said one witness twenty years later. "It did not have on any clothing. Its eyes glowed like a cat's in the headlights, and there was a strong, indescribable odor in the air. It literally walked over a six-foot fence without using its arms or hands - like it was just a step or something. It seemed so unreal." The witness was impressed with the creature's exceptionally long arms, and the fact that it seemed to be in no hurry at all, even though it knew it had been sighted. It stopped for a second, the witness claimed, turned its head to look at them, then stepped easily over another six-foot fence and disappeared into the night.

One of the first counties formed after statehood in 1792, Scott County is located in the north-central part of the state and has a population of fewer than 45,000 people.

SIMPSON COUNTY

A Simpson County policeman reportedly saw a large, hair-covered humanoid creature cross the road in front of his cruiser one night in January 1977. Other such sightings had previously taken place in the area. Although the incident is somewhat scarce on detail, it does show that all types of Kentucky citizens are prone to have sightings of these creatures. They appear, it would seem, to both the official and unofficial alike.

Another large, hairy, manlike beast was seen by a Simpson County family, but this one was truly bizarre in its appearance and may not be related to the Bigfoot creatures at all. "The first sighting was back in August of 2006," said the parent of one of the witnesses. "Our children thought that one of our goats had gotten out of the fence and went to get it. They came running inside, terrified about what they had seen. They saw a white, longhaired, horned, sharp-nailed creature. They said that it looked like a white gorilla with a smashed face. It was in a crouched position, like it was sleeping. It had shoulders much larger than a man's, very muscular and big boned. Its hind legs were shorter but just as strong. It had four canine teeth that stuck out of its mouth even when closed. It didn't have normal gorilla fingers or toes. It had nubby like fingers and toes with claws. It looked like it could have easily weighed 500 pounds. It was lying down, but from the rear to the head was about five feet. If it stood, it would have been much larger. It was sleeping with its arms crossed like when schoolchildren put their heads on their desks."

The area has a history of animal mutilation, and nighttime yowler activity. The family considered abandoning their house and moving away in order to escape the frightening activity.

"Me and my boyfriend [sic] at the time were riding his four-wheeler in the creek," said another Simpson County Bigfoot eyewitness. "We had just got to a deep spot so he was trying to make sure he didn't drown it out. I glanced to the left and thought I seen something [sic] big and furry standing in the cane weeds. I am 5'3" and the weeds were about two foot [sic] taller than me and it was about two foot taller than them. I was about fifteen to twenty yards from it. I looked back over there, hoping it wasn't what I thought it was, and it seen me [sic] and turned, hunkered down and ran off. Its back was about three feet wide and it was a light brown in color."

During their ride, she said they had noticed four or five dead deer, each about a half mile from the last, and thought it strange that they should see so many of them. She further added, "The creature appeared to be between eight and nine feet tall, based on the height of the weeds it was walking through." She did not see any facial features. The arms were swinging like a human's as it walked away. The creature's ears were visible on the sides of its head and she described them as slightly pointed and covered with hair. The incident allegedly took place in August of 2007, at dusk, just off Hwy. 100, near the ruins of a small bridge in Franklin.

SPENCER COUNTY

One Spencer County resident claims that he has had repeated sightings of a Bigfoot-type creature over the last several years, beginning in 2002. "The first time I saw it," he said, speaking in 2005, "was approximately three years ago. It was squatted down in a tree when I got home around 10:00 p.m. At first I thought it was human. I yelled at it, "What are you doing?" and it jumped out of the tree. It was at least fifteen feet up in the tree, yet it jumped out of it and landed with what seemed to be no injuries. When it landed, it stood up on two legs and took off through the woods. I knew then it wasn't a human because it was too tall. It seemed to have a rather stocky upper body build, but a skinnier lower body."

"The second time I saw it was a few days later," he said. "I got home around 1:00 a.m. or so and when I got out of my car, I saw a bipedal animal standing to the left of me, watching me. It was only about fifteen feet from me, standing next to my mom's truck."

Using the truck as a reference, the witness stated that the creature was at least eight feet tall. He was reluctant to tell anyone about his sightings, until his mother told him she had seen a very tall figure when she parked the truck earlier. He said his third sighting took place in the same general area. "It was right next to our house, walking toward me when I pulled up," he said. Again it was around 1:00 a.m. He said he got out of his car and yelled, "I see you!" The creature stopped in its tracks and stood, unmoving, as the witness hastily entered the house.

"The fourth time was the most dramatic and the most clear observation I had to date," he said. "My Australian shepherd was barking crazily at the back door. So I walked outside with him. He took a left off the porch and headed to the tree line along our side yard." Still barking, the dog stepped a few feet into the woods where he was no longer in view. Then the barking stopped and the dog backed out of the woods wagging his tail and looking up. "The brush began to move and out came a really long, slender, yet muscular left leg. The floodlights were on so I got a really good look at it. It was hairless and seemed to be a light beige color with a slight grayish hue to it. The most abnormal thing about it, in regards to human terms, was that it had a groin at about the height of my chest or higher. It made me immediately think of the [way] that most people describe aliens as looking. My dog looked at me and the creature stopped moving. It slowly moved its left leg up and moved it back toward its body and then took off through the woods."

The fifth sighting, which happened in 2005, occurred in broad daylight as the thing was running swiftly down the hill. "It looked like the upper body was hair-covered and the legs were not," he said. "It was at least eight feet tall." The dogs, usually fearless, did not give chase. The witness admitted it was possible that the thing's legs could have been covered with hair as well, just of a much lighter color than the brown-colored, stocky upper portions of its body. Strange noises, which sounded like a child howling have been heard in the area as well.

TAYLOR COUNTY

Does Bigfoot walk abroad in Taylor County, as well? My guess would be a resounding yes. The following account of a nighttime yowler comes from Campbellsville, just off Spurlington Road, near the Pittman Valley area:

"In 1977 my husband and I bought a small hobby farm in Taylor County, Kentucky just outside the town of Campbellsville. Our farm was surrounded by neighboring farms, but no one lived on the land bordering ours; the owners all lived in town. So, our little farm was fairly isolated and I liked it that way. In the summer of 1978, I believe the month was July, my husband, while alone at home, heard a sound one evening that frightened the daylights out of him, and he doesn't frighten easily. He called me at a friend's place, screaming at me, 'Where are the shotgun shells?' His attitude, his nervousness, scared me. I didn't know what was going on and he wouldn't tell me, he just kept screaming, 'Where are the shotgun shells?' I finally told him and he slammed the phone down. It wasn't until later that my husband related the story of what he had heard. He never did see anything and years went by with no answers to that cry he had heard that evening. Although, for the first several years, as we watched nature films which had various wildlife cries, I kept asking him, 'Did it sound like that?' He always replied 'No, it was like nothing I had ever heard before.'

"In 1988, again in the summer, the month was August, and it had just started to turn dark in the evening when my husband came in from outside and all he said was, 'Do you want to hear that sound?' He didn't have to say any more. I knew right away what he was referring to, so we both went back outside and stood outside our kitchen window. I was standing there listening when I told him, 'I don't hear anything'. He quickly replied, 'Shhh.... Just wait.' So I continued to listen. All of a sudden this horrible cry came up from our woods where our two creeks merged. It caused chills to run up and down my spine! My first reaction was shock. Then another cry was heard. This time I felt myself slowly edging backwards toward the house. Whatever this 'thing' was, the cry was like nothing I had heard from any wild animal before, and I remember starting to shake with fear. Then another cry was heard; this time it came from across the road in the woods where the creek continued to flow. This cry hadn't even crescendoed when there was another cry heard from our side of the woods again. I thought, *Oh my God! There are two of them!* That was it for me; I turned and ran into the house. My husband came in with me, but he grabbed the shotgun and went back outside. He wanted me to hold the light for him as he investigated the woods. I stated, 'You're out of your mind, I'm not going back out there!

"That basically was all that happened that night. My husband never saw anything, nor did I. But I did smell something! It was a very strong musty odor that wasn't pleasant. Actually, the odor was wafting across with the gentle breeze, so sometimes it was very light, and sometimes much stronger. I remember wrinkling up my nose when it was strong, and thinking, *What on Earth is that smell?* So now, after ten years, I had heard the same sound that my husband had heard alone back in 1978. The next day I did go down to where the two creeks meet and walked along the banks looking for strange prints, but didn't see any. Even though it was broad daylight, and a gorgeous sunny day, just being down there gave me the creeps. What had happened the night before had really shook me up and never again did I enjoy being down there anymore. Just the replay in my mind of those cries was enough to make me jumpy whenever I was close to the woods and the creeks area again," she said.

"The sound of those cries stuck in my mind and I had a gnawing feeling that I had heard that sound before...but where? I was a video collector back then and I quickly went through all of my videos to see if anything would jog my memory. I have many natural wildlife tapes, so I thought maybe that is where I had heard it. But when I came across a movie entitled *Sasquatch*, a feeling inside of me told me to watch this tape. So I did. I sat in my living room and watched all the way through that movie, until close to the end. They had the sound - the very same sound - that my husband and I had just heard a few nights ago! As soon as I heard it chills again ran up and down my spine. I quickly rewound the tape to the beginning of where that sound was and left it there until my husband came home from work that evening. As soon as he came home, I told him I had something I wanted him to watch. So within a few minutes he was seated in the living room and I played the tape. As soon as that cry was heard on the tape he jumped up yelling, 'That's it! That's the sound!!' We replayed that part of the tape over and over again trying to allow all this information to sink in. We now felt, we knew what we had heard. It was a Sasquatch. Or actually, two of them, in the middle of Kentucky! An experience like this, you don't ever forget. You can't! It'll stay with us for the rest of our lives!"

TRIMBLE COUNTY

Bigfoot was being seen in Trimble County in 1962. Farmer Owen Pike described a creature about six feet tall and covered in dark hair that attacked his dogs and fled on two legs. Other sightings of the creature also allegedly occurred there subsequently and the year became known for the "monster scare." The last reported sighting took place on September 15, 2008 near Bedford, just after a violent windstorm, with sustained gusts of up to 75 miles per hour, had swept through the area.

"On Sept. 15th, 2008," eyewitness Thomas R. states," I went out to check the damage after the windstorm. While standing on my porch I noticed movement in the field across the road." He could see a large dark figure as it moved east to west across the field about 300 yards away. He hurried back inside, grabbed an old rifle scope, and stepped back out onto the porch and trained it on the figure. He said that what he saw, "was no bear or man or deer." It was a seven-foot tall, manlike creature covered in dark-brown, shaggy, dirty-looking hair." He couldn't believe what he was seeing. "It began to move toward the woods, which were south of the field. I didn't tell anyone of this. Later the next day a friend of mine came to the house acting weird and asked if I could come to his house to check something out." Once there, according to Thomas, his friend explained to him that, as he was sitting in the living room earlier, his dogs had started barking furiously and acting agitated. Then, a large figure had walked in front of the picture window out front. "From what [he] stated about the size it had to be at least seven feet tall. This happened around 3 p.m. on the 15th, the same day I had my sighting."

He said his friend also admitted that his sister had also seen the creature that same day, walking in a field behind the house. "I have seen this creature several times since I've lived here in this county," Thomas said, "And so have other people around Colbert Lane, Milton, Bedford Pike and U.S. 36."

TRIGG COUNTY

The following, written by David Roeck, describes an incident that happened in 1972 while he was camping at Land Between the Lakes. He calls it, "An Unforgettable Night in the Woods."

Nearly four decades have passed since my autumn car trip to California from upstate New York in 1972, the first of numerous journeys to come in the intervening years. I was a free-spirited youth yearning for travel and adventure, which eventually took me to the far reaches of the continental U.S. This journey, like others before and after, was a solo trip of self-discovery. That year I left Rochester, N.Y. on a rainy early morning in October, heading southwest toward West Virginia, where I spent my first night at a rural farmer's field-type campground.

The next day I made my way through the winding roads and mountains of West Virginia toward Kentucky to the west. I felt inspired to seek out a large, pristine forest to camp in that night -- ostensibly to immerse myself in nature and drift off to sleep by the sound of wind in the trees. That is how I used to view camping in the scenic woods and wilderness areas; I saw it as a rejuvenating retreat from the over-developed, fast-paced world into the restful and rejuvenating forest.

As the day progressed, I made my way across Kentucky, stopping only for lunch and fuel. At one of these stops, while looking over the road atlas, I noticed a sizeable wooded state park at the western end of the state called Land Between the Lakes, so named because it was bordered on the east and west by two large lakes running north and south, and straddling the Tennessee border. That seemed a good place to consider, even though I would be short of covering the distance I had planned.

Upon reaching the area in late afternoon, it seemed ideal for my purposes. The open paved road leading into the park appeared inviting, with no gate or entrance booth to be seen. Being off-season, it appeared to be deserted, although some distant boats dotted the lake. I followed the road back into the woods as it climbed the hills and curved around into the interior of the park, glimpsing as I went the receding lake through the trees until it was out of sight. I continued on deep into the woods, driving several miles before I arrived at a remote area and an abrupt end of the pavement. There was no continuing dirt road; the asphalt simply terminated at the edge of the trees.

I stepped out of the car and surveyed the area, noticing a pathway off to the left leading to a small clearing in the woods, perhaps 25 yards away. It appeared to be a camping area made to accommodate a tent. As I looked around, I had a sense that something felt odd about the place, and the usual feeling of peace and refreshment I had felt in the past [from] being in the woods, was now curiously absent. But I dismissed it as simple road fatigue, and proceeded to unload the car and set up my tent in the nearby clearing.

During the repeated trips back and forth to my car, I became more aware of the earlier feeling of an inexplicable strangeness in the air, which for me was unusual, but which I continued to dismiss. It was now dusk; soon it would be dark and I would be busy in my tent preparing dinner. The preoccupation of attending to those immediate functions was helpful, and I focused on that. But after dinner, while studying the maps for the next day's journey, a distinct feeling came over me of being watched. I had heard from others about this strange sensation, but I had never experienced it until now. It was a definite intuitive awareness, clear and unmistakable. Then, involuntarily, the thought came: There is someone or something out there! I felt an accompanying involuntary shiver and quickly reviewed my situation. I came to the conclusion that there was nothing to be done about it now; it was pitch dark outside with no lights anywhere except my tent, which when internally illuminated with a lantern, glowed brightly in the forest like a bright orange jewel that could be seen from a great distance. My general outlook had always been that I tended to put trust in the universe and my place in it -- whatever the circumstances might be. And it was this fatalistic attitude that allowed me to turn off the lamp and go to sleep. But I was not to sleep for long.

A few hours later, in the middle of the night, I was suddenly shocked awake by the beastly sounds of something growling, grunting, and snarling, loudly and aggressively, crashing through the brush from a distance and advancing directly toward my tent. I sat bolt upright in my sleeping bag, terrorized, my attention locked on the strange and menacing sounds approaching, and instantly, intuitively knowing: That is what I have felt watching me! For long moments it came on until it stopped abruptly and fell silent, perhaps twenty feet or less from my tent. It was then, at that peak moment of panic that something even stranger happened.

I have thought about this next occurrence for years and do not know what to make of it. As if it wasn't strange enough for an unknown beast to storm toward my tent in the middle of the night making weird and threatening sounds, abruptly stopping short and becoming completely silent -- then, at that exact moment, before I had a chance to think about it, I felt a sleepy wave of peace come over me from some unknown source, and I felt I was being guided to simply lay my head down and go off to sleep like a baby, which is exactly what I did! I saw no angelic vision nor heard any inner voice, no instruction nor promise of protection, just the bizarre notion to simply lie down and go off to sleep. I have never understood how that intense moment of terror could be instantly transformed into a night of peaceful sleep, but that is what took place. Was it a protecting angel? Was it an example of supreme denial? Whatever it was, it remains a mystery.

The next morning I awoke with a start, and the frightful experience of the night just hours before, came flooding back into my consciousness. My mind raced but I could not account for it all nor make any sense of it. Even more unsettling was the realization that I never heard the thing leave! But it was now a sunny morning and as I cautiously looked out through the tent flap, everything seemed quite natural, with no sense of danger at all. I inspected the area around the tent and could not see any obvious evidence of anything having been there, as the forest floor was covered in fall leaves and brush. I quickly packed up my gear and was off, promising myself to find a KOA campground that evening, and hopefully set up my tent between two motor homes!

This event prompted much thought and reflection, and left numerous lessons and implications to reflect upon. I do acknowledge so-called supernatural forces, i.e., angels and spirit guides, and if it wasn't the timely assistance of a supernatural helper at that critical moment, then I have a new respect for the power of denial! But the nature of that presence, or "wave of peace" that came over me was as vivid in its own way as was the sound of the approaching beast. It was powerful enough to bring to awareness that quiet inner spirit that resides in each of us regardless of circumstances. Again, I have always traveled with a sense of belonging in the world, wherever I chose to adventure, to have faith in the situation, and to be open to a higher source of guidance and protection. Certainly, for me at least, allowing for this trust or sense of abandon into the larger scheme of things was verified and [was] quite useful in this strange event that I will never forget.

I have since taken a different view of the deep woods and wilderness in general, and while it is still beautiful and compelling, I no longer go off by myself to camp in its depths. Based upon my subsequent reading on the subject of remote areas and strange encounters, I prefer to view it from a distance.

Perhaps this brief account illustrates an important point about life in this world and the conditions therein, and how we might enlarge our awareness and appreciation to include the benevolent but unseen presence that seems to be with us wherever we go. It is a reminder, in more ways than one, that we are not alone.

Roeck attributes the fact that he inexplicably fell asleep during what sounded like the approach of a terrifying wild beast to the intervention of a supernatural helper, but what if the creature that he heard charging his tent was responsible for his seemingly magical slumber? It has recently begun to be believed by many Bigfoot researches that these entities may be able to use sound inaudible to humans in order to subdue, terrify or even paralyze. If this is true, who knows what really happened after Roeck fell asleep?

The Cadiz Record, Thursday, January 15, 1981

HAS BIGFOOT BEEN SPOTTED IN STATE?

Cadiz, Kentucky (Associated Press) -- Folks in southeast Trigg County at the edge of Lake Barkley are waiting for the next snow to see if, "ahem," Bigfoot shows up again. Linton residents haven't seen Bigfoot. At least they aren't saying so if they have. But they spotted, took pictures and even trailed large humanlike tracks made by somebody (or something?) walking barefoot during the recent snow. Bigfoot has been the source of endless speculation in the community near the Tennessee state line.

One person even went so far as to nail up a placard on a highway sign proclaiming: "Slow Bigfoot Xing." The sign marks where the tracks crossed KY-164 at Linton. E.S. Lester, a Linton resident who examined the tracks and took Polaroid snapshots of them, said the tracks exhibited some of the characteristics of a human foot except they are much larger - 18 inches long and up to six inches wide. "The only thing is, in some places it had a four and a half foot stride! I tried to do that and it is hard to do. I don't believe a varmint did it," Lester said.

Lester also said the tracks appeared to come down a hill to the old Ferry Landing, then around the restrooms and a parking lot and other areas near the lake's edge. The trail went around the edge of the lake for quite a distance, then climbed to and across Kentucky 164.

Trigg County Deputy Sheriff J. R. Smith also took a look. "I don't know, I'll be honest with you, I did see the tracks and I'd put it that way. My personal opinion is I think it was a prank," Smith said. However, Lester and others say the prankster put some time and thought into his endeavor. First, the tracks appear to be made by someone heavy enough to leave impressions in the snow deeper than those of a normal person. If a prankster, he also rambled through some briars nearly impossible for an average person to get through. Smith agreed that whoever made the tracks was a serious prankster, attentive to all the elements involved in pulling off a good hoax.

However, Lester said a close examination of the footprint/s reveals that the shape of the foot where the toes join is perfectly straight. On a human foot, Lester observed that the area is rounded. He said the tracks are not the first discovered at Linton. Local residents discovered similar tracks about three years ago. In the event of another snow, Lester added, he and others will be ready to trail the creature.

Two mussel poachers, however, weren't afraid to come forward and claim that they saw Bigfoot in Trigg County, 1996, while sitting in their car at the edge of Lake Barkley. The monster disappeared into the woods when the headlights were turned on. Vocalizations were then heard and a large, heavy log was thrown forcibly against the car. The next day they returned to the site and examined the log, which, they claimed, was so heavy that both of them could not lift it.

Another hirsute humanoid was allegedly seen by a passing motorist in July of 2005 on Kentucky State Route 164 in Canton. It was about 8:30 a.m. on a clear sunny morning. The witness claimed that he was driving along listening to the radio and looking for deer when he passed a figure standing by the edge of the woods beside the road. He later described it as ten feet tall and covered with thick, black hair. "I've watched for it ever since then," he said, "and have yet to see it again."

Friend and fellow Fortean enthusiast, Jeffrey Scott Holland writes in *Weird Kentucky*, (Sterling Publications, 2008): "In September 2006, a Trigg County woman was surprised to find a Bigfoot-type apeman on her rooftop in broad daylight. Not being a believer in Bigfoot, she assumed it had to be some crazy person in an ape suit and attempted to talk to it by yelling things like, 'Okay, you're funny. Joke's over, now who the hell are you?' which elicited no response. 'It was like something from a bad old movie,' she said. 'It didn't look real at all. It totally looked like a man in a really fake gorilla suit, and I didn't think he was doing a very good job of acting like a gorilla either.' But as she was rummaging through her purse looking for her cell phone so she could call a neighbor for help, the apeman rolled backward, did a sort of somersault, leaped an incredible distance off the corner of the roof to a utility pole - something no human could have done - and deftly swung from the pole to the tops of nearby trees with great speed. It was out of sight in seconds. Good work for a guy who likes to put on an ape suit and scare people."

UNION COUNTY

The following is an eyewitness report from June 1982.

"My brother and I were fishing in a farm lake and decided it was getting late so we started home. I felt like something was watching us. I turned and saw something standing at the edge of the woods. It was big, black, and hairy, and just stood there observing us. I told my brother at once to get down, and he also saw the creature and exclaimed, "My God, what is it?" We sat there in awe for about ten minutes observing it. We were pretty scared and puzzled about it. Suddenly we jumped up and started running home. When we got home we told our mother about it. It looked as if it was getting out of a tree and was leaning with its arm up against the tree."

The witness said he was also involved in another encounter with what he believed was the same creature while he was frog gigging in the river bottoms with four friends. All of them were allegedly chased from their gigging hole by something large and heavy as it ran toward them through the woods. Luckily, they were able to make it to their vehicle and escape before the creature revealed itself.

A woman experienced a late-night sighting of Bigfoot near the Uniontown boat dock on Dike Road in November 1996. The creature walked unhurriedly across the road in front of her vehicle and disappeared into the tree line that ran there along the Ohio River. She described it as around ten feet tall with long arms and covered with long, wooly hair. It was broad shouldered, narrower at the waist and had a gorilla-like head with no neck. She said her husband and son, both commercial fisherman, had heard this creature many times as it splashed about in the shallow waters just off the shore of a large island in the river.

Bigfoot investigator Tony Gerrard interviewed the witness in question. "In 1996 the witness's husband and son worked as commercial fishermen on the Ohio River," he wrote: "The witness would drop them off, and then pick them up again at a point farther down river. On the night of the sighting she was waiting in the parked truck with the headlights off. She said her son was mistaken about the creature walking in front of the headlights. Although the moon was not full, there was enough moonlight to make things fairly visible. The creature came out of the woods about 50 feet from the truck, crossed the road and a field, and entered the tree line along the river. At one point it stopped briefly and looked around. She estimated it was over eight feet tall, stating "it wouldn't have fit through a regular-sized door."

The body was broadest across the shoulders and narrower in the waist area, the woman told Gerrard. The head was "shaped like a gorilla's," she said, with no real neck visible. The witness described the creature as "woolly-looking." While she could not see any facial details, she said it had hair all the way down its arm and on its body. It did not have on any clothes.

According to the witness, "It walked at an unhurried pace, swinging its arms, just like a gorilla or a monkey would do." She said its arms were long compared to a human's and probably hung down to knee level. After the sighting, the witness said she rolled up the windows, locked the doors and turned on the headlights because she was frightened. No vocalizations or odors were associated with the sighting. The witness' son added that he and his father heard the log-breaking noises on the island on four or five different occasions.

The area has a long history of monster activity. Interestingly, it is also the site of the largest concentration of desecrated Native American burial mounds in the world and the largest known burial site in Kentucky. Over 800 graves belonging to the Angel Medina culture were looted at this location in the late 1980s. The crime garnered national attention and, consequently, massive protests from Native Americans across the U.S. Hundreds of Indians soon descended on the area to hold rituals and sing sacred chants as they re-interred the remains back into what they considered sacred land.

In the late 1990s, I was able to gain access into the area, known locally as the Slack Farm, and have a look around this magical place. Some stealth was required. Since the grave desecrations of the previous decade, which resulted in the nation's first lengthy prison terms for Indian grave looters, the area was highly restricted and trespassers faced immediate jail terms. This was not the first time, nor the last, that I would

(Above) The Slack Farm as it looks today. This area has been the scene of many strange events, including cattle mutilations, UFO sightings and Bigfoot reports. Local folklore holds that the forested hill in the background, and all of the surrounding bottomland, is home to huge hairy beasts that locals simply call "gorillas".
(Photo by Kaleigh Duncan)

Bigfoot in Kentucky -- Page 151

find myself risking much just to stand on one particular piece of ground for a little while. Nonetheless, my wife and I were able to spend several quiet, uninterrupted hours there completely unnoticed as we walked the far end of the ridge, which sat below a large, forested hill. This hill, like so many others in Kentucky, was reputedly home to large, hairy, manlike animals known locally as "gorillas."

As we walked close to a small creek at the base of the hill we unexpectedly came upon the carcasses of around ten dead hogs. They were ripped to pieces and strewn over the entire lower end of the ridge. They appeared to be fresh, despite the curious absence of blood, and none of the meat looked as if it had been eaten. After this, an extremely uncomfortable feeling came over both of us, almost as if we were being watched, and we decided it would be best to leave. I have no doubt at all that "gorillas" exist in the area.

WARREN COUNTY

On July 23, 2005, at 8:30 p.m. a man who was hiking around a large lake in Warren County saw Bigfoot chasing a deer across a game trail. He yelled out in fear, which caused the beast to stop and look at him. Then it ran back into the woods in the direction from which it came. It was very large and walked and ran on two legs, the witness claimed. It had a muscular body covered with brown hair. He also described it as having humanlike eyes and a bad smell. Warren County is located in southwestern Kentucky and has a population of around 105,000 people - and at least one monster.

WASHINGTON COUNTY

A group of Washington County youths got the surprise of their lives on October 17, 2008. Ben C. (full name on file), his brother and two of their friends had set up another friend that evening to take him "snipe hunting," an age-old prank designed to take full advantage of an unsuspecting person's gullibility. They found no snipe, of course, since snipe are purely imaginary, but they did find something much more frightening.

At 2:00 a.m. the group was on a wooded hillside in Springfield. "After setting up my friend halfway down the hill," Ben states, "myself and my two friends [sic] were circling around to 'drive the snipes' to him. My brother stayed behind at the top of the hill to watch the event unfold." Things went from humorous to serious, however, when the trio stopped at the edge of the woods and were pelted by rocks and sticks being thrown at them by an unseen assailant. They automatically assumed it was Ben's brother, as they didn't know exactly where he was positioned. But they were wrong. Scanning the woods all around them, Ben spied a "bipedal, humanlike figure" as it walked between the trees. "I thought my brother was behind us following us up the hill," Ben said, "but once we entered into the open field we realized that he was still at the top of the hill, watching us."

While they stood at the top of the hill waiting for the friend who was the subject of the hoax, who was innocently holding the bag in which to catch the snipe, they continued to be pelted by rocks and branches. "While watching my friend walk up the hill to our left, we looked down into the woods where me and my friends came out. Near a forked tree we saw something crouched down next to its base." They watched the figure for a couple of minutes debating who - or what - it could be, then the group went back to Ben's house, *sans* snipe but in possession of a larger mystery.

"There was no possible way there was another human being in the woods that night with us," Ben said. He described the figure they saw as bipedal and humanlike with broad shoulders. "Even though it was crouched down," he said, "it was still very tall."

WHITLEY COUNTY

Nancy O. (full name on file) claims she watched a Bigfoot for about twenty minutes one afternoon back in the summer of 1997 in Rockhold, near Williamsburg. "It was summer. I was sixteen years old. My younger brothers and I wanted to go camping but we didn't have a tent," she said. At their mother's suggestion they set out to find some small trees to cut down in order to build a fort on a huge rock in a field above their house.

"We went out to find some small timber to cut down," Nancy said. "My brothers found some before we reached the top of the mountain and began to cut them down. They sent me on ahead to scout for more up above the field around the cliff's edge." Nancy had been in that field numerous times and knew just where a stand of suitably sized trees was located. She reached her destination under the cliff and took a good look around at the trees. She decided to start chopping down the nearest one at the edge of the thicket and put the small hatchet she carried to work. The sound of metal striking wood echoed along the mountain. She was only about halfway through the tree when the heat began to get the better of her and she sat down beneath it to enjoy its shade for, perhaps, the last time. She had only rested there for about five minutes when she heard a peculiar banging noise above her on the cliff.

"At first I thought, 'well, that's the echo of the hatchet where I was hitting that tree a while ago,' but the noise kept on and I began to get curious." She got up and turned her gaze upward, backing away from the cliff face to get a better look. She could see nothing, however, and soon gave up and walked back to the tree she was working on. Suddenly, she heard rocks sliding down the cliff. She turned and looked up again. "And then I saw it. At first I thought 'what in the world is that?' Then, when I realized that what I was seeing didn't match up to any animal I knew of I began to get scared. There, standing about fifteen feet above me on the cliff was this manlike thing with shoulders about four feet wide and long, shaggy reddish-brown hair all over its body. It was huge. I had never seen anything like it."

Her first impulse was to run away screaming, but her mother had always warned her that wild animals would instinctively chase running people. She began to back away slowly. Her mother had also told her that, if she were to ever run into a wild animal, to pick up two rocks and strike them together to scare it off. "So I picked up two rocks and started beating the crap out of them," she said. "It wasn't working." To her surprise the figure bent and picked up two rocks, as well. Bizarrely, it began imitating her actions. Nancy quickly decided to give up on trying to intimidate the creature and continued her calm, slow retreat toward the hill above the house, keeping her eyes glued to the creature on the cliff. She feared that at any moment, it might come after her. Imagine her horror when the hairy beast began to follow her! When it reached a spot on the cliff where it could climb down she broke into a terrified run toward the bottom of the hill where her brothers were.

"I met up with my two brothers screaming and crying," she says. "I have never seen anything like that before, but I've watched TV, and read, and listened to other people's stories of similar encounters, and the only thing remotely resembling what I saw that day [is what] people call a Bigfoot." Nancy further describes the thing as standing eight feet tall, four feet wide at the shoulders, with dark-brown skin beneath six to eight inches of shaggy, reddish-brown hair. According to her, it was muscular with hands that were over ten inches long. It had an "almost human face with primate features," she said. As for its striking the rocks together, she said, "It was almost like it was mocking me or trying to communicate with me, like it wanted me to know it was there or was trying to get my attention."

Another Whitley County incident, this one ending in gunfire, also took place near Williamsburg on March 22, 2008. "Me and my sister [sic] were hunting," says Josh T. (full name on file), "and we heard a loud noise." The two turned toward the sound, later described as "a horrible, screechy roar," and saw a huge, hair-covered, manlike creature standing in the woods not far away. Frightened, the two said they did what most Kentuckians would do in this situation - they fired on the thing. Instead of frightening the beast off, however, the shots had the opposite effect. Seemingly unhurt, the creature roared again and charged the two hunters who, quite understandably, turned and ran.

Josh said they were relieved when the thing jumped into some tall weeds and disappeared, but not enough to quit running. They made it back to their vehicles and immediately left the area. One of them later described the figure as eight feet tall, covered with dark-colored hair and having "huge hands." A fisherman saw a similar creature the previous year, on June 14, 2007. He reported that a tall, hairy, manlike monster emerged from the woods and began drinking from the stream. The anonymous fisherman said he quietly left the area.

CONCLUSIONS

Whatever these gigantic, humanoid creatures turn out to be one thing is certain - they are here. They have always been here, and contrary to what most people believe they are not trying very hard to stay hidden from the eyes of modern man. They tend to step out onto the highways in front of oncoming vehicles instead of waiting until the vehicles have passed. Sometimes they even chase vehicles, almost as if they are making sure that they are seen.

They do not confine themselves to the tracts of unexplored wilderness that the state has to offer, but rather seem to mostly inhabit the fringes of civilization where they are easily observed. They do not avoid the isolated country farms but seem to delight in trespassing and causing havoc and fear. Ignoring the abundance of local fauna, it would appear that these creatures relish our livestock and domestic animals, stealing and/or killing and consuming cats, dogs, pigs, goats, chickens and all manner of other creatures that live out their existences in pens and pastures.

Considering the alarming frequency of hairy hominid sightings in the Bluegrass State, why do its citizens only rarely find their footprints or tracks? Given their tendency to announce their presence with the loud and unsettling cracking and breaking of underbrush, tree limbs, and even entire trees, the forests of Kentucky should be littered with these things' trails of destruction. They are not. They build nests and teepee-type structures and snap the tops off saplings along a well-used route to mark their territory for any and all to see. Their actions are entirely contradictory to the notion that they are shy and passive creatures, only wanting to be left alone to live in peace. The Native American population, long ago, knew of and accepted their existence. Yet we cannot. As we have seen, they are observed time and again by frightened witnesses, yet they leave behind only fear and mystery to slap at the collective face of academia.

In the end, we can only point out that Kentucky is ideally suited for creatures such as these for a number of reasons. The thickly forested Appalachian mountain range runs through the eastern parts of the state. Isolated and remote, seldom intruded on by modern man, this region still has many miles of unexplored wilderness that could contain any number of unknown creatures.

In south central Kentucky we find Mammoth Cave, the largest cave system in the entire world. With over 350 miles of underground tunnels and passageways that have been discovered so far, who knows what may lurk in the darkened recesses of this subterranean world? The Bluegrass State also boasts more miles of navigable waterways that any other state in the Lower 48, second only to Alaska. In western

Kentucky alone, Kentucky Lake and Lake Barkley have a combined total of well over 3,000 miles of shoreline. The various creeks and rivers that run through this part of the region add thousands more miles to that total. So, we have massive amounts of untouched wilderness and nearly endless systems of caves, creeks, lakes and rivers for these entities to utilize for concealment and a means of travel. Small wonder, then, that they may come and go as they please and disappear, seemingly at will, very quickly when they choose to do so.

Long ago this region was called the "dark and bloody ground" by the ancient Americans. Although literature explaining this ominous moniker is scant, the Indian name, "*Kaintucke*" has been translated to mean '"The Land of Tomorrow." Who knows what that tomorrow may bring? Perhaps the discovery of a completely new species of hominoid awaits us within the boundaries of the "dark and bloody ground." Only time will tell.

B. M. Nunnelly
Fall 2010

SELECTED BIBLIOGRAPHY

Every search into the mysteries of the unknown should begin at home or in your local library. Many of the incidents contained in this volume can be investigated further by reading the following distinguished works:

Books and Magazines:

1. *Mysterious America* by Loren Coleman - Faber & Faber, 1983
2. *Mysterious Kentucky* by B.M.Nunnelly - Whitechapel Press, 2007
3. *Monster! The A-Z Of Zooform Phenomena* by Neil Arnold - CFZ, 2007
4. *Weird Kentucky by Jeffrey Scott Holland* - Sterling, 2008
5. *The Complete Guide To Mysterious Beings* by John Keel - Doubleday, 1994
6. *The Locals* by Thom Powell - Hancock House, 2003
7. *Tragedy At Devils Hollow: And Other Kentucky Ghost Stories* by Michael Paul Henson - Cockrel, 1984
8. *Mothman and Other Curious Encounters* by Loren Coleman - Paraview Press, 2002
9. *Alien Animals* by Janet and Colin Bord - HarperCollins, 1985
10. *Strange Creatures From Time and Space* by John Keel - Fawcett, 1970
11. *The Bigfoot Files* by Peter Guttilla - Timeless Voyager Press, 2003
12. *Mysteries of Time and Space* by Brad Steiger - Dell, 1973
13. *FATE* magazine
14. *Fortean Times* magazine
15. *Bigfoot Across America* by Philip L. Rife - Universe, 2000

Websites:

1. *Kentuckybigfoot.com*
2. *Cryptomundo.com*
3. *Bigfootencounters.com*
4. *Bigfootsightings.org*
5. *BFRO.com* - Bigfoot Field Researchers Organization
6. *GCBRO.com* Gulf Coast Bigfoot Research Organization
7. *Strangeark.com*

ABOUT THE AUTHOR

Author, artist, filmmaker and well known Fortean investigator, Bart Nunnelly has been studying all aspects of the unexplained in his native western Kentucky for over 25 years. His wanderings throughout the Bluegrass bottomlands have brought him face to face with such creatures as Bigfoot, black panthers, water monsters and several other curious Kentucky cryptids including a Thunderbird in 1998 - something no other living researcher can presently claim.

In addition to legendary beasts, Nunnelly has also experienced spectral phenomena and UFO activity on multiple occasions.

His first book, "Mysterious Kentucky" was published in 2007 by Whitechapel Press to much acclaim and his next work, "The Inhumanoids! Real Encounters With Beings That Can't Exist," is due out in 2010 by CFZ Press. His crytpo-art has been widely featured in everything from children's books to television shows throughout the world and his first documentary, "Hunt The Dogman," a rousing investigation of Kentucky's werewolf sightings, was released in 2007 by Grendel Films. He is currently working on his second crypto-documentary film project, "The Spottsville Monster," with McGill Media Llc, out of Louisville.

Whitechapel Productions Press is a division of Dark Haven Entertainment and a small press publisher, specializing in books about ghosts and hauntings. Since 1993, the company has been one of America's leading publishers of supernatural books and has produced such best-selling titles as *Haunted Illinois, The Ghost Hunter's Guidebook, Ghosts on Film, Confessions of a Ghost Hunter, The Haunting of America, Sex & the Supernatural* the *Dead Men Do Tell Tales* crime series and many others.

WHITECHAPEL PRESS

With more than a dozen different authors producing high quality books on all aspects of ghosts, hauntings and the paranormal, Whitechapel Press has made its mark with America's ghost enthusiasts.

You can visit Whitechapel Productions Press online and browse through our selection of ghostly titles, plus get information on ghosts and hauntings, haunted history, spirit photographs, information on ghost hunting and much more. by visiting the internet website at **www.americanhauntings.org**

Founded in 1994 by author Troy Taylor, the American Hauntings Tour Company (which includes the Illinois Hauntings Tours) is America's oldest and most experienced tour company that takes ghost enthusiasts around the country for excursions and overnight stays at some of America's most haunted places.

AMERICAN HAUNTINGS TOURS

In addition to our tours of America's haunted places, we also offer tours of Illinois' most haunted cities, including Chicago, Alton, Decatur, Lebanon, Springfield and Jacksonville. These award-winning ghost tours run all year around, with seasonal tours only in some cities.

Find out more about tours, and make reservations online, by visiting the internet website at **www.americanhauntings.org**

I dont believe those who insist that North America has no new secrets. One day Bigfoot will be recognized as a living creature. I hope to see that day soon. In the meantime, the sightings continue, the number of Bigfoot seekers keeps growing, and the search is still afoot.

Loren Coleman

Lightning Source UK Ltd.
Milton Keynes UK
174252UK00005B/34/P